NYC Horse Power

AN ORAL HISTORY OF FAST CUSTOM MACHINES

MICHAEL MCCABE

Schiffer Publishing Ltd
4880 Lower Valley Road • Atglen, PA 19310

Other Schiffer Books By The Author:
Japanese Tattooing Now: Memory and Transition, 978-0-7643-2142-0, $29.95

Tattoos of Indochina: Magic, Devotion, & Protection, 978-0-7643-1679-6, $29.95

Tattooing New York City: Style and Continuity in a Changing Art Form, 978-0-7643-1388-6, $29.95

Library of Congress Control Number: 2012931565

Designed by Justin Watkinson
Cover by Bruce Waters
Type set in Velvenda Cooler/Aminta/Minion Pro/Gill Sans Std

ISBN: 978-0-7643-3961-5
Printed in China

Schiffer Books are available at special discounts for bulk purchases for sales promotions or premiums. Special editions, including personalized covers, corporate imprints, and excerpts can be created in large quantities for special needs. For more information contact the publisher:

Published by Schiffer Publishing Ltd.
4880 Lower Valley Road
Atglen, PA 19310
Phone: (610) 593-1777; Fax: (610) 593-2002
E-mail: Info@schifferbooks.com

For the largest selection of fine reference books on this and related subjects, please visit our website at **www.schifferbooks.com**
We are always looking for people to write books on new and related subjects. If you have an idea for a book, please contact us at proposals@schifferbooks.com

This book may be purchased from the publisher.
Include $5.00 for shipping.
Please try your bookstore first.
You may write for a free catalog.

In Europe, Schiffer books are distributed by
Bushwood Books
6 Marksbury Ave.
Kew Gardens

CONTENTS

Lenny's '51 Chevy Bel Air under Bronx elevated

ACKNOWLEDGMENTS

Many people have contributed their time, energy, and thought to this project. I knocked on a lot of doors and I rang a lot of phones as I worked my way through the long list of people's names I accumulated. I appreciate everyone's openness and guidance which helped me to get my bearings and stay on track. I was invited into very special and also very private shop spaces where people paused in their work, put down their tools, and permitted me the opportunity to burden them with my questions and my camera. Thank you.

Jeffrey Schad and John Copeland, Bushwick, Brooklyn

NY Coliseum, c. 1967. Photo: William Gedney, Duke University Library Collection

Frank Voto, Staten Island

For me, the people, machines, and private workspaces that I have been fortunate enough to experience represent an ongoing social process of creative stylization. This process has its own unique personality that is guided by both a sense of history and a sense of place. Beautiful machines represent bundles of highly imaginative information that is contextualized by the sensibilities of the creative people that work on and also appreciate them. For the most part, the horsepower world in New York City is a closed and specialized world. The viewers of this book have been given the rare opportunity to take a look at it and learn from it.

Paul Cox and Keino and Alex Lerner and Joe and Ed Serino and Frank Voto invited me into their respective workshops, generously moved heavy machines around, and spent a lot of time with me to help educate me about the history and depth of this movement. Ron Lopez of Staten Island helped to connect me with important people like "Big Daddy" George and Vinny; Angelo Scotto of the Bronx did the same in his borough. Sal Pepe of Brooklyn spent a lot of time explaining the dynamics of timing, push rod and cylinder angles, torque, and horsepower. Dougy, Izzy and Ricco, Charlie Krause, Ray Ray, and Steve Iacona generously invited me into their Brooklyn workshops as did Craig Hoffman and Jeff Rogan on the Island and Mike Palazzo in Jersey. Ralph Torres met me in Coney Island and Bay Ridge and was patient as we waited for the light and the correct position of the sun. Bobby Whalen made suggestions about who might be interesting to talk with on Staten Island and made the introductions for me. Lenny Donghia of the Rumblers Car Club volunteered valuable suggestions like Jimmy JAR in Queens. Brian Darwas, Willie, Lil' Chris, Big Mouth, Eric, and the other members of the Rumblers CC were very generous with their time and insight. John Copeland, Wes Lang, Neil Fenton, Jeffrey

Paul Cox, Brooklyn

Schad, AJ, and Andy Camay of the White Knights were very helpful and encouraging. Vince Szarek and Aaron Frank invited me into their High and Tite studio and let me bother them with my camera as did Bobby Garey, Ray Abeyta, Erik Green, Pete Ranko, Timothy White, KAVES, and ION.

We are all in debt to people like Bonge. He spent a lot of time with me to make sure I understood the depth of this subject. As I came to realize, the culture of cars and motorcycles is a private one that is only now receiving some mainstream attention. Bonge has been way ahead of any notion of a curve with his passions about cars and bikes since his early days and was scrutinized heavily by "squares" who suspected that he was only up to no good. Bonge, Mel Bernstein, Eugene Zandomenego, Krazy Kevin Argus and his wife Sue, Austin Johnson, Spade George, Frank Voto, and Mark Kmiotek took photographs and saved them over the years. They knew it was important to preserve them and their insight to do so has enriched a more complete sense of history. I appreciate the generous opportunity to use some of these photos in this book.

I would like to thank my wife Tzyy Jye for her encouragement and support. I was MIA most weekends for the better part of a year as I visited with people, and I appreciate her sense of patience.

Keino, Brooklyn

INTRODUCTION

TAKING IT TO THE STREET

I experienced weightlessness for the first time a few years ago in the back seat of my friend David Gray's '67 Pontiac GTO. As he power shifted from second to third the torque of his 389 V8 threw me up against the ceiling and I hung their motionless in mid-air for what seemed like several seconds until he dropped the car into fourth. His girlfriend sat next to him inhaling slowly on a cigarette with the calmness of a test pilot who regularly cracked the sound barrier on routine maneuvers.

Ace

I didn't have a clue about the physical force that had grabbed me in the back of Dave's car, but it definitely scared the hell out of me. He understood the extremely intoxicating relationship between torque and horsepower and the experience forever changed the way I thought about him. He was intimate with machines and knew how to get what he wanted from them. I got a lesson that day about the aesthetics of velocity. His deep purple, almost black, GTO which he had built from the ground up was iconic American muscle. Each element of the car, from the engine size to the gas cap was an intentional statement of some kind that spoke of Dave's values and passions about going fast. The personal and somewhat esoteric sensibility that he introduced to me during that experience continued to inform me throughout this oral history project.

The people I have interviewed for this book are all passionate about their machines and the challenge of making them in a place like New York City. There are many different perspectives about how it should be done that range from high-cost show cars and bikes to vehicles for the rough and tumble streets, but for the most part people in the city do not pass judgment. A builder might be a tree wrench who cannot afford the luxury of a garage, parks in certain known places, under certain strong trees, and uses rope and a limb as a winch. Or a kitchen mechanic, who with the help of a few friends stands their motorcycle on end, drags it into the building elevator, and then works on it in their apartment kitchen, living room, or even bedroom. In a city like New York the issue of space is a critical factor that everyone understands. Garages become second homes that reflect the personal aesthetics of the people working in them.

Horsepower is not an easy thing in the city and the process surrounding it asks: Can you build something under these conditions, and most importantly, can you bring it to the street? The answer to this question appears as fast bikes and cars continuously scrutinized for both their style and performance. And reputations develop around the people that have used their knowledge and aesthetic sensibilities to build them.

The people and machines in this book are not necessarily all about the show. There is a private history of street racing in New York that started to take shape in the 1950s as a by-product of both an increase in specialized knowledge about fast cars and motorcycles and the development of the city's parkway system.

Many notable New York City wrenches have raced for paper (title, registration, and/or money) over the years and turf racing between legendary neighborhood builders has always taken place on narrow residential streets crowded with galleries of thrill-seeking onlookers. As speeds climbed to serious levels, illegal racing shifted to notorious stretches of various parkways. Cars and bikes were called out at locations like the abandoned access roads at the far end of Kennedy Airport in Queens, the Connecting Highways, the Belt (the Circumferential Parkway) a series of highways that form a complete circle around New York City, and also along favored stretches between certain exits on the Hutch (Hutchinson River Parkway in the Bronx). Xeroxed flyers announcing the late-night times and locations of races between notable cars and drivers were distributed among in-the-know people and momentary crowds would appear mysteriously on bridges and overpasses along the race routes. Today, increased police awareness and enforcement has put street racing under pressure but it certainly still exists.

New York City had its own NASCAR-sanctioned fifth-mile asphalt stock car track that operated on Staten Island from 1953 to

AJ

Benji, Bronx

Chris, Rumblers CC

Benji, Bronx

Bobby and Beryl Whalen, Staten Island

Bonge

John Copeland, Brooklyn

Coney Hot Rod event

Doug, '41 Ford Coupe

Drew

EZ

1972. Track historian "Big Daddy" George LeBlanc used to race there and will explain that the Weissglass Speedway opened seasonally between May and October and featured drivers with local and national reputations. In the early days of the track, the best drivers ran late 1940s Ford coupes with classic Flathead V8 engines. During its heyday, the track attracted thousands of spectators who enthusiastically attended a mixture of weekly races.

Drivers and cars ranged from top-level competitors to local personalities like Tiny Milano who had a reputation for flashy, perfectly maintained red and black cars and matching black team racing outfits with red pinstripe trim. Rather than jeopardize the well being of his car Tiny would intentionally hang back, avoid the thick of competition and lose in style. The crowd loved it. Some of the most popular local drivers specialized in raucous free-for-all demolition derby contests that were a popular part of the show. At intermission time, fans were encouraged to mingle with their favorite drivers and cars down in the pits.

"Big Daddy" George became friends with Ed "Big Daddy" Roth and the two worked together for several years at seasonal auto shows in the greater New York City area. George candidly reflects about his experiences with the pivotal American hot rod and motorcycle legend.

To a large degree, the story of building fast cars and motorcycles in a place like New York City is an outsider's tale. During the 1950s and 1960s, cars and motorcycles gained momentum in the public's psyche in places like sunny California, which had been literally built around the concept of wide freeways and individual mobility. New York City was from a different era; the old streets and urban layout were behind the times. City planner Robert Moses dragged the people of New York into the twentieth century with his grandiose ideas about the integration of the automobile into modern life, but there was unwillingness to surrender completely to the new regime of progress. It was a hard sell in a place like New York that still had miles of cobblestone streets.

During the mid-1960s, the annual auto show held at the New York Coliseum at Columbus Circle attracted mostly mainstream automobile and motorcycle tastes. The automobile represented social and economic ascendency in the post-war world. A fledgling outsider/outlaw sensibility about cars and motorcycles was just taking shape in America but it was blurry and undeclared at best. When *Harper's Magazine* published Frank Rooney's short story, "The Cyclists' Raid," in 1951, the scene started to become a little more clear. Rooney's story, of course, led to Brando's classic 1953 role as the rebel Johnny Strabler in *The Wild One*. It was Brando's legendary and insubordinate quip, "What ya got?" that stereotyped the attitude of wheeled rebellion forever.

The 1965–66 William Gedney photos of Mel Bernstein and his early biker sensibilities were also on view at the Coliseum Auto Show and complete with Nazi swastika WWII German flags and chromed German military helmets. They seem anachronistic and passé by today's standards but at the time they certainly turned heads with a mixture of disgust and confusion. "People didn't know what to make of it at that time," Bernstein reflects. "None of this stuff had been stereotyped at that point. It was definitely outsider, strange behavior, but no one knew what it was all about. In a place like New York there were some people building impressive bikes and cars but the process was very private."

Today there is both a real and unreal quality to fast cars, motorcycles, and the people that build and fly around with them. Reality television productions have keyed in on the intimate relationship between America and its machines. These shows are made as mass-market dramas that miss the point for the most part and clumsily exploit a mixture of sensibilities which bounce between weekender store-bought superficiality and dedicated, original ground-up building. These kinds of productions fail to explore the real process of style and regionalization and the flow of information and influence as it passes through places and people.

There are of course foundations to making and using stylized and fast machines, whether in New York City or elsewhere. As Brooklyn motorcycle builder and leather specialist Paul Cox will tell you, there was a time when specific parts of the country were known for their own specific design and fabrication strategies. Long before our day of the Internet and before mass-marketed motorcycle or car magazines, people had to travel to see these different styles, or the machines travelled to them. Mostly men but also a few women drove their machines around for a mixture of reasons, and the stylistic idiosyncrasies moved with them and influenced people.

Mel Bernstein and Steve Bonge remember that during the 1960s there wasn't a whole lot of information to go on. They were both operating in a marginalized cultural vacuum for the most part. To get involved in making and changing cars and motorcycles was a precarious outsider's statement which was way ahead of any notion of a curve. Ed Roth first published *Choppers Magazine* in 1967, but on the East Coast it was available by subscription only and rarely seen. The machines featured in it were just beginning to be codified among people who were a part of the subculture but they were completely invisible to mainstream America. This was radical, outsider behavior that was not just going against the grain but, more importantly, was creating its own sense of grain which in turn was creating a mystique.

Under BQE, Rumblers summer event, 2010

Iggy with guns

Iggy

Spade George, NYC, c. 1969

Jason, '49 FL Pan

Kyle and Brandi, Lead Fist Cycles

Lee Quinones

Mechanic's Alley

Jim

Austin Johnson has been riding in New York for over thirty years, Sal Pepe for more than a decade. Before bikes they were both involved with building and illegally racing fast cars on the street. They are from different generations but will tell you that when you break it down there is a story behind every impressive machine in New York City. Names are connected to the machines—on four wheels: Coney Island Ralph Landolfi, Jack Merkel, Broadway Freddy DeName, and John Lobranco. On two wheels: Eddie Reed, Harry Lang, and Mardo Bennett and his Cycle Circus and Custom and Chrome shops in the Bronx. There was also an important motorcycle club called the Aliens that has a lasting legacy.

What I have learned from the people I have spoken with is that there is diversity to the making of machines in a place like New York City. It continues to change but to a large degree what goes on has a historical depth that remains nuanced and somewhat privatized. It is a story that reflects people and their projects as they are shaped by time, neighborhood, culture, race, ethnicity, class, and the mystery of accumulated personal sensibility.

In recent years a groundswell of interest has developed in New York City among younger men and women who are exploring custom cars and motorcycles as a way to reconnect to a hands-on narrative of making things. There are garage spaces now in the out-of-way areas of Brooklyn, Queens, Staten Island, and Manhattan where creative people work together to explore the process of expressing themselves with tools, metal, vehicles, and the nuances of the internal combustion engine. For some of these people, getting their hands dirty while wrenching on something answers new creative questions. For others, this is an older discussion grounded in traditional working-class sensibilities.

Many of the people I talked with work by choice on older machines and for them there is certainly a dialogue with the past. The conversation goes deeper than just romantic nostalgia and reflects a committed sense of understanding about historical forms, design strategies, and processes. John Copeland, Jeffrey Schad, and Wes Lang are accomplished, represented artists that balance their creative life between their studios and garage spaces. Erik Green, who runs the large Works Engineering garage in Brooklyn, has created a dynamic resource center for the growing community of enthusiasts who need to take their interest to the next level. Pete Ranko works from a small garage behind his home in Ozone Park, Queens. The Serino Brothers' historic shop is located in Long Island City, Keino Sasaki works near the waterfront in Brooklyn, Brian Darwas and Willie Gee wrench in the Bronx. These people have different backgrounds and sensibilities but they share similar passions and mutual respect for each other and their projects.

During the warm summer months there are a number of motorcycle and car events where people come together. Dick Zigun of Coney Island fame was early to key in on the connections between people, their machines, and popular culture. For two decades he has provided a platform for enthusiasts to meet each other and show off their work. The Rumblers Car Club has worked hard to create an event schedule in New York City. Their annual car show under the BQE (Brooklyn Queens Expressway) in Brooklyn continues to grow in size and is widely supported. The Indian Larry Legacy Shop in Brooklyn has its annual summer event as does Works Engineering in Brooklyn. For the second year, the White Knights have organized a very important and highly successful one-day-only custom motorcycle invitational show. In Bedford Stuyvesant, Brooklyn, the Head Hunters dragster club has a street fair that features a very impressive line-up of very powerful cars.

The sense of dedication to New York City horsepower continues to take shape and gain recognition at the same time that it reflects on its past. In Frank Voto's shop located in Staten Island, you are reminded about the process of time and the human texture that accompanies a personal sensibility about machines. As a young man, Frank found his milling machines in scrap piles and spent countless hours resurrecting them. He is intimate with his machines and their tolerances, but as he explains, his art and skill with his tools has been redefined today by a changing world. He wonders about the longevity of the knowledge. Young builders in the city, like Paul Cox, Keino, John Copeland, Jeffrey Schad, Andy Camay, Sal Pepe, Pete Ranko, Brian Darwas, the Rumblers, and others like them answer Frank's question with the uncompromising quality of their work and a respectful nod.

Rumblers event under BQE

Ray Abeyta, Brooklyn

As I started to work my way into this project the issue of organizing the material became a process in itself. After a few of the interviews I realized the one thing that connected all the people and their stories was a sense of making things during

Paul, Rumblers CC nomad

periods of time. For the early people, they built their machines with a tactile sense of the unknown and took risks; for the later people there was a vigorous sense of nostalgic realization. Each of the people in the project related to building and appreciating their machines within the context of the time when they made them. I decided to explore this process and to put everyone's histories into a sequence of time from oldest to youngest. The reader should be sensitive to this progression of ideas and efforts and should appreciate this flow and these connections.

Tim White

Rumblers summer event under BQE

Joe Serino, Sr.

Joe Serino, Sr.

SERINO HOT RODS

Long Island City, Queens

During my early days, the very first Hudson step-down I saw changed the way I thought about cars. They called them step-downs because you opened the door and you stepped down into the car. You did not step up and climb in. They were low and they were designed for the car to be lower. They made two-door, four-door, and convertibles, too. I had a convertible. Hudson was a superior car in every respect. The body, the chassis, the front end, the motors, the steel that the motors were made of, everything was better quality. It cost them more money to make and that's why they didn't sell like a Ford or a Chevy. I got a '54 Hudson Hornet convertible. If you talk to anybody that knows old cars and you mention that car, you will get a rise out of them.

The Hornet only had a six cylinder motor in them. A Flathead. But the motor was such a superior design and it didn't blow up. Each cylinder had its own intake and exhaust port. The engines breathed in easily and burned all the fuel and then the exhaust got out. It was a superior design to every other motor made at the time. It absolutely produced more horsepower. The engine could breathe when it revved up without blowing up. I still have two of them that I am working on: A sedan that I have had for a long time—it's my everyday car—and I have the convertible. These cars are moving memories for me.

My dear dad started the business in 1935. We got a little sign up there on the wall to remember that date. He started it over on 12th Street and 35th Avenue. There's a housing project there now. The city came in and put Dad out at the time so they could build the projects. But luckily he found a place over here which was empty land. He started with a two-car metal garage and a little office building. As time went on and things were working, he built the front of the shop up here. His three sons are working with Dad now. We all followed Dad. We built the back of the shop and we all went along like that for the longest time.

We get some work on every day cars but most of the work is on older cars. Special jobs, body or paint; engines. Everything around here is all special jobs. We got some old customers that have come to us for a long time. We try to accommodate them. Sometimes they bring in a late model car. That's an accident. We lost the old trade in fixing regular cars. We specialize now in hot rods. Putting bigger engines into cars. Things change you know. March on. My son Joe does most of all our big jobs. He's got his dear father's genes [laughter]. And his grandfather's genes, too [laughter]. A lot of this kind of thing about working on things is inherited.

Old Serino Hot Rod photo

Garage wall, Serino Hot Rod

Old Serino Hot Rod photo

As a young man I grew into this kind of work. It's one of those long stories. At 12th Street, where we were was a very big piece of property. It went from 12th to 13th Street—from 35th Avenue to half way to 36th Avenue. My dear grandfather...Here's some history for you. Before movie theaters like we got today there was organ theaters. My dear grandfather Tony, he had an organ theater. It was kind of a good sized building made like a movie theater with the rows of seats in it. I was just a kid but I remember the organ with the big pipes and a tremendous keyboard. I was just a little guy but some things stay with you. You know? People would come to the theater and sit and listen to the music. That was it. There was no movies then. This is in the '30s.

I was just a little guy and we lived in a house over there. A two-family house. It would be night time and I'd ask my mom, "Ma, what's that sound?" She'd say, "That's grandpa playing the organ."

Serino Hot Rod garage

Joe Serino, Jr.

My interest in all this started when I seen my very first Hudson...'48 it was…A good friend at the time lived on 12th Street over there. He bought a new car and came over to show us. I looked at it and said, "What in the world is that? It stood out amongst all the other cars. It wasn't just different, it was different! It was a superior car in every way. It performed very well and so they took a lot of them for stock car racing in the early '50s before big V8 motors. The suspension was superior to everybody else's. The steering was solid. They could drive the car fast without having it go all over the place.

It was a smaller car company. The auto industry was very different in those days. Oldsmobile and Pontiac merged later and became General Motors. There was a lot of good cars in those days, but the Hudson just stood out.

I got a Hudson pick-up…a '46—two-tone blue with white wall tires. We recently got a call from video people. They needed an old pick-up because they were making a video for a young singer, Cindy Lauper. I figure what do you got to lose.

Joe Jr. working

Recent build for TV build competition

Serino Hot Rod event

Joe Jr. working

Serino Hot Rod garage

Anthony White pinstriping Jeff Rogan Triumph build at Serino Rod event

Old Serino Hot Rod photo

Serino Hot Rod garage

Old Serino Hot Rod photo

Now, there are these TV shows about all this car culture. Competitions between different shops. Everything has changed so much. Now, there are all sorts of modern technologies inside the car. This is how it is today. It has become very different. Times change, cars change but I remember many of these old cars like it was yesterday. That's the way it goes in our world today.

Cars have been in my family for generations. Serino Hot Rod goes back quite a ways.

Serino Hot Rod card

Bob Germino

Bob Germino

WE GOT OUR SENSE OF STYLE FROM LOOKIN' AT THE CARS

Williamsburg, Brooklyn

I was born in Williamsburg. It's a neighbor of Greenpoint. I married a girl from Greenpoint. I've always had cars since I was younger. I was sixteen when I got my first car. I was livin' on Meserole Street between Union and Lorimer in Williamsburg. I wanted to quit school, I always had a problem with school, I never liked it. My father said, you're not going to sit home. You have to get a job and do something.

I had a brother-in-law out on Long Island. His uncle had a junk shop where he had all old cars and parts. He said, look—I'm going to take this boy out to my place for the summer and I'll get him a car and get him his license. So I said, "OK, this is good." I got a little job. Sixty dollars a week. My brother-in-law brought me to a junk yard and I bought a 1938 Plymouth for forty bucks. He said, "Every night when you come home, I'll let you go get five gallons of gas. I want you to drive around my junk yard until your gas runs out. That's all you can drive for the day." I said great. I was learnin' to drive and this was a junk yard. Perfect.

In the junk yard there was a big circle so I drove this '38 around and around. The car was a stick shift. I smashed into everything. I hit everything. I knocked everything down. It was like a demolition derby. Nobody cared, it was a junkyard. It was great. That's how I learned to drive. I drove around every day. I saved my money from my job. I bought my mother a washing machine for her birthday. The whole experience helped me build my moral character.

So I had this beat up car and I got my junior license at like seventeen. The '38 I had was a gray four door. It was nice. Every day I burned through the five gallons of gas I was allowed to buy. My sister had a fit every day. I would kick up a huge amount of dust drivin' around the junk yard. The whole yard was full of smoke, the house was full of smoke, the neighborhood was full of smoke, dust, whatever. That car burned oil like you wouldn't believe. I kept drivin'. That was 1953.

In those days things were very different with cars. Around '53 there were very few car commercials. It was a very new idea to own your own car. People didn't consider it. Commercials were rare. Later on in '57 I can remember things started to change.

After that '38 I had maybe a dozen cars. I had a '48 Hudson, an old "cockroach car" we used to call them. They were brown and long, just like a cockroach. When I was about eighteen I had a '49 Mercury convertible. That was a beautiful convertible with rainbow seat covers. I was goin' out with my wife at the time. We'd go to Rockaway and ride the Cross Bay Boulevard. I'd be speeding down there and burning up rubber. There wasn't a cruise scene that I can remember. A bunch of guys would get together at the Bow Wow and get some burgers. They'd go and speed around. You have to remember, the whole thing of speed was a very new thing. To control your own speed? That was a whole new idea. A guy would challenge you, "I got a faster car than you." He'd try to make it to the next block before you. You'd be at the light and you'd hit it. A lot of times I'd be comin' back Cross Bay Boulevard and on Cross Bay and Woodhaven there's a tunnel. It's a sharp turn. You can't go more than like fifty miles an hour without hittin' the walls. I used to do like sixty-five, seventy and I'd be scrapin'

Bob and son's Chevy

Bob and son's Chevy

and I'd see sparks comin' off the front of the car. That was nice.

Back then, there were very few cars. I still remember when my father got his first car. When his father died he got a little money and he bought himself a '36 Packard. The old gangster car. He loved that. It had the big spare tire on the front fender there.

The car I have now is a '57 Chevy Bel Air. My son and I have been working on this car for some time. I bought it about 50% restored. It looked like a plumber's car. It had wires hangin' all over the place but it had a nice engine in it. It had a TPI (Tuned Port Injection) engine. Some people call them alley rats. They took all of the works out of an '89 Camaro and they put it into this car. When I got it, it needed a paint job and it needed restoration. Somebody had put Oldsmobile wheels on it. Me and my son brought the car back as a Bel Air. We put Kraigers on it. Later on we put a bigger engine in it. We changed the carburetion. I got a Chevy small block that came out of a '86 Camaro. But the engine has been worked. It's a race engine. It's been bored out sixty over. It's got sixty over forged pistons with polished rods. It's got a three-quarter cam in there. It's really hopped up. The engine's doin' about 490 horsepower. My son had it out a couple weeks ago on the highway to see what it will do. He was hittin' one-forty and it still wanted to go. He had plenty of room left with the pedal. I got Nitrous on it too. It got Nitrous one-hundred and fifty shot. This gives another 150 horsepower. I don't use it but I just like to know it's there.

Nitrous gives you a feeling of power. You know, you're out there talking to some body and they see the bottle, "Oh jeez, he's got a bottle in there." They say, "He's got the juice." If you need it, it's there. My son drives the car sometimes late night on the LIE (Long Island Expressway) and he'll give it a shot to see what the car will do. He's been through quite a few bottles of that.

A few years ago my son said, "Dad, why don't you get yourself a hobby. Get yourself a classic car." I grabbed this car for a good price and we've been working on it ever since. You see, the way these Chevys are made and particularly the '57, you can do anything to them. Now, the TPI its good but they can be trouble. We changed the engine to carburetion. We put two, four-barrels on the engine. They are five-hundred each. That's one-thousand carburetion on the top. The car is really hooked up now.

I was born in '37. At that time there was very little traffic in New York. There might have been two or three cars on the block where I was in Williamsburg. As a matter of fact, if a person had a car they were considered rich in those days. As young kids we would keep our eyes out for cars and we noticed the people that had cars. It was not all that common. We'd hang around on the block and we'd notice the cars. It was not something you took for granted. It was special. As kids we kept track of who and what; "Did you see that guy Joe? He's got a '59 Cadillac." We'd pay attention. We noticed and learned about a sense of style. We got our sense of style from lookin' at the cars.

I've always had a thing for style on the cars. I think that is very New York. You associate your style with your taste in cars. Me, I always liked the fin. The high fin in the back. And that's what got me with the '57 Chevy. If you notice, some of my cars I've had in the past: I've had a '59 Cadillac with the big fins, the double lights. I've had a '59 Chrysler, again with the fin. I made sure that my cars had fins on them. It gave me that rocket look. It was talkin' about airplanes and rockets. Years ago that's all you'd hear on TV—"Ride the 88. Ride the rocket." As a young kid that burned into my head. "Ride the rocket. Ride an Oldsmobile."

In the '30s and '40s people didn't worry much about speed. They worried about style. But in the '50s things changed. Young people came into the picture; they were worried about speed. You always thought about the speed—who's faster with their car. But back then doin' seventy or eighty was fast. Very fast. Now doin' one-hundred forty, one-hundred fifty is fast. Now they are race car drivers in the street. They are going two-hundred miles an hour.

When I was younger and you'd race on the streets you would set up at the corner under the traffic light. When the light changes you'd hit it. There was a little prism you would mount onto your dash. If you pulled up too far under the light you couldn't see it. So this prism it would reflect the light and you'd get the jump on the guy. That racing prism was an option that came with the '57 Chevy. There is a hole in the dash for it. Kids at that time were into racing that car. The prism gave you an advantage. But imagine a car company that is promoting speed and racing with a prism option! You would never see something like that today.

In those days you didn't race on tracks you raced in the street. And the best place for racing in New York was Cross Bay Boulevard. That was the longest stretch from Rockaway over the bridges. Rockaway Boulevard you had a long strip, maybe two three miles without cross streets. In Queens it was Woodhaven Boulevard. Once you got to the water you could really open up. Under the BQE you could really open up.

Years ago the cars were made different. The bodies, the steel—now it's all plastic. Now kids go out and buy a car for $60-70,000 and its all plastic. The steel alone in my '57 is unbelievable. It's a tank. That's what you want. Somethin' if you ever do get in a crack up, you won't end up bein' a part of the car.

When I was a kid, if you had an accident there were gypsies who would come around with a hammer and a piece of metal and they'd bang out the dent for $5. They would wander around neighborhoods looking for dents to bang out. A lot of the time they'd create more damage than they'd repair. You'd have to be careful with them.

In Brooklyn years ago during the '50s and '60s you'd see guys that pulled old cars apart. Maybe they'd have an old '29 Ford and they'd rip the hood off it. If you did see it, it was rare. In the '50s we'd get stories about the West Coast. California especially. They might have been ahead of us on the hot rods. We heard about the cars out there. But it was very far away. You never saw what they looked like. There was no way to see it. We'd have to try to imagine what people were talking about. Maybe we'd get our hands on a magazine. A guy would come back from out there and tell us how they went to a place at night and there were all these hot rods. You always looked at it as, that there is the place. Then you'd see it at the movies. *Bikini Beach* and all that.

My car is important to me in that way. It brings me back to the younger days. Just to park and see people react to it. To show it off. And also, something in my mind is to leave it down to my son and my grandson and so forth. They can enjoy it. So, it's like a lifetime thing. When we bought the car we took a picture of me, my son and my grandson wearing leather jackets. My grandson was four at the time. Now he's twelve. When I go to visit him, he always says, "Hey, where's my Chevy? Bring my Chevy back." That's nice.

A car is something you can pass on. My son has put a lot of work into this car. When I take it out if it's raining, my son says, "Be careful, that car's fifty somethin' years old. You'll rust the bottom out of it. When I am out with it, I enjoy the people's reactions. Especially the older people. They always say, "I used to have one of them. I rode in one of these."

I keep photos in the trunk; James Dean, Elvis. I set up photos from different decades when I go to car shows. I play certain music from the '50s. My wife thinks I'm crazy. My son likes the car for racing, I like the car as a way to travel back. People come over and they remember something that happened to them back then. They remember what they did on the back seat. It's roomy back there, if you know what I mean. They associate themselves with the car and what they did in the car.

The '50s were an ideal time for a lot of Americans. It was after the Depression, after the War. I remember then. My father drove a cab all his life. Times were bad years ago. Then after the War things started to boom. The '57 Chevy stood for something. It was American made. The style, the shape. It showed the force of America. It brought back a relationship America had after the War. That sense of power we used to have. Pure steel from America. When this car came out, America didn't depend on foreign countries. Ride a '57; the fins, the style. The future, the space age, prosperity. I set the car up two ways: the speed and the nitrous, the flames are for the younger people. I set up the interior for the older people. They remember what they did in that car. I play music from the '50s. Many times older people will start dancing around my car. My car is a time machine. I try to relate to young and old. I set up everything in that car to relate to people. My car has the power to do this. Cars have certain lines, a certain look. The GTO, the Camaro. Certain years, certain styles. They hit you. For my father's era it was the Packard, gangsters. For me, I think about the '59 Cadillac with the fins, the '63 Corvette Stingray.

Bob and son's Chevy

Interior of trunk time machine

"Big Daddy" George LeBlanc

DRIVING AT WEISSGLASS SPEEDWAY AND PINSTRIPING WITH ED "BIG DADDY" ROTH

Staten Island

The Weissglass speedway had opened in 1953. This was spring 1964. A friend who was thirteen years old had built a '55 Chevy for an older guy to drive at Weissglass. He asked me to letter it. I had my mother drop me off every day and I spent all day lettering this '55 Chevy for a week. It was horrible, but it was the first car I ever did. I ended up doing a lot of lettering of guy's cars at the track. For the next ten years I lettered almost every car at the track.

Big Daddy George with Weissglass stock car

Weissglass closed in 1972. Back in those days, that track was a part of people's lives on Staten Island. Back in that era, after World War II stock car racing grew all over the country. Guys were building race tracks but they had no cars. NASCAR had been established as a way to supply cars and divers. Weissglass became a NASCAR track. The owner, Gabe Rispoli, had the stadium that was a sporting facility. Baseball and horses. Gabe paved it to capitalize on the craze of stock car racing but he had no cars. So, he signed up with NASCAR, but it was your partner. You had to pay their officials; you had to pay a sanction fee every week. They were your partner and they were strict with their drivers. They weren't allowed to race on a non-sanctioned track. If you did you were banned for life. So, the drivers would run under different names because there was too much money to be made then.

Guys made fortunes then. Back in the early fifties guys worked for $50–60 a week. If you were a real good mechanic and a good driver and you were able to win, the main events at Weissglass paid $100. And you could run seven nights a week. For example, Bruno Bracky. He was an exceptional talent as far as a mechanic. He knew how to set

Big Daddy George racing, 1969

Big Daddy George opening night, 1969

Weissglass race

Weissglass poster

Weissglass poster

Weissglass stock car

Weissglass poster

the cars up to make them handle. He was a great chassis man, a great driver, and he was a great business man all in all. He built race cars and sold them. At that time everything was a flat head four. That was the standard stock. Thirty-seven Ford was the standard stock car. It was small, it was light. That was the car everyone wanted to use.

Bruno became very good with the flat heads. He ran Freeport Tuesday, Friday, and Saturday. Saturday was the big night. Drivers raced for forty percent of the gate. So Saturday night there were 6,000 people there. A $1.50 admission. Freeport paid well. Back in the late fifties that track paid $700 and Bruno won a lot. He did everything himself. There were no pit crews. You did everything yourself. When I raced there I'd get a flat tire and I'd have to fix it.

Back then Weissglass ran on Thursday night; Roosevelt stadium in Jersey City ran on Friday night. They were NASCAR sanctioned. Freeport ran on Saturday but it was not NASCAR sanctioned. So there was Bruno at Freeport and Johnny Frank at Weissglass and Jersey City. Sunday he would go all the way to Hightstown, New Jersey, and he was a mailman. He had a regular job. And a lot of people would show up to watch. Freeport regularly had 3500 people.

Alan Weissglass was very active in the community. It was a big family run dairy on Staten Island. They built ball fields for little league. Gabe took over Weissglass stadium in 1952. He was a baseball and football promoter. There was a racetrack that came up for sale and Gabe jumped on it in '52, paved it, and opened up a stock car track in '53. Then Alan Weissglass gave Gabe $700 for some improvements and that's why it was called Weissglass stadium. At the end of the races, Alan would come down and present the winner with a trophy. As time wore on you'd see less and less of Alan.

The main event started with eighteen cars. You had to run a ten lap heat. You'd have as many as fifty cars show up to make that heat. In 1958 Gabe started a jalopy division for bone stock street cars. They were very affordable. Back then you could buy an old car for $10. Take the glass out and you had a race car. In those races there were no rules. You could spin guys out. They also had a demolition derby that was very popular.

With the main event you had to run a ten lap heat. They took four cars out of that for a semi-final race that took two cars, then there was a consolation race which only took the winner. And that car got into the main event. If you didn't get into the main event you didn't get any money. It was a big deal to make the main event. The bulk of the racers were from New Jersey. Then Gabe started a Staten Island division to develop local interest so local guys would build cars. Gabe would have the NASCAR event and then he'd have a NASCAR-Staten Island event. Within three years he had enough drivers so he didn't need NASCAR any more. He

Weissglass stock car

Weissglass stock car

dumped them and started to sanction the Hollywood style stock car race.

There was a TV show back then called *Jalopy Racers* from Hollywood. A half hour show in the 1950s. They had really violent crack-ups. They'd show a '32 Ford flying through the air and then they'd interview the guy stumbling around. Gabe capitalized on that. People came in hopes of seeing cars flipping all over the place like the TV show.

Back then all the cars were pretty much the same. They were '35 to '41 Fords. There were guys who were on the ball and knew how to handle their cars. There were guys who got tips from New Jersey guys and NASCAR guys. They'd buy parts from Jersey guys and get some driving tips. Guys who had a few dollars to spend, businesses, junkyards, body shops. Those guys made it to the top. The best cars came from shops. Mostly Ford Flatheads. A couple guys ran Plymouths with Chrysler engines in them. They were all Flatheads. Gabe didn't allow overhead valve engines until 1965. The track was small and wasn't that wide. Chevy had the V8 in 1955, but you weren't allowed to use it. It was all Flatheads. Pretty much the rules were the engines had to be stock in appearance. They had to have one carburetor. You could bore them out, you could put racing cams in them, you could put big valves in them but they had to look stock.

By 1964–65 the drivers were complaining that they couldn't find Flathead engines, so Gabe finally let them run overhead valve engines in 1965. So most guys ran 283 Chevys, 292 Fords, and 312 Fords. They were the most popular. With all that power they had to put bigger tires on the cars and they were faster. It was a very tight track. It was only a fifth of a mile and it wasn't that wide so it hurt the racing. You couldn't run side by side. With the Flatheads with eight inch slicks on them you could run side by side. You could pass and this made for good racing. When the cars got too fast, it was follow the leader. It was too hard to pass. The guy on the inside, unless he's trying really hard to hold his car down to allow you to be out there all he's got to do is slip six inches and you're in the fence. So, the quality of the racing suffered and spectators dropped off.

They had a driver's strike in 1965 and all the name drivers that had a following went on strike. The cars were getting expensive and the drivers wanted more money. Gabe refused to give in and the top drivers left his track. There were three divisions: the top; the middle division, class B, which was a stepping stone from the Jalopies to encourage those guys to move up. It was tough because it was expensive. The jalopy guys wanted to stay jalopy. Gabe had a rule, if you won three jalopy races, you had to move up. So guys intentionally held back. It was too fast and too expensive. The class B division allowed one slick on the left to try to improve the quality of the racing, but it was never the same after the strike.

I had graduated high school in 1964 and I had no intention to go to college. There was a postgraduate automotive course you could start immediately and it was free. I got in that program and that's where I learned how to build engines, body work, and welding I learned on my own. Back then nobody had any money. You couldn't pay anybody so you had to do it yourself. I got a welder and learned how to weld; I got a grinder and body tools. I learned how to do body work. I had always been drawn to metal. I was attracted to this kind of thing from a very young age. I always liked painting. I got pretty good with a brush.

I went in the Army in '66 and I didn't start racing until I got out in '69. I was getting ready to buy a car in '66. This guy had a really decent car for $300. A '36 coup with a 6-cylinder Flathead Chrysler engine. That was the hot set-up for a Plymouth—if you ran a Plymouth you took a big Flathead six out of a '54 Chrysler—it was 265 cubic inch. It was the biggest Flathead six you could get. You put it in the Plymouth and it ran pretty good. My parents said, "You ain't bringin' no stock car in here." So that was the end of that.

So, I got drafted that September in '66 so it didn't make much of a difference. I was in the service for two years. One year in Vietnam. The only thing on my mind that year in Vietnam was getting back to Weissglass, getting a car and racing. In the Army I did K.P. duty and guard duty for guys who didn't want to do it. They would pay me and I'd put the money away to build a car when I got out. I had a few car parts catalogs in Vietnam and every month they got orders from me. When I got home from Vietnam my basement was full of boxes of stock car parts and I started building my car—it was a '32 Plymouth coupe. I built the engine myself. I spent the whole winter building that car. I had a brand new car ready for opening night 1969.

I was twenty-two. I got out on the track that night and realized I had a lot to learn. I had all good equipment on it, brand new slicks and racing shocks. I tried to use some of the knowledge I thought I had learned from reading the different scarce publications. The Weissglass track was a fifth of a mile. The main event had eighteen cars. In the old days you'd have fifty cars show up but towards the end you'd be lucky if eighteen cars showed up. It took a lot of experience to tweak the suspension and drive the car. It was a flat track. It took me that first year to learn how to keep up with the pack. The following year I changed a few things. I changed the camber on the front tire; you had to tilt it in a certain amount so when you went into the turn the car leveled up. I changed the rear end ratio—I started with a 486 in second gear and it was too much for the engine. I put in a 411 and it was better. When Fords had sixty horsepower engines there was one gear ratio. As the horsepower got higher the rears changed.

The early Fords—'36, '37—they had 941, which was a 456 ratio. Then they had a 940 and a 937, which was a 411. Guys had the second gears figured out with the cluster gears and the rears right down to a T. Most guys were running 937s in second gear. You had to stagger your tires; your right rear tire had to be no more than two inches larger than the left rear tire. That's what makes the car turn. Like when you roll and ice cream cone. It turns. You would have the gas pedal pushed all the way down for the whole track except when you came off the first turn. You would hold the car to the floor for as long as you could without flipping over. You could feel the car going up on two wheels most of the time. At the third turn you'd be up off the ground so you'd let up for a second, crash back down and then to the floor again. You had shoulder straps and an open face helmet. You raced in a t-shirt. You had a roll bar. The safety equipment was minimal. Nobody thought they were going to get hurt. I saw cars flip, the roll bar would break and the car would keep flipping and the broken roll bar would be beating the driver as it kept flipping. He'd be better off without it.

Races were structured. At Weissglass drivers and cars were positioned for the start of the race depending on their points and how they had placed at the race the preceding week. Cars that had finished badly the week before started at the front. They would try to hold on to the lead but the fast guys would work their way through the field and take over the race. The track was narrow. If two cars ran side by side, there was no way anyone could pass unless they hit you hard. In those days you were allowed to bang into other cars. One car would hit another a couple times to make them move. If you didn't move, you'd get spun out. You really had to pay attention. You were constantly turning around the track. There was no straight away. You were constantly driving that car. The centrifugal force was intense. Things happened quick. You would be looking one turn ahead of yourself to look for trouble. This was physical racing. I had worked a lot on my car and I didn't want to wreck. Guys would run up over you and then squeeze down on you. They'd rub their tires onto yours. They'd try to shake you up so you would back off.

You'd race with the same guys every week. You got to know who you could beat who you couldn't. Who was a clean driver and who wasn't. Who you could trust on the outside; who you couldn't. You would not want to get on the outside of some people because they'd push you right into the fence. Being a fifth of a mile and running in second gear, top speed was probably sixty-five or seventy. This doesn't sound fast but remember you are running on a tight track and you were really flying around. Some cars were set up so that the left front tire was always in the air. It never touched the ground. Back then the thinking was if you had one tire up in the air the other three had to be down pretty good.

What determined if the left front lifted was the stiffness of the right front spring. If you had a tight right front spring the left tire lifted. Some guys would chain the axel to the chassis and this would lift the left front. If you were running a torque tube '37 Ford you put a model A spring and cross member in the rear which lowered the car down. That was a popular set up. There was a center bolt on the spring and the cross member had a hole in the center where the spring bolt was located. Guys would drill another hole off to the right and then set the spring there. It would offset the rear of the car and offset the weight to the left. Guys would drill into the cross member and tighten the springs. The whole idea was to form a wedge in the car that would transfer the weight to the right rear when you went into the corner. It was crude by today's standards. To measure things, you'd set up the car and then jack it up to see if the left rear came off the ground before the right rear tire. If you could put three fingers under the left rear tire before the right rear came off the ground then the car was good. This was setting the wedge in the car.

At Weissglass, one of the most popular drivers was Tiny Milano. He drove very nice looking cars for that era and he always had white wall tires, and his cars were always black and red. He wore a black and red outfit and driver's gloves. As years went on, the cars evolved more into race cars that were built by local body shops. He was careful with his car so he didn't win too many races but he was flashy and popular.

The guys ran different kinds of gasoline. I ran pump Sunoco 260. But everyone had a little secret. Some guys would put brake fluid in their gas. Some guys would put castor oil in the gas. Make it run hotter and get more power. There were two local engine builders on Staten Island that worked on Flatheads. You went to Gus the Greek or Pop Carlson. Back in those days very few guys had the money to pay Gus the Greek to build an engine. Carlson would build an engine for what it cost. He wanted to be there and watch a car go around with his engine in it. Then a lot of guys built their own engines. They were good mechanics. They got the Flathead blocks and bored them out and put different cams in them and they got a lot of good power out of those Flathead engines.

In 1965 the track finally allowed overhead valve engines and Flatheads were pretty much done. You could get more power out of a stock 283 or a stock 292 Ford. You had six cylinders and guys would put 223 Ford six-cylinder engines in there. Put a cam in there with a couple carburetors and they ran good. Guys were putting in 283s with adapters bolted up to the '39 Ford transmissions. Of course there was a lo

Weissglass race

Weissglass race

more power. Guys were blowing up rears. Their transmissions were designed for a ninety horsepower Flathead and now you had a 250...300 horsepower engine. So they tended to blow the first or second gear. There were guys changing transmissions in the pits who had it down to like twenty minutes.

Being a torque tube car you'd have to drop the rear end and pull the rear back. It was a job to change the transmission in an old Ford. There were guys changing two or three a night. Back then the old Ford transmissions were getting scarce. Weissglass was one of the last raceways that favored the torque tube drive shaft. The rear ends were all bolted solid. Ford used that set up from the Model T days to '48. With racing, the rear end would not get wrapped up. Ford kept that buggy spring suspension until '48. It was the last company to go to an independent suspension and the overhead engine in '49. He wanted to save money—keep that proven and cheap method of building cars. He kept the Flathead until '53. It was up to 200 horsepower but it was the same.

In 1972 the promoter waited until half way through the season to tell us, but we all knew that was it. We had a meeting in the pits but we almost didn't believe it. He said don't sell your cars but I knew all the parts I had stashed would be worthless. I sold my car and all my parts and Gabe never opened a new track. According to him he had the only license to operate a racetrack in New York City. He thought about partnering up but that was about it.

I got into pinstriping. I'd be at a show pinstriping a car and I'd have sixty people watching me. During the 1980s there was a pinstripe craze on Staten Island. All these guys drove the same kind of car—Firebirds, Iroc Zs, Monte Carlos. It lasted about nine years. It started around '82 until about '91. I thought the next generation would pick it up but they didn't. Maybe leasing cars had something to do with it but it just went away.

I was very lucky that I had the background. Guys would be working on their cars and I'd be lettering them. During the '80s I had cars lined up to Forest Avenue seven days a week. The first car would pull in at nine o'clock in the morning and many nights I'd be in the Pathmark parking lot lettering till two o'clock in the morning. I'd be painting these guys' cars and drinking a beer and talking. At one point I lined the cars up like an assembly line. Names, dates, nick-names, stripes. It got intense. I never measured, I never used a grease pencil. I just did it. It came out centered. Roth, Von Dutch, there was a symmetry. A mirror effect. It's got to be the same on both sides.

When I worked with Roth he always commented that I was a "snapper"—snap the job out and go to the next one. A lot of time Roth needed to use a grease pencil to help him lay things out. I didn't need it and it helped me with the speed. When I worked with Roth he'd comment, "What are you doing?" about me not using guidelines. Years later it got back to me that Roth had said a lot of good things about me. For a while Roth and I were pretty good friends. I helped him and he helped me. We were both broke. It was a novelty thing for me doing pinstriping. This was the late '80s. He was trying to get back to the swing of it—he was printing how-to books. He restarted his mail order business. He got a contract with a toy company doing plastic models of all his cars. His attitude changed after that. He started wearing a sport jacket at the shows. A white shirt and a tie. He told me I had to wear a jacket.

When I was working with Ed Roth, he was in the process of trying to own all the copyrights to Rat Fink. He didn't own any of them. Even going back to the '60s when Revell was making all the models. He didn't own any of it—candy, toys, comic books, t-shirts, models. Each one was a separate thing. He sold it to the Japanese. He got royalties. Then his five sons from his first marriage and his wife from his first marriage pooled their money and hired a lawyer and sued him. They wanted Rat Fink. One of his sons backed a truck up and cleaned the whole place out. Ed finally won the suit for the rights to his Rat Fink. It was not a good story.

I remember when Rat Fink first came out in 1962. I didn't find it very interesting. I still feel the same way about it. Ed's monster shirts were great. The only access you had to this stuff was *Rod and Custom* magazine. There was no cable, no Internet, no nothing. I bought my first *Car Craft* magazine; it was the May 1961 issue. I still have it. On the cover are Ed Roth and Beatnik Bandit. I still consider that the best hot rod going. The first car Roth built was the Outlaw. It was a fiberglass take off of a T. He made the mold and the glass body. It was a wild take off of a T. Revell liked the car and they made a model of it. With Revell the deal was once they made the Outlaw, he had to have a new car ready by every January first. The car would start touring and then they'd make a kit. He was under a lot of pressure to have a new car ready every January. He had a very good artist, Joe Henning, who drew the cars for him. Roth would make a plaster mold as close as he cold to the drawings.

The first Joe Henning drawing of Beatnik Bandit was a tall T coupe. A wild looking body with a unique roof. Darryl Starbird, who made the Predicta, showed Ed how to make a bubble top. Ed named one of his sons Darryl. He put that top on Beatnik Bandit and that changed everything. A lot of young guys started to pay attention to Roth's cars. The twin engines, Cyclops headlight. That was pretty wild for the time. Then he built the Road Agent. It was a Corvair powered car.

I was always a fan of Ed going back to 1962. I was racing go-karts down the street from where I lived at the Weissglass stadium. I was building model cars like most of the kids back in those days. Revell portrayed an image of a beatnik guy with the beard and "Hey, man," the Beatnik talk. It attracted a lot of rebellious teenagers. He had full page ads in *Rod and Custom* of all his t-shirts. All his classic designs. I started copying his monster shirts with a magic marker. I started doing t-shirts when I was fifteen.

Things changed for Roth as my age group started to grow up. From model cars and hot rods to girls and the Vietnam War; getting drafted. Going to college to avoid the draft, getting a job. Roth's entire fan base of rebellious teenagers went away over night. He told me he got a penny a kit in royalties. At his peak he told me he got a check for six thousand a month. That's a lot of kits. Plus he had his t-shirt business and he was building cars. The Outlaw ran, the Beatnik Bandit ran but it had a hydraulic stick steering set up with a center stick that controlled the whole car. It worked. You turn the stick and the car turns. Push it forward the engine accelerates; pull it back, the car brakes. Roth was a concept guy but he was also a craftsman. He knew his stuff. He built most of the stuff himself. He did hire guys who were experts for upholstery, Larry Watson did painting; he painted Beatnik Bandit, he painted the Outlaw. In fact, he painted most of his cars. He had guys working around the clock—sanding and plastering. Getting that mold ready for the fiberglass. He'd come in the morning and there would be a guy sleeping on the car. They'd throw that guy on the ground and start sanding. It must have been pretty intense.

He built several cars where he got half way through and he didn't like it and he busted it up and threw it on the scrap pile. One particular vehicle he called the Wishbone; it was a Volkswagen-powered thing with crazy looking forks coming out. He finished it and took it to Revell but they took one look at it and said no, the parts are too thin. We can't use it. So he brought it back to the shop and cut it up into pieces. One of the workers, Dirty Doug, he took it and put it all back together and took it to another model company and tried to get them interested. Roth's whole life was treachery and betrayal.

When it was finally over with Revell, he started riding bikes. He claimed he was the first guy who ever made a VW trike. He even patented it. When the show car scene was over and the model thing was over he got into motorcycles. He published a magazine, *Choppers*. He sold it to a big publishing company. Then he started

Ed "Big Daddy" Roth business card

Druid Princess build by "Big Daddy" George

Arial photo of Weissglass Speedway

building three wheelers. He made fiberglass bodies for them. He was going around, all over California buying Volkswagens. Then he started building V8 trikes. The foot pegs came off the valve covers. He made fiberglass bodies for them.

He got into drag racing. He built a rail dragster called the Yellow Fang. He spent a ton of money on that and then he got sick of that. He said he got the idea for the V8 trikes because he was looking at the narrow rear end of one of is dragsters. He took the engine and transmission and rolled it over and put it on the rear end. Then he made a frame and a body. They actually looked pretty nice. But they were very unstable. They couldn't corner even with the big back tires. When you went to turn, the whole thing flipped over. A lot of guys got killed. So, he was doing the triking and then he got into the Hells Angels. Revell told him stop with the Hells Angels or we will cancel your contract. He said no and they cancelled his contract. In fact MPC did build a model of one of his Mail Box choppers. That was the last model any company made. That was a bad period for him. At some point he became a Mormon and he said that's what saved him. Then he got a job as a sign painter at Knotts Berry Farm and he worked there for ten years to get away from his crazy friends and that whole lifestyle.

He continued to build three wheelers for himself. One was a Honda powered thing called Rubber Ducky. He went very low key. He disappeared. Then in the 70s there was a documentary made about him. In the mid 70s there was resurgence about the 60s. A lot of guys were older, settled down, married. By the mid-70s there was a new interest in hot rods and vintage kits. I started selling them. One day I got a letter in the mail from Ed Roth. I organized shows of model cars. I always had it in the back of my mind to ask Ed to do one of these shows. So I called him up and told him, "I am having a model car

Raceway sign

show on Staten Island, you want to come?" He said, "get me a tuxedo and we'll do it." He had all his cars at Cars of the Stars at Knotts Berry Farm. They were all in pretty bad condition. Then the museum closed and he sold all of his cars, all the motorcycles, everything for $5,000 to Harrah's Casino.

Ed and I did a lot of shows together in the New York area. We started with Lead East in New Jersey, Nassau Coliseum Thanksgiving weekend. Then we hit Syracuse. Wherever he got invited. It was something new for me, even though I had been doing pinstriping and lettering since I was a teenager. When I was a kid I didn't know anything about One-Shot. I was using whatever I could find in a hardware store. Rustolium. I did know enough to get my hands on a pinstripe brush. I struggled and learned.

I restored antique cars. I had three guys working here April to September for several years. This place was jumping. I built a Druid Princess car. It took me four years between everything to build the car. Finally, when I finished the car, Roth saw it but he didn't say nothing about the car. He never thought I could build it. He got mad. We were still doing shows together airbrushing t-shirts. Ed would paint the monsters and I'd paint the cars. Initially it was gratifying. It was an opportunity to work with Roth. He taught me things about hand lettering that I needed to learn. As years went on the bubble burst. Back in '60-'61 Revell had given him that Big Daddy name. In those days of the bohemian coffee shops, the Big Daddy was the guy behind the counter who made the coffee and ran the place. It was a beatnik thing. I use Big Daddy George because Roth was a big influence for me. Ed and I worked together and it was good. I remember that May 1961 issue of *Car Craft* with the Beatnik Bandit on the cover. That was a huge influence. I have the same feeling today as when I looked at that for the first time. That was a great car.

Window decal

Museum card

Ray Ray

Ray Ray

I LOVE BIKES, I LOVE JUST THE SMELL OF THEM

Brooklyn

I was upstate from like '71 to '80. That's a long time, but that saved my life, bro. I was so fucked up in the street that I was going to end up the way all my friends did. They didn't die of old age. I lived two lives. I got a good life now. I'm just chillin'.

When I was a kid I loved cars. My father used to take me to the New York Coliseum. I must have been eight or nine years old. Every year he bought me the book that showed you every car that was in there. The weight, the wheel base; you know, all that bullshit. I loved cars. That was my first love. I was six years old; I had a motorcycle jacket on; a motorcycle hat. You know? What kid don't like motorcycles? This is '56 maybe.

I grew up on a block where there were bookies who ran a candy store. Me and my friends used to rob the candy store. At night we'd take $20 worth of quarters and go shoot pool in the pool room. But the guy who owned it and his friends are what I call "knock around guys". They did crazy shit. They both had big fucking Harleys. I rode on 'em with the guys. I'd jump on the back of the big fucking seats. They'd say, "Come on Ray!" I loved it man. I loved just the smell of it.

I consider myself a street guy, but I was a good guy. When I graduated high school I worked construction. Good money. I used to fix up my cars. Oh man, I had some bad cars. I had a '69 Thunderbird; I had a '77 Buick Regal. But see, I'd get a regular car and I'd make somethin' look really fuckin' nice. On my Thunderbird, I put gangster

High School photo, c. 1962

Early photos

Ray Ray incarcerated

Gangster white walls, c. 1970

Gangster white walls, c. 1970

Punch you out

white walls; the real ones. This is over thirty years ago. You didn't see fuckin' cars with gangster white walls. I used to go out there every day with a fucking Brillo pad. They were the whitest white walls you'd ever want to see. I'm tellin' ya. People used to, "Wow! Wow! Wow!" The car was black, it had a T top. You know, you take the glass off. It was a beautiful fucking car.

Then I had an orange pick-up. Thirty-three inch high wheels. Twelve and a half inches wide. I put a big roll bar on it. Big spot lights. That fuckin' truck was bad. I just ran around the street crazy in it. It was really nice.

I didn't do it but I grew up watchin' street racing. I was too young. But on 1st Avenue and 37th Street, every night they had fucking races. Guys used to come with their race cars on fucking flat beds. They'd race for registrations. The firemen used to come hose the street down so they wouldn't race. As soon as it was dry? Wow! What a fuckin' race track that was. I was like twelve years old but I loved that. That got me into the cars, too.

They were racing stock cars. Then you'd get cars that were suped-up. They'd race for each other's cars; for registrations. Put up your registration. Whoever loses, loses their car. That's some serious shit. If you lose, you give up your car. You back out of it, you wind up gettin' fuckin' killed. There'd be more than a hundred people watchin'. You couldn't get down the fuckin' avenue. It was dangerous too. Whenever you'd fly down the street there's always a hump. A guy got killed. The Corvette came off the ground and when he was up he had turned the wheel, when he came down the car went ba-boom, knocked over the Johnny pumps. The motor came out of the car; the guy was dead. Then they really started breakin' balls down there. I think that ended it; after that guy got killed. Along the Belt Parkway by Kennedy Airport—I forget what they call

Standing with bike

Bike scene

photo of Ray Ray
taken by a friend

Bike at Brooklyn Bridge

that stretch—that was a fuckin' famous raceway over there, too.

First bike I bought I was eighteen. And I've had a bike ever since. It was a '69 Sportster. All stock. It was 1,000 cc's. It was an Iron Head. All engraved. I did a ton of work on it. I'm not a mechanic, I'm lucky if I can change a sparkplug. But I am into detail. I like to do spike nuts instead of acorns. The way I hook things up; people like it.

I rode around like I do now. I hang out with a couple guys who own bikes. We go to the feast in Manhattan. To the feast on 18 Avenue. We go to Coney Island. Maybe go upstate. That '69, I didn't have it too long. I learned on it. I sold it and bought this one.

It's fucking dangerous riding around Manhattan. Especially the cabbies. All they want to do is race around and get the next fare on the corner. The pot holes, the traffic, the cops. You need to look around at ten different things before you pull out. It's a challenge. I love it.

I changed a lot of things on the bike I got now. I had a 3-inch-wide, 21-inch-high tire on the front. Then I seen a bike like mine with a low 16-inch tire and wide like the motorcycle cops. I liked the look of that. It's a fat heavier look. I changed it.

I've had offers to join a few clubs but I'm not into that. I like to ride when I want to ride. You know. These mother fuckers call you up three o'clock in the morning: "Yo, we're goin' on a run." Fuck you, you're goin' on a run. Go ahead, I'll see ya. Not me. And when you're a prospect you're like a fuckin' jerk. Go get this, go get that. Go watch the bikes, go clean my wife's ass. Get the fuck outta here. I spent too much time in prison and had people tell me all them years what to do, when to do it, and how to do it. That's not me bro. I'm a man. This is my home and I do what the fuck I want. Any way I want to. I've been deprived of that for ten years. I do what I want when I want to do it. If it's illegal I keep it to myself. I live a straight life. I don't fuck nobody around. And that's how I expect them to treat me. I like being an independent rider.

To be honest, I think there's more clubs now than before. When I was a kid, all you knew was like HA. Now that I'm older and I see all these clubs. Just in Brooklyn you got the Bridge Runners; you got the Non Knights; you got the 69rs; you got the Crazy Pistons; the Filthy Dirty Mad Dogs; you got the Low Riders; Carribe, a Spanish club; the Hidden Faces, they're in Manhattan. I don't know why there would be more clubs today than in the old days. I'm not really into that club shit.

They talk about paying dues. These are grown fucking men, bro; they're still paying fucking dues? Grow out of that shit, bro. I don't know, everybody's different. These guys follow guys around. Can I get you a coffee? Can I wipe your bike down? What are you crazy? If I do that, I do it to my own bike.

I am always thinking about my bike. If I had a couple extra thousand dollars I'd have the bike stripped down. Whatever ain't new on there, I'd make it new. I'd have a new wiring harness put on it. My bike is thirty-three years old. I got an electrical short now. I want to put my blue lights on and there's a fucking short. It bothers me. Even if it's the fucking day time and you don't need the lights, it bothers me that the blue lights don't work. I like my shit to be 100%. I get upset. Most definitely, besides my family, that's the only thing I think about and worry about. If I had a $1,000 in my pocket and it was going to cost me $1,002 to fix my bike and I was hungry; I'd borrow the $2 and go hungry. It's a passion. I'm fucking obsessed. When I ride around the city, my heads that big. I've been riding forty fucking years. A lot of people know me.

Bikes can change you. I had a friend; he's dead now. He was a super technical guy. He had a high tech job at a water plant. Nicest

Ray Ray in his van

guy you could ever meet, but when he was riding you could never see his teeth. No smiles. It was strange. On the bike he was Mr. Mad Man. Just a mean fuckin' look. Off the bike he'd be smilin'.

I ride around; I don't smile at people because you gotta give these mother fuckers a mean look. They are two inches away from you. I look like, "What the fuck? You wanna go up my fuckin' ass?" One day goin' along Fort Hamilton Parkway, the mother fucker behind me with his horn. I see the red light a couple hundred feel ahead so I go even slower. I get to the light; the bitch comes along side of me. It turned out to be a woman. So I'm lookin'. I say, "Open your window." She cracks her window and I say, "If you were a guy, my bike would be off and I'd break your mother fucking face." I said, "You got balls!" Know what she did? She closed her window and pulled away like I didn't even say nothin' to her. I'm lookin' to go to blows with this guy and it's an old lady. She looked at me and closed the window like nothing happened. I thought, "*You got balls lady*." She blew my mind. I need a girlfriend like that.

It's like when I was a kid I went to Prospect Park where they have the horses; where you get on the horse and they trail you around the park for an hour. When you're on that horse you feel like a king. Like you are fifteen feet high. That's how I feel on my bike and I'm not a kid no more but I still get that feeling.

It's nice, especially when you have a nice place to go to. Like when Indian Larry had his events at the Hard Rock Café on 43rd and Broadway. We'd all park right on fuckin' Broadway. Talk about tourists and girls?! You'd meet people from all over the world. People like motorcycles. Most definitely they like the excitement. Yeah, I'm hip. I did a video with Latoya Jackson. The director came up and said, "Give me that fucking mean look that you got." That makes me feel

Ray Ray at his garage

Ray Ray in his workshop

Ray Ray's bike

Ray Ray with bike

good. I love that shit. They used my bike in a Revlon commercial.

It was a 1200 when it was built. Now it's got a 96-inch stroker motor. You know, the whole nine yards—high performance spark plugs, a new coil. You know, all the good shit. I've changed the paint job in the last twenty years maybe five times. Changed my tires, changed my rims. I've changed everything. You get tired of the old stuff. You want to be creative. I can change my bike everyday. Whether it's like changing the position of a skull that I put on the bike. Puttin' another skull somewhere else where there was none. I just like being creative and doing my own shit like everyone else. Everybody is the same way. No matter what bike you're lookin' at or who you're talking to, everybody wants to do their own thing. And they think it's cool and so do I.

Somebody might come up and say, "Why'd you do your floor boards like this?" Hey, that's the way I like it, bro. What, you don't like it? Don't look. You gonna tell me how to shave? How to trim my beard? You gonna tell me what side to hang my cock on? Left side or right side? What's the deal man? I think it's up to the person. I might say, "Why the fuck did he do that?" It's stupid or its crazy or its endangering your health. Whatever it is. If he likes it, it's fine.

I'm riding forty years. Since I'm seventeen I'm riding. I don't care who you are, bro. I know lawyers riding, I know cops that ride and I know outlaws that ride. Who ever's on that bike if they are enjoying it; no problem. I see women riding. They can ride with me; I don't care.

I rode in Florida, South Carolina. I rode in Jersey. It's all good except for the roads. You know, when you're out of New York you can ride with your eyes closed. You don't have to worry about pot holes. Or metal plates in the road where you're going to go down or something. You go in them southern states you can ride with your eyes closed. So smooth. You can enjoy it so much. In Manhattan you gotta be on the ball, otherwise you're dead. You gotta watch out for the potholes, gotta watch out for the people ridin' in the summer time with their windows closed with their air-conditioning on, radio blasting. They don't even know they run you over and they keep goin'. So you gotta really be on the defensive mode when you're riding. Especially in Manhattan. I hit a pothole once; good thing I saw it and I slowed down to the point where my front tire went in it and I was holding the bike up. Half the tire was in the hole. It had to be two feet deep. If I woulda hit it without seein' it I'd be dead. My front wheel woulda went in there and I woulda went north. Probably landed on my skull. You're a dead man.

I like goin' fast. I don't do it all the time but I do it when I know I'm on a familiar road. Where I don't have to worry about holes. I don't want to hit a hole doin' ninety. I'll pick a particular part of the parkway where I can go and get my shit off. Other than that I don't mind just blastin' around the streets.

When somethin' happens to my bike it's my attitude. You can't talk to me. My wife don't even want to look at me. I'm a different guy. When my bike is down, I'm down. Don't even say hello to me. Until my bike is fixed, then I'm in a better mood. It could be the slightest thing but I won't be able to sleep. I take it to that extreme. Look I got a heart condition. If I don't take my medication for my heart, I say, "I'll take it tomorrow." What's the big deal. But if something's wrong with my bike I won't be able to sleep. I'll be calling people up trying to fix it myself. I'm telling ya. It's not just a passion but it's somethin' more. Somethin' a lot more than passion. You have to find a new word for the feelings I get outta my bike. It ain't even human. Can you dig that? I don't have another feeling that can compare to that. I can have an orgasm; it's the greatest feeling in the world. Shooting a bag of dope is the greatest feeling in the world but my bike is a completely different thing. To me it's the greatest feeling in the world. Can you understand that, bro? It's down to the point exactly where I want to get at.

In my own mind I am talking to a higher authority when I'm on my bike. Definitely. Whether other people see it that way or not, I really don't care. That feeling of passion, but it's a bigger word that I can't explain. That's the way it is.

Ray Ray

Ray Ray with bike

Ray Ray's bike in garage

I only work on the Harley Davidson's. They come out with an Evolution in 1984 and they used it up until 1999. You can still buy a new one if you want from Harley. The parts are all interchangeable for all the Evolution motors. Now, the Suzuki's and Kawasaki's you would have to have a warehouse as big as Macy's just to keep all the parts. I am not going to be doing inventory on all these parts, son.

Honda and Kawasaki, every year they are doing more research and development and everything else. Harley is not doing this. Maybe they refine the ABF brakes. The Evolution engine is probably the best engine they have made. Before, things were different. The Sportster engine had four cams. Each pushrod comes up from the cam. All the Shovels, or the Panheads, Knuckleheads they have one cam in the middle. The pushrods were designed in such a way and they could bend. Instead of going straight up and down. The Evolution is different. No more cast iron cylinders and they use aluminum heads. Everything is aluminum on an Evolution motor. Better air flow, better cooling, better everything. Then they come out with a twin cam. Each cylinder has its own cam and now the pushrods are straight again. No flexing.

That's the way they did it in 1903. Two cylinders with a cam in the middle. This didn't make much of a difference when you're only making fifteen horsepower.

JAR Choppers, Queens

JAR shop

JAR shop

But, as the horsepower comes up and the technology comes up you need to have more of everything. You've got valve timing, lubricating the cylinder walls. When you are making more horsepower you are making more heat. When you got a lot of heat you have to get around the heat. So they make the all-aluminum motor. And you have to remember that Harley did not design the Evolution motor or the twin cam motor. Porsche designed these for Harley. Harley told Porsche what they were looking for so they made a beautiful motor for them. They are the experts for air cooled motors. They pay Porsche for every motor.

I don't know. Maybe I have rebuilt fifty motors so far. Harley is going to sell you a bike that's not going to have any kind of special stuff on it. Harley will sell you all sorts of accessories to make your plain Jane thing special. Guys like to have their bike look different. You'll spend 20,000 on the bike and then you'll spend another $4,000 worth of shit to make it what you want to have. They are not selling custom bikes. They are selling bikes that you can ride on the road. It is very difficult to take a custom bike with a long rake and ride it from here to Florida. Harley will make a motor that runs seventeen part air to one part gas so they can pass the EPA emissions test. There's no horsepower there. That bike has 96 cubic inches but it's only putting out 65 horsepower. But, this engine has the potential to put out a lot more horsepower. It's up to you to do it. If you want it.

Humans breathe fifteen pounds of pressure. 14.875. What I'm doing is changing the ratios and mixtures in the cylinder. I am putting a box more of air into the cylinder. A supercharger pushes more air into the cylinder. Theoretically, twice as much air, twice as much cubic inches. The movement from the top of the piston to the bottom. That's the cubic inches. So I am taking an eighty cubic inch motor and putting twice as much air into it. Two atmospheres. So the motor thinks it's got 160 cubic inches. With more air you have to richen up the jets. Your sucking more air so you gotta suck more gas but you have to keep the ratio thirteen and a half to one.

JAR shop

JAR build

They are making a 96-inch, 1800 CC motor that puts out 65 horsepower. They are looking for longevity. So that you can ride from here to fucking Texas and back and never have to do anything to it. They are trying to make a heavy bike so in case you go down you can go home. Years ago, if you had and old Shovelhead big twin, the motors and the transmissions were separate. Theoretically, even if a front piston was broken off but the back piston had compression, spark and gas, it would get you home.

I'm making all this stuff myself. A lot of guys have four mechanics doing the work. I do all the work myself: How to make things; how to make it look good. That's

JAR build

what I do. Every bike in my shop is my work until it leaves. For years I was an electronic engineer. I figured a lot of this stuff out. I have sat and read all the manuals backwards and forwards. I had a good mechanic here for a while but then he decided to shoot drugs between his toes. On the Fourth of July he borrows $500 from me. He was mixing up some kind of something. "OK, I'll see you on Tuesday." Then I get a phone call on Sunday afternoon, "Can you come identify a body?" He was a good mechanic but what?

The guys, they come in and say, "This bike hasn't been run in six months." I go over the bike and make it right. I have been doing this for a while and I know where to get any part I need. I can see where there's good and bad. What needs to be redone and why. Harley cut corners on their bearing assemblies. It saved them money but the engine is weaker. So I have rebuilt a lot of these engines with the old bearing assemblies. This reduces heat and improves reliability. You got to understand that you don't rebuild these things like they do on two, one-hour episodes on TV. To do it right it could take months.

Motorcycling has changed a lot. I started with all this in the early 1970s. But you know something? Things have changed a lot but I think the kids who are into it now they appreciate the old stuff. A lot of these kids cannot afford a new bike and the Harley dealer doesn't want to talk with you unless you have a brand new motorcycle. They are not into doing motor jobs or anything like that on an old Shovelhead or an old Panhead. So the Harley dealer sends them down to see me.

Other than that, the kids that are out there now, there is a whole different thing going on. Ya know? They want to ride and enjoy themselves. It's not like the old days and the whole club thing. These kids are not into these heavy duty clubs. They're out to ride and have fun. For me, that sounds like a good thing.

I have an appreciation for some machines more than others. My Road King is similar to the FLH. I know it's all in my mind and we're only talking a difference of a few pounds, but the FLH is too top heavy. I'm older now and I'm more comfortable with a Road King because I'm closer to the ground. Everybody is different. Some bikes are more physical and some people like that ride. It's a bike; you're going to hit every bump. It's the difference between being in a sports car or not. A hard ride or an easy ride. A lot of the young guys are into the hard tail Bobber style. A part of this is based on looks and a part of this is also because Bobbers are inexpensive. They are stripped out. There's nothing there and it has been a certain style and way of doing things.

I am an inspection station here. Guys come in here with straight pipes, and their handlebars are too high. I tell them to drop their bars to shoulder height. Push a baffle into the pipes. Guys come in here with bad tires. "No, you can't modify that. You gotta buy new tires. What are you nuts? You wanna get a blow out at 90MPH? You wanna take a corner on a wet patch? That'll be the last time you ever ride a motorcycle. That'll be the last time you ever do anything but lay in the ground. Come on, son, use your head."

For a lot of guys the ride becomes a horsepower game. The thing with straight pipes is for noise but also for more horsepower. There are ways to get around the noise problem and the police. I make something you can put in the pipe that you can swivel to reduce the noise if you need to. The cop pulls you over; you lean over and turn the thing and, "What noise; I didn't make any noise?" A lot of guys are wrapping their pipes now to increase horsepower. To tell you the truth, with a Harley this doesn't really matter. With a Jap bike that's putting

JAR build in progress

JAR tank

JAR customer working on his bike

Jimmy's wife

JAR engine build

JAR build

out 150...180 horsepower, that engine is super tuned. When these guys are racing a new Suzuki, these guys take the whole engine apart and do what is called Blue Printing. For example, bearing clearances can be between two and five—they make it five. Maximum clearance for everything. They make everything flow easy. Maximum horsepower. From Suzuki, the engine is like 175 horsepower. When these guys are done its 275...300 horsepower. They put an expansion chamber in the pipe. This lets it build up some back pressure so everything is working just right. Harley doesn't need an expansion chamber. It's a whole different ball game. Harley de-tunes everything so it will last. If you want to add all this stuff to the motor, it's up to you. You can't give a powerful engine to any asshole. He'll get on that bike and blow it up.

The whole thing with motorcycles can get ridiculous. I used to take best of show for my motorcycles at the ISCA [International Show Car Association] events. Then they started to want chrome-plated brakes as a feature to win best of show. But these bikes don't really have to run. They need to travel ten feet at the show to qualify. These are show bikes that only serve one purpose. It sits there and people look at it. It comes down, gets pushed on the trailer and goes home to sit in the living room. I don't make motorcycles like that. Everything I make has to work. If it's not working then there's no sense of doing it.

When I was building bikes back in the 70s and 80s, you could build a show bike for twenty or thirty thousand. In the 90s, these guys were spending two, three hundred thousand on building a bike. For me, I want to build a bike that handles. I am not interested in building a show bike. As far as I'm concerned, there is no combination of both. You cannot make something that looks fucking outrageous and still performs on the highway. That just isn't my thing, son.

JAR card

JAR build

JAR shop

Vinny

TOP SECRET STREET RACE DAYS

Staten Island

Vinny driving

Ever since I was a kid I needed to be around cars. I used to ask older guys who had nice cars if I could wash and wax them. I remember on Sunday mornings I used to sit by the Belt Parkway and whoever would come by with a cool car I used to beg and plead with them, "Please I'll do anything; I'll wax your car for you." That's how I met Freddy DeName—Broadway Freddy [Frederick DiNome was a 1970s East Coast underworld drag racing legend]. I was like twelve, thirteen. I didn't know the guy but I was at the track waxing his car. He was a total maniac but he had a race car. I didn't give a shit. I went to the track and cleaned his car and I learned. He was into some heavy shit. He chopped some people up and went to jail in Texas. He got killed in there. He had a funny car and he brought it to Coney Island and he did a burn out by the Cyclone. It was pretty much staged but it was big. That was cool.

Vinny in Garage

Young crew

Eugene's father's Erooklyn street rod, c. 1953. Note pinstriping

Brooklyn street rod, c. 1966

Brooklyn street rod, c. 1966

Early New York pinstriping, c. 1966, West Coast influence

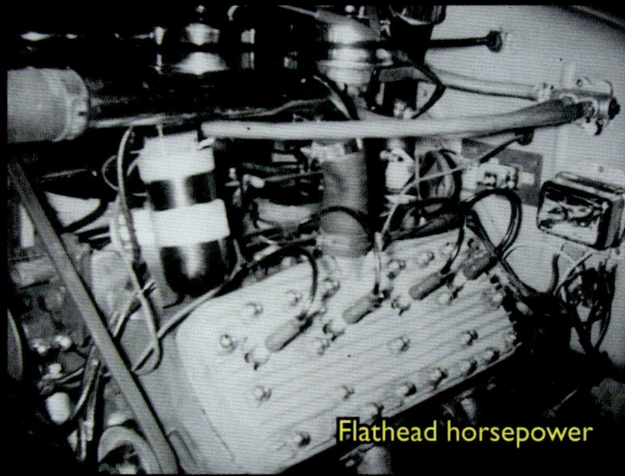
Flathead horsepower

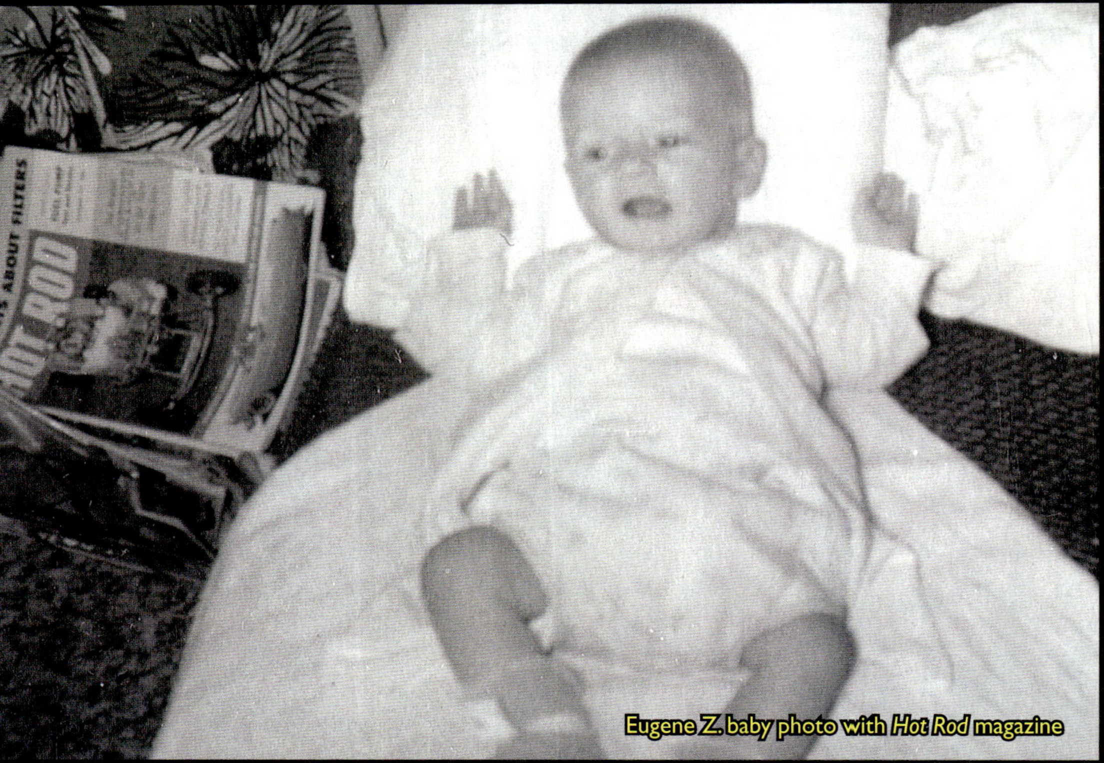

Eugene Z. baby photo with *Hot Rod* magazine

I just needed to be around this kind of thing. You know, it's the speed, the power, being part of the cool crowd. If you had a fast car in the neighborhood you were the king. In my day the cars were getting a little faster and they were starting to get a little more sophisticated. I'm talking from '50s to late '60s. Things came in like fuel injection, supercharging. The jobs became better. We were making a little more money working on guy's cars. So, you could build a little better car. This was New York. All the West Coast guys, they were actually letting their secrets out. We were reading magazines and thinking, "*Hey we can do this, we can do that*." We built faster cars.

At that time the West Coast was always a little ahead of what was going on. In the 1950s the West Coast guys started moving away from the Flathead eights to the Chevy small block. Man, when they got a Caddy engine or a Chevy engine or an Oldsmobile! See, when I was sixteen I had a '55 Chevy. I bought it off a wacko guy that died. I bought the car for five bucks. Yeah, five bucks. A gorgeous '55 Chevy. I was going to Grady, the vocational school. This guy around the corner, Dirty Ernie, he's dead now, he was into cars. Jaguars, Oldsmobiles, and he had an Oldsmobile engine so I said, "Ernie, I'll sand your car down for nothin' if you give me that motor." He gives me a Six Deuce [six carburetors]. Now. I could probably get $50,000 for that motor.

Man, keeping all those carburetors in tune was interesting. You didn't. Back then, as young guys we didn't know what the fuck we were doing. We tried our best. I always wanted a Flathead and I had one in my '53 Ford. Then I had a Chevy and so I put that Oldsmobile engine I got from Ernie into it. Everyone thought I was nuts. I started my cutting and fitting. That was actually the first car I ever built. A '55 Chevy with an Oldsmobile engine. It was a 394. I put it together and I'd tell my teacher, "Yeah, I'm making a car." My teacher says, "Stop the bullshit, you'll never get anywhere in life if you keep bullshitting people." I said, "No, teach, I'm really doing it. It should be ready in a week or two." I was sixteen years old. My teacher says, "Cut it out, it's no good."

So, I say to myself, fuck that, I don't give a shit; I'm driving this car to school. I finished the car but I'm young and I don't even have a driver's license. I had one bogus plate on it. I take the car; I drive it from my house on West 7th where I built the car. I drove it the twenty-five blocks to the Grady High school and pull it into the parking lot, park the car and go into class. The teacher says, "Where you been?" I tell him I was getting my car, it's parked outside. He says, "Yeah, yeah, yeah, right." I finally get the teacher outside for a look and the guy's mouth drops open. He says, "I can't fucking believe it, you built this car?" It was a little ratty but it was done. It would run. The teacher pulls me aside and says, "Hey, I'm going on vacation next week; take care of the class." I'll never forget that. I went home and said, "Ma, I'm going to teach the class." She says, "Are you fucking crazy? You didn't even want to go to school, now you want to be the teacher?" I told her I brought the car to school. She yelled at me, "You brought that car to school?" What a beating I got. My mother used to beat me with a broom handle. She'd go through fifty brooms a week.

I guess I had a knack at this. I remember the family would be eating Sunday dinner and everyone would say, "This kid, I don't know where he got it from? He worked on the guy's car down the block. He got it runnin'." It was all down-hill from there.

Now in New York there are some very talented younger guys. I like knowing that they are out there someplace. I met Paul Cox at a show. He is very talented. He saw my car and liked it. We had a good talk. Then there is a young guy Keino. Him too. That kid is very cool. These guys are making stuff that is very special. They are in their own little world.

When I was young I would hang around some of the older guys in my area. It was the same kind of feeling that I have when I see Paul's and Keino's work. I'd look at the Brooklyn guy's work and, Wow! It impressed me to see that a guy could make something like that. I remember saying to myself, what the hell is going on here? I got to get my shit together. You have to remember that it was different back then. The fast guys; everything was secret. They would never tell anybody nothin'. That's how I grew up. I'd ask, "What size it's the motor?" Secret. "What size is the cam?" Secret. You wanted to be the fastest but all the information was guarded; top secret. There would be a street race. People would ask, how's he run so fast? The answer would come back, nobody knows. You would have to get close to the information. Talk to the right people, read the right magazine. If you wanted to know how to really tool a cam you would have to spend time.

It took me forever to make the right connections. I used to go to this guy Bobby Lombardi. I was a kid and this was a special speed shop. Because of my cousin, I would be able to go in the back. I would see things back there that would blow my mind. I would concentrate and do my best to absorb all that shit. Most guys would be, "Yeah, yeah, yeah." But they didn't pay attention and learn. Me, I'd try my best to pay attention. I'd see certain names, certain stickers. I'd watch the car run. I'd listen to it. I'd put two and two together. A lot of these special cams were coming out of the West Coast. I had no idea where to get them.

I would hang out with a few guys and we'd try to figure it out. We'd go around and if I could, I'd look in guy's garages. I would have six or seven projects going on at one time. By then I was maybe twenty years old. I'd be drag racing to make money. A friend, his dad had a body shop. They called him Red Bob. He was a beatnik. He was big time into Big Daddy Roth. He was the coolest guy in the neighborhood. Most of the other guys were pretty square and they were a little afraid of Red Bob. To hang out with Red Bob meant you were cool. I jumped right in there. Red Bob was customizing cars during the early '50s. He worked at a body shop and then he had his own body shop. Back then, nobody knew anything about this stuff. It was all secretive. Red Bob was way ahead of his time.

Back in those days, this whole thing about cars and horsepower and speed was an underground thing. We were like cavemen. Really. We had to hunt down anything we could find. We'd hear about some bit of information or we'd hear about a car and we'd have to go scavenging for it. We'd have to literally hunt for it.

To know about this whole thing you had to be a part of this underground thing. There were a few magazines out at that point in the 1970s. There was a place called Mitchell's on 86th Street in Brooklyn. That was the hot hangout for the cars and bikes. You see, there were different groups. There were guys from the East Side and guys from the West Side. Whoever had the fast car in your neighborhood, you'd hang out with that guy. And he would turn you on to other guys. Every guy would have a little garage behind their house. Hey, secret. The street I lived on was two lane and a little wider. It became a drag way. This was a small world. Maybe three dozen guys, maybe more. It was a neighborhood thing. West 6th Street was my personal track.

I had a drag bike and I used to test it. All the guys would line up on a side street and I'd test my bike before I'd take it for a run. We'd race up 86th Street to Avenue U, make a U turn, and then we'd race back. Back

Vinny's Comet on the street

Photo courtesy Eugene Z.

Brooklyn street racing, c. 1969, photo courtesy Eugene Z.

Brooklyn street racing, c. 1969, photo courtesy Eugene Z.

and forth all night. "Hey, Vinny's racing today, he's taking his car out; he's taking his bike out." People would line up. The street would turn into a track. It was our personal track. That was during the day. At night things changed. If you wanted to run for money or somebody would come in from a different neighborhood. We'd go to Cross Bay Boulevard or we'd go to the Connecting Highways. I had two motorcycles. Pure stock Kawasaki. I used to ride up and I'd ask if anybody wanted to run. Somebody would step up. $500, $100, whatever. I'd tell them I'd be back in an hour. I'd go home and get my race bike which was the same exact bike but it had wheelie bars and a slick. I'd put it on a trailer and bring it back. The competition would say, "That ain't the same bike." I'd tell them it was and we're gonna run. It went over OK. This was a way to put money together to put into projects. We didn't make much money but it all went to building.

Vinny's '31 Ford five-window coupe, Vinny build

Brooklyn street racing, c. 1969, photo courtesy Eugene Z.

Brooklyn street racing, c. 1969, photo courtesy Eugene Z.

Vinny's '31 Ford five-window coupe, Vinny build: all-steel body, 1957 Chrysler Hemi, 500hp, '69 T-10 4-speed, '57 Olds posi-rear

Butch's 1941 Willy's, Vinny build

Butch's 1941 Willy's,
Vinny build:
502 blown and injected,
900hp, all chrome engine,
custom box frame

There were a few speed shops with good reputations. Eastern Automotive, that was Bobby Lombardi. He had a machine shop. He had the fastest Willy's on the East Coast. Eastern Automotive. That was a top shop. Just to get in the door you had to know somebody. He knew how to tune a car. If your car was tuned by him you were running. He was strictly professional. He wasn't street racing. Exotic fuels and stuff a regular guy couldn't understand. He was a step above us.

There were all different levels. At one level guys can kind of figure out how to make a high performance engine. Then at the next level guys are experimenting with modified fuels and supercharging. Those were the big guys who we looked up to. They had more money and they knew what to do with it. They were older than us and they would go just to the track. For guys like me at my level, our ultimate goal was to get off the street. Just to have a track car. If you owned a track car and a regular car man, you were it. That was my ultimate goal.

Things have changed so much today. There is so much available information about all this kind of thing. You know, sometimes I don't want to move ahead. I'd like to stay where I'm at. If people want to move forward, that's their thing. Me, I'm stuck in the era. I had such a great time finding information, innovating and building cars and bikes in that secretive world. That is my thing. I don't necessarily want it to end.

We were all drag racing in the neighborhood for money. My friend had a '54 Corvette and he put a big block in it. That was unheard of back then. He was street racing and he made the cover of the *Daily News* after the cops got him racing on 1st Avenue. I had two garages. I had one where I used to build the cars and another where I used to keep them and bring them in and out. The guys in the neighborhood

Stevie's 1969 Camaro, Vinny build: 383 blown small block, 650hp, T-10 4-speed, 12 bolt, 3.90 posi rear

Vinny's Chevelle, real SS street racer, Vinny build: big block 900hp, posi rear

would never steal the neighborhood cars. They'd go to a different neighborhood to steal a car. If I needed something, I'd go out of the neighborhood to get it. It didn't get too rough. There was no gun play. Everyone knew their place.

We would know which roads were good or bad. Some were good for cruising, some good for racing. The roads back then were not as beat up as they are now. There was a cruise scene in Brooklyn that centered around that place called Mitchell's. When that place closed in '72, that was one of the saddest days in my life. I was there on the last night with my Comet, my race car. I had a '65 Comet with a straight axle. That place was *the* car hangout. They had car hops. That's where all the hot guys would go. On a Friday night that place would be cool. The older guys like Sandy and his crew, they had Flatheads, Oldsmobiles with four-barrel carburetors. They were the hot thing.

In my day, people started to get into muscle cars—1969–70. If you had a modified car like my Comet, most guys wouldn't run me. That car was all out. They'd see the car was wild. There were also factory engines on the street—327 Chevys. I used to race this guy Ronnie Caputo. I used to race him every Friday night and beat him. He never knew who I was. One time he saw a photo of my car and asked, "Who's car is that?" I told him that it was my car. He had no idea. I would always race secretive. I'd have my windows rolled up. I lived only three blocks from him but he didn't know me. That's how secretive it was. He had no idea where I was coming from. We'd line up and race every week but he had no idea I was his neighbor. I never got out of my car. Top secret. I'd run him, beat him, make the turn, get on the highway and go home.

In those days, you'd never open your hood. Top secret. That was cool. People would snoop around waiting for you to open your hood. I never did. Somebody would ask, "Whatya got?" No answer. You'd say, "Stock." The guy would look at you. You'd say again, "Everything's stock." They'd ask, "Can we see it?" You'd say, "You open yours, I'll open mine. Then we'll run." That would be a condition of the race. We all had what are called Door Slammers. A fast car but with a stock body. You could open the doors.

The whole nature of car culture has changed in recent years. Used to be, you'd see old cars on the road. Years ago you'd see people driving older cars. No more. Now if you want an old car you have to pay. Forty years ago I was fourteen years old. I didn't even have a license. I happened to find an old hot rod sitting in a guy's yard. I bought it for two-hundred bucks. An older friend dragged me home with a piece of rope. I put it in front of my house. My mother went nuts. "You don't even have a license," she yelled. I had it chained to the tree in front of my house so someone wouldn't steal it. You see, car ownership has all changed. In the old days, people owned their cars. Now everyone leases their car. It's a very different thing. Every two or three years people get rid of their cars. Plus, you gotta realize that after the '70s all the cars looked the same and they were all junk. Who wants a '77 Chevy? The cars from the '60s, '50s, '40s, and '30s are all in garages. Every once in a while they come out.

My first several cars, when I was a kid, I never paid more than $300 for one. I used to hide my cars in the back of my house in the dirt alley. The alley where the guys would take the stolen cars and cut them up. It was our personal junk yard. The older guys were stealing the cars, cutting them up and dumping them. Then we'd pick through what was left for our cars. Guys would steal a car just for the transmission. A set of seats. And they'd leave the rest of the car there. It would be a '67 Corvette that they'd steal for some little thing. They'd leave the car and we'd be sitting in them, playing in them.

Vinny's garage (L-R): Eugene Z., Vinny, Stevie, Butch

These cars are worth half a million dollars now. That dirt road was our personal junk yard. This was normal behavior for us. We never even considered that we could get arrested. This was just something we did. Some of these guys would steal a brand-new car just for the hub caps. They'd leave the car behind our houses on the dirt road. We'd check it out. Leave it for two days then we'd be all over it. That's where I got most of my parts. Then the older guys got married and got jobs. That hurt. No more stolen cars to pick over. That hurt. I had to get a job.

Eugene Zandomenego and 1950 Shoebox Ford, 401 Nailhead

Vinny's and Eugene's back alley car stripping zone

Eugene Z.'s 1950 Shoebox Ford

Eugene Z.'s 1950 Shoebox Ford

(NEWS foto by Leroy Jakob)

Driveway which serves homes on W. 7th St. is blocked by bodies of stripped cars.

Call Car Stripping Naked Shame

Vinny's and Eugene's back alley car stripping zone

Austin

1970s NEW YORK RIDING

Brooklyn

With me, I was always into cars. My first car was in 1965. It was a 1956 Chevrolet 210, two door with a post; a three-speed 283. I had it for about a year and a half. I think I raced that car every day that I owned it. In 1966 I bought a 1966 Chevy 327...350 horsepower, four-speed with a 373 posi (Positraction) rear end, 220 first gear. Raced that car every day I owned it. I got it brand new and I raced it every day since I got it from the show room. We'd race for free, we'd race for money. It didn't matter. Just race. I'm tellin' ya, that car had zero miles on it. I'd run into a kid with a Mustang and that was a race. This was Bath Beach, Brooklyn. Avenue U and 86th Street. Over by the Marlboro projects.

Austin, c. 1969

Photo from unknown 1970s Biker film, courtesy Austin

Late '60s to early '70s style NYC choppers, Brooklyn

Late '60s to early '70s style NYC choppers, Brooklyn

'70s style NYC chopper

Austin, c. 1971

Later in '66 I went to see Peter Fonda's *Wild Angels* and seeing that movie changed my life. In the movie Fonda is talking to a priest and the priest asks, "What is it you guys want?" And Fonda says, "We want to be free to ride our machines without being hassled by the man." I said to myself, I gotta get a bike. That's what I want, a bike. I didn't want a family, I didn't want a job, I wanted a motorcycle and I wanted to be free.

This whole thing about cars and engines and bikes was a part of my life. When you were a young guy you were reading car magazines. You knew what's out there. When I was in high school, instead of studying we'd listen out the classroom window to the cars go around the block. We could tell what kind of car it was just by the sound of it. Oh, that's a Plymouth; oh, that's a Ford; oh, that's a Chevy. That's a small block; that's a big block. He got headers; he got straight pipes. Whatever it was, that's how we entertained ourselves.

I bought my '66 because Bill "Grumpy" Jenkins, who was a famous drag racer, that was the car he was using. He was using a Chevy with a 327 and he ran it in A stock class. He ran it against street hemis. If he was beating the hemis, I knew it was a fast car. If he could do it, I could have fun with it on the street. I was no heavy wrencher but I could get my hands dirty. We did all our work under trees. We'd take motors out under a tree. Use a big limb as your winch. Back in the mid-sixties they didn't have alternate side of the street parking. So, you could park a car on the street for months. Not like today where you have to move things around or you are going to lose it.

You gotta remember that there was very little traffic in the city in the sixties. We used to race on the Gowanus and we'd close the highway down. We'd get cars to block all the lanes and the two guys that were racing would be out in front. Once the traffic in front of you cleared there would be a drag

Aliens, 9th Precinct Manhattan, c. 1968, photographer unknown

race. There was so little traffic it didn't matter. That was a regular thing. This is '66-'67.

The first bike I bought was a 1967 Honda 305 Scrambler. It was a nice little bike. At the time it was Honda's second biggest bike. Their biggest was a 450. So, I bought that little bike and instantly I started taking it apart. I took the front fender off and threw that away. I put ape hangers on it, a Pat Jones peanut tank, I sent out to a company called Cheetah that was one of the first accessory companies. This was the sixties and there were no companies selling parts. I put a Cheetah seat on it and as soon as I got it, I started hanging out in the Village. I knew bikes hung out in the Village. Then I started meeting guys with bikes. One of the first guys I met was Spade George. He was riding a '53 Panhead. Then I met this other kid Red who was riding another small Jap bike like mine. This is 1967. There were a lot of nice people; a lot of clubs were down there then. This is the West Village. The original hang out was actually 3rd Street between 6th and MacDougal. That was the original bike hangout. The Aliens used to be there.

At that time I was twenty-two. Nobody really took me under their wing, but the guy who influenced me into getting a Harley was Spade George. I was happy with my little Honda, but from being with George he was always, "Get a Harley, get a Harley." He kept bugging me so I decided to sell the Honda and get a Harley. I figured if I had any problems with it George would help me out. Well, as soon as I bought the Harley, George moved to California [laughter]. The summer of 1969 I sold my Honda for $500 and I bought a '51 Panhead for $500. It had an extended Triumph front end on it and a half Jones tank. I sold the front end to a kid with a Triumph and I went down to 3rd Street and bought a Wide Glide front end for $40. That was the start of it. Actually, I changed the fork tubes to eight inch over fork tubes with a Sportster tank, pulled back handle bars, ribbed rear fender, Cheetah seat, and a sissy bar.

I had developed a bit of an aesthetic and sensibility from hanging out with Spade George. I was hanging out in the West Village and some guys came through who were making a movie. It was an exploitation type of a film. Hippies against Bikers. They used a lot of the guys who hung out in the Village. And they used the Aliens. That's when I started to see custom bikes. The Aliens had a lot of custom bikes. They were influenced by a gentleman named Mardo Bennet. It was a Grease Monkey type looking bike. Mardo was a guy in New York who knew more than most of the guys. He was a painter and a designer and an engine builder. He could do it all. He was very influential.

The Aliens were known for their style of bike. They had a look. A lot of their bikes looked like bikes you would have seen in San Francisco. Basic stripped down choppers. Nothing extra on them, just what you needed to get down the road.

I am African American, but at that time I didn't know anything about black clubs. When I started riding I didn't know anybody who rode. I just got into bikes because of that movie I saw. One thing I did know was that guys with motorcycles hung out in Greenwich Village. There was always bikes there. That's where I gravitated to. So my motorcycle lifestyle was an integrated lifestyle. It would have been different if I was born in Bedford Stuyvesant or something. Sometime in the '70s I ran into a club the Harlem Knights.

There was a whole style to the kind of bikes the Knights rode. FLH full dressers, rooster tails, cherry lights, the owner's name in a pattern of cherry lights. They did a lot of scroll work, seat rails, anything and everything they could do to bikes. But, I never got into dressers. I never owned one. We'd see one and it didn't impress us. The only thing we were really concerned with was choppers.

Choppers had not been around too long at that point. In New York I would say that I first noticed them in the mid-sixties. There was one kid in my neighborhood that had a custom Triumph rigid frame. A nice candy-blue paint job. I didn't see too many choppers. New York bike culture started in the West Village and then moved over to the East Village. The East Village was cool. There was the Electric Circus, the Fillmore. I saw a lot of good shows at the Fillmore.

I started working for Brooklyn Harley Davidson in the mid-seventies. I worked for them for about three years. We started hanging out in the East Village in 1969. Between St. Mark's and 7th Street and 2nd Avenue. When I got over there, one of the first people I saw was Spade George again. I hadn't seen him for years. This time when I saw him he had colors on. He was in a club called the Rat Pack from Brooklyn. I took a ride with him to the club house and the president of the club was another guy I knew from '67. His name was Red. Now he was riding an Indian and his name was Indian Red. One thing led to another and next thing I know I joined the club. That's how I got in the Rat Pack.

The Rat Pack was an Italian and Irish club. Irish and Italian and me and George. Then in the mid-seventies we started the South Side Shifters club. This was also an integrated club. We had Dominicans, Puerto Ricans, Italians. We even had one Arab in the club. Back in those days there were a lot of clubs in New York. Different territories. You had to be a little careful if you were wearing colors, but basically I didn't run into that kind of thing. Especially when we had the Shifters because we didn't wear colors. We wore t-shirts. We didn't flag the club and we had no beef with anybody. We'd go any place and every place. At the time there were a few outlaw clubs and they were sensitive to the issue of colors. If you were disrespectful and you were in their territory, they would take people's colors and tear them up and sew them on the asses of their pants. They would wear those pants when they went to parties.

Curbed bikes, St. Mark's Place and Second Ave., c. 1970

Spade George, Brooklyn, c. 1970

Austin, c. 1971

Austin's bike, c.1972

Austin's bike, c. 1972 (close-up): brass pushrods and springer

Rat Pack bike club NYC, c. 1970

Back in the summer of '69 there were a couple Rat Pack chapters. One in East New York, one in Queens. A couple guys from the Ridgewood chapter were in a bar drinking one day and all of a sudden one guy said to another guy, "Hey, do me a favor cut my trigger finger off." He put his finger on the bar and his friend took out a knife and chopped off his finger. So, then the guy who did the chopping told his friend, "Hey do me a favor. Chop off my finger." So they cut off each other's trigger fingers so they wouldn't be drafted. This was at the height of the Vietnam War. They put the cut-off fingers into their vest pockets. When they'd see you, to say hello, they'd take out this green shriveled-up finger and poke you with it. That completely freaked people out.

You had to be aware of the areas you were moving through so you wouldn't piss anyone off. One time I remember that my bike had broken down. I had my rear wheel off because I had a flat. This guy I didn't really know said he'd ride me someplace to get it fixed. This guy was a 1%er but he was also an artist. He had graduated from art school. We were in the middle of nowhere and I had no idea about what was going on there in terms of clubs or alliances. So, we're riding to get my tire fixed and four or five guys from another club ride up on us. The guy who was giving me a ride pulled over, got off his bike and immediately went off on these other guys. He was beating them down very intensely. I was standing there like, *"I thought you were an artist?"* Oh shit, I don't even know this guy but now I go to cover his back? I jumped in swinging but I had no idea why I was swinging, what the beef was or who the other guys were. I was just kicking these other guy's asses. Whoever they were, they must have done something pretty bad because the guy that gave me the lift was really kicking their fucking asses. So I just did the same thing. This is how it went down sometimes. Man, we left those guys all over the street.

Our club the South Side Shifters was different than a lot of clubs. To be in our club you had to ride a Harley, preferably with a jockey shift. But we did not want to be portrayed as outlaws. We were a bunch of guys that loved Harley Davidsons and loved to ride and loved to party. We didn't want any trouble from anybody. This was in the mid-seventies and we were active for about five years. We had a couple dozen members. It was a decent sized club and we would always ride together. We had planned rides we would take and we had mandatory runs just like any other club. We had round robins with our brother club so we partied at our

South Side Shifters club house, Brooklyn, c. 1971

Austin (center) with friends, c. 1972

Austin, c. 1972

Austin and wife

brother's clubhouse. One week we partied at our club, the next week at our brother's club. It was good and every party we had was a success. Good food and good music. It was a nice lifestyle. A very nice lifestyle.

I got the chance to go to California. I took my bike out there in a truck. A friend of mine was moving to north Hollywood. We went down the East Coast, down the Gulf into Mexico. Coming out of Mexico, they stopped us because it was me, a black guy, and two hippies. So of course they stopped us. They stripped the truck. They told me to get the bike out of the back but I took issue with that. It was pretty heavy. The border guy said, alright leave the motorcycle in but everything else comes out. So, we took every damn thing out of that truck. It's all over the ground. The cops start to go through everything and they find a little brief case that my friend had. There was all kinds of drug paraphernalia in that case. He had rolling papers, roach clips; everything you could think of except drugs. The cops looked at this collection and then they looked at us. They said, "Who owns this?" My friend says, real bold, "That's mine." They took him away and did a cavity search on him [laughter]. But they found no drugs, no weapons. Oh, they did find a gravity knife and said it was illegal in the United States. They confiscated that.

We drove from there up through California and then to north Hollywood. The house that the guy was going to live in was a rooming house that was filled with motorcycle guys. There were two clubs that lived there; one was The Choppers and the other was The Chosen Few. They tried to convince me to stay in LA with them, but I said, "No, I got people waiting on me in San Francisco. I got to make it up north." These guys were talking about a movie they had just seen called *Easy Rider*. They said a black guy had built the bikes for that movie. They also told me that they had just made a movie, *The Black Angels*. That was probably the worst motorcycle movie there ever was but the bikes were gorgeous. I finally saw that film in the mid-eighties. They had a biker film anthology over on 2nd Avenue. I saw it there. It was terrible.

I stayed out in California for about a year but I got homesick for New York. I had never left New York before and I was twenty-five years old. I just had to come back to New York. So, I jumped on my '51 Panhead and rode across the country. That was an interesting time. I was thinking of that movie *Easy Rider* all the way across the country. All the way I am thinking of that last scene in *Easy Rider* and I was saying to myself, "Oh, this is not going to be good." It was intimidating. All in all it was a good trip.

I was a New York, East Coast guy. I was used to congestion and crowds. I remember feeling very strange out west. It is a big place. I remember I got into Wyoming and I'm on the highway and a guy pulls up next to me on an old Knucklehead. Every part on his bike you could see it was handmade. He had done everything himself. We are riding side by side and he looks at me and pulls me over. I was wearing old engineer boots with the soles falling off. The guy says to me, "When I seen you there with your shoes flapping in the wind I said I got to take this guy home and get him some boots." So I followed him home and he and his wife lived in a little house out in the middle of nowhere. I looked around and there is nothing there. Just this wide open space. He gave me a brand new pair of engineer boots, a twenty-one-inch inner tube, he filled my gas tank, his wife cooked me something to eat and he was just the nicest guy. His first name was Bill. Then, I went back on the road.

I was riding a '51 Panhead with a stock Sportster tank so every sixty miles I had to stop for gas. I ran out of gas twice—once on the Bonneville Salt Flats and another time at a gas station at the pump. On the Salt Flats we had to start pushing the bike. I had a girl with me. As soon as we started pushing, a guy pulled up and gave us some gas. He didn't want any money. Then I got to Lincoln, Nebraska, and the bike ran out of oil. I parked the bike and started walking. I found a gas station and walked in and asked for some sixty weight. The guy didn't have any but another guy heard me and said, "You must have a Harley. My brother's got a shop at his house. You wanna go? I'll take you to the house and get you some oil." Sure enough, the guy had a full shop in his garage. We changed the oil and the guy says, "Where you goin'?"

I said, "New York."

"Where you comin' from?"

I said, "California." The guy looks at my bike and says I think you need a rear sprocket. He says I'll give you a 26 on your transmission that will be a lot better for you on the highway. I get back on the road and, yeah, I was really cruising nice. Seventy-five, eighty miles an hour, just cruisin'.

I finally get close to New York and my body starts aching. The closer to New York, the worse the roads. With my rigid frame, every time I hit a bump I felt it. Aches and pains. I got to the Delaware Water Gap area and the roads all went to shit. By the time I got to the bridges to cross the river into the city, my ass hurt. I had forgotten how bad the roads were.

Back in those days you didn't get stuck in traffic jams like you do now. And there wasn't a light at every corner either. But compared to when I had been riding way out in America, the streets were crowded. I remember when I was riding across the country I kept thinking about all the western movies I had seen as a kid. As I was riding out there I remembered the dialogues between the characters in some of the movies. They talked about the cattle and the sheep. When I was riding out there I remember passing through cattle country. Man, the cattle ranches smelled horrible. The cattle shit. Unbelievable smell. Cornfields and cow shit. Comin' from California. I rode up 101 to Sacramento and then I hit Reno and that was it. There's nothin' until Nebraska. As a guy from New York, this was a total trip. There was so much open space in this country. But that was a long time ago in the '70s. There was 2,000 miles of open space. It's a beautiful country. I rode sun-up to sun-down. If it wasn't raining I slept on the side of the road. If it was raining there were bikers collected under the overpasses. I got a hotel room. It was only $10. I can't figure out why people leave this country when they travel. They go on vacation to other countries. There is so much to see here.

Back in New York I worked a little for Mardo Bennett. He was from up in the Bronx. He had two shops. One was called Mardo's Cycle Circus, the other Custom and Chrome. The bikes Mardo built for himself were strictly stripped down to the bare bones. Small back fenders, eighteen-inch back wheels, hopped-up motors, small gas tank. He was the first guy I saw who axed a tank. He took stock Harley tanks and split them and welded them back together. He is the originator of the axed Harley tank. When you see a tank with two caps on them, that's an axed Harley tank. After I worked for Mardo, I took some ideas from him. Especially the eighteen-inch rear wheel. After him, I always ran an eighteen-inch wheel.

Mardo and another guy named Chucky Hubbs. These guys were riding straight choppers. Even in those early days there was plenty of choppers around. Bobby Cool from Brooklyn. A lot of choppers were around. Most of us back then were riding old bikes. Knuckleheads, Panheads. Flatheads. Very few guys were on new bikes. I can't remember seeing guys with new bikes. This was because of both cost and style. In terms of style, guys didn't want Electra glides. Guys wanted those rigid frames. No shocks on the back. They wanted choppers. When I was buying my bike in 1969 I had the opportunity to buy a '47 Knucklehead dresser, all original for $500. But I wanted a chopper. I didn't want a stock bike. I turned it down. The guy rode it over to my place. But I wanted a chopper. I bought a '51 Panhead for $500. This was I call B.E., before the movie *Easy Rider*. After *Easy Rider* the prices more than doubled. After that movie came out my bike was immediately worth $1200. *Easy Rider* was that influential. Everybody had to have a chopper. African American builders Cliff Vaughn and Ben Hardy are credited with building the bikes for the movie. That movie was very influential. To see those bikes moving down the highway and to hear that sound track. "Born to be Wild."

Working at Mardo's I met this guy that had a shop a few doors down named Billy Midnight. He got that name because he didn't open his shop until the middle of the night. Midnight Motorcycles. This was cool. If you broke down and you needed a part, you'd go to Billy Midnight. He was in the Bronx. Billy introduced me to this guy who had a shop and tells me, "OK, we're just going to go in the guy's shop and get what you need and leave." Billy said this guy was a bad ass and he don't like nobody and he was the president of Bronx MC. They called him Big Alex. So, I go in there and meet Big Alex and got what I needed.

The next time I go to see Big Alex by myself because I needed some stuff. It turns out that Alex was a really nice guy. He was one of the smartest motorcycle guys I had ever met. Alex had this friend Jimmy These. He was an old dresser motorcycle guy from New York. If you wanted that fancy stuff you went to see Jimmy. He made all that scroll work and he was a polisher and a chromer. So Alex and Jimmy and I became very good friends. This was like 1975–76. Back in those days there were not many shops. So when you did find a good shop, you went there.

We were working on our bikes and changing things on them. I didn't have a torch but I did all the other kind of work. Spade George turned me on to a guy B&D that was a Harley dealer in Rahway, New Jersey, on Route 1&9. You could go to B&D, ride your bike up and if there was a part you wanted to chrome on your bike, they had the part in the store already chromed. They used to do a chrome exchange. They would lend you the tools to take the part off your bike. That was a really cool thing. Everybody used to go there and hang out. You'd save up your money until you had enough for whatever it was you wanted. At B&D you could put the chromed part on right in front of the store.

Those days, the Village was a bike hangout. It was clubs plus independent guys who used to hang out there. Any day of the week you went there was at least twenty, twenty-five bikes curbed there. When you went on the weekend, now you are talking seventy-five to one-hundred guys. There were so many bikes over there on the weekend you couldn't find a parking spot. That's both sides of the street between St. Mark's and 7th Street. Both sides of the street would be bikes. There was just guys hanging out, drinking, picking up girls, and figuring out where they were going to go. Those were the days.

After that scene at St. Mark's and 7th Street, we went back to the West Side. We used to hang on Bleecker Street around Sullivan Street. Early seventies, that was a big biker hang out area. Everybody was pretty much well behaved. So well behaved that one time when we were all hanging out on Bleecker there was a local police officer that patrolled the area. He was standing there talking to us and a green and white patrol car pulled up with a sergeant in it. The sergeant rolled down the window and asked the cop if there was a problem. So, the cop says, "Problem? No, these guys are all right. Let me show you how alright they are." The cop unhooks his gun and puts it in my hand. Now, I am standing on the street in front of three cops with a police officer's revolver in my hand on Bleecker Street. He gave me his gun! It happened so fast I didn't realize what was going on.

In those days, riding a bike in New York was very neighborhood. Like in a place like Bensonhurst, there were a few guys riding. Gangster guys riding Sportsters with $50,000 into them. They rode them around and did wheelies and parked them in front of the gym. They didn't leave the neighborhood. Their big thing was to go into the city one day and ride up on the sidewalk and blow up girl's skirts with their pipes and ride back to Brooklyn.

I like a quick bike. I always like to go fast. A clean, simple stroker. I prefer the Shovelhead. That's what I've had for so many years. The bike I'm riding now is a stroker

Austin and son, 1985

Austin and son, 1990

Shovelhead. It's a hot rod. It might not be the fastest thing out there but it's a hot rod. That bone shaking, jaw aching thing. Just like the cars. That's what an old Shovelhead is with a stroker; it's a hot rod. You get on that thing and you are in for some fun. It's not for everyone. The Shovel was the first Harley motor when they went to longer rocker geometry. Better heads. It is different than a Panhead. The throw on the rockers is very short on a Pan. A Pan will run worse when you do performance work to them. A big Pan will never run as good as a big Shovel. The motor has been out since the forties so there is tons of aftermarket stuff out there. The Shovelhead was the first motor Harley did that changed the rocker situation that helped the pushrod angle a little.

I'm not sure that you can say there is a New York City style bike. In the early days most guys were influenced by what was being built on the West Coast. We saw the movies. We saw what they were riding. That's what we wanted to ride. Once the movies came out, that's when bike culture changed and it changed in a couple ways. First, it changed in the attitudes that the bikers themselves had because they saw how these guys were acting on the screen. That's the way they wanted to act in real life. Movies like the *Wild One*, *Wild Angels*, *Easy Rider*. These were influential in terms of creating something. They say that art imitates life but it's also life imitating art.

Back in the '60s, when I started with my interest in bikes, the behavior was different. Back then any time a biker saw another biker, it didn't matter what kind of bike they had but they always spoke. They would wave to each other. You don't see that any more. If a guy broke down other guys would always stop no matter what kind of bike you had. Guys would stop and see what help you needed. I have broken down recently and I hear a bike coming and I'm hoping the guy will stop. These days the guy might slow down and look at you but he keeps going. These are young guys who could give you a lift somewhere but they blow past. Nothing. No help. I have a friend that tells a story about one day he was broken down and three or four guys blew past him. Man, he fixed his bike real fast and he chased these guys. He was on his way to Daytona and he broke down in Georgia at like three in the morning. So its bike week and there are a million guys blowing past. He's on the side of the road and guys are going past with looks like, "Ah ha, fuck you." Man I just wasn't taught to behave like that. Now, everybody is too cool.

Back when I started riding, everybody used to speak with each other. When you pulled up next to a guy you would speak. If a guy was broken down you would definitely stop. You might see it today with guys that ride older bikes. Now a lot of young guys just don't get it. I can't tell you how many times I have pushed my bike down the highway and nobody—bikes, cars, nobody stops. Not anymore. And I don't think it's a tough guy thing. I just think that a lot of guys riding don't know anything about what they are doing. They know nothing about bike culture. Back in the old days things were different. You could not become a biker in two days.

I do see a resurgence of the old style choppers like we used to ride. Today, younger guys are finding those bikes hip. That's what they want to ride. Now my Shovelhead gets a little respect because I've been riding the same bike for 25 years. When these young guys look at it they might not realize it. They think my bike was put together a few years ago, but when they find out I built my bike the way it is and have ridden it the way it is for 25 years then that kind of blows their mind. They stop and look at my bike. It's an all blacked out bike which is very popular now. Avoid chrome at all costs. But this bike looked like this 25 years ago. It has a 98-cubic-inch motor. It's a fast, black bike.

Austin and son, 2010

Austin's Shovelhead

Austin and his Shovelhead

Austin and his Shovelhead

As an example of how things have changed. Back in '68 we were hanging around the Rat Pack clubhouse and a guy comes rolling up with a station wagon. He says, you guys want to get into the movies free today? We ask, what's playing? He said he was playing a couple motorcycle movies. So we say, "OK, we'll come." So the guy pulls out a big loudspeaker and puts it on his car and he's driving through his neighborhood blasting out that he's going to have a real live motorcycle club come through the theater. So, our whole club jumps on our bikes and rides to the guy's theater. The guy tells us to bring the bikes inside. So we bring our bikes in, right down the aisle and park them in front of the screen and we get carte blanche at the concession stand. So we're sitting on our bikes eating popcorn, watching the movie. The whole neighborhood came out to see us.

We are in there for about an hour but then we hear something. We hear very loud pipes coming. There is something about fishtail pipes and the sound they make. From the sound of the bike I knew who it was. I knew it was Spade George. And here comes George flying into the building, down the aisle, hits the breaks, skids and smokes the rubber. That was crazy. There's a biker film playing and the whole theater smells like George's burned rubber. There were about 25 motorcycles parked up front by the stage in the theater. We're all just relaxing eating popcorn, eating candy, and drinking soda. That was cool. That was just an interesting thing to do. The neighborhood girls found that very interesting. Back in the day we used to call our Harley's Milwaukee vibrators. Those big twin rigids. Forget about it—those girls loved our bikes.

Spade George

I DO WHAT I DO
AND THAT IS WHO I AM

Brooklyn

Spade George with chopper build

When I was young and riding in New York it was not always a pleasure riding around. The streets were rough. I had to build a very tough bike to handle those streets. We all rode day-in, day-out rain or shine. It wasn't really an issue. Nothin' would really stop us from riding. Now I live out in the Bay Area and the streets are getting like New York. It's not quite as bad but it's not a pleasure riding around. I still build a bike that is pretty hard core. You can bounce around with it and beat on it if that's what you got to do.

I am not a chrome freak any more. We do a lot of powder coating. This has become more popular now. It holds up. You don't have to worry about it when your bike gets beat up. I never was one to wash the bike. I'd get on it and ride and come home. If someone wanted to wash it for me that's okay but I never got into that part of the motorcycle thing. If I build a bike that has chrome then it's going to get rusty. Back in the day in New York we might put a few pieces of chrome on our bikes but chances were it was used chrome. And that's a problem. We started to black out the chrome parts because it was more practical. New York is next to the ocean, it's humid. Chrome doesn't like this.

Now everyone is going into this stealthy black look. The Hollywood version of an outlaw now is changed considerably to what an outlaw biker was. To me, too much black is not where I'm coming from. I'm in between. I still have that old style, old school outlaw feel and that's how my bikes are. Most people don't understand that and they just see it as "Old School." But they don't understand where it came from.

You look at the style bike the Aliens ran in New York City during the 1960s. They were all rigid frame and they rode the dog

Spade George, Brooklyn, 1969

Spade George, Brooklyn, 1969

Spade George on steps, Wanted Dead or Alive

shit out of them. I learned from those bikes. That's how I learned to build a bike. If it breaks you make the parts stronger. Finally, then you understand how to build a bike that will hold up. Things have changed—now days with these show bikes.

You know there was a group of Aliens that rode out of an area in the Bronx. Those guys and their bikes; a man named Mardo Bennett gave me the biggest inspiration. They had the coolest motorcycles. They worked out of a small shop in the Bronx. Their bikes were in all the shows. We would see their bikes on the Lower East Side all the time.

People of color have a little bit of a harder way to go. I do good work and I am very conscientious of what I do. I see how a lot of people do their work and it is not what I am comfortable with. I know, because I spend a lot of time going over and fixing a lot of this kind of work. I am not the kind of guy who is into this for the credit. It matters but it is not the number one reason I do this. I do what I do and this is who I am. Whether no one comes into my shop or a thousand people come into my shop this doesn't change things. This is the way I am.

The motorcycle world has changed over the past couple years. The Internet has opened things up and people now have the option to go direct to suppliers. Stuff is now being sold on the Internet that is cheaper than I am buying it wholesale. Today there is no quality control but people don't necessarily care. If you had been in the business for as long as I have you would be able to see the difference between the past and now. This includes the style of the parts and how they fit on the bike when you are putting them on the bike. In terms of your labor time it is difficult to estimate how well things will or will not work out. All I do know is that when I am done everything it's going to be one-hundred percent.

I was originally brought up in Brooklyn in Bedford Stuyvesant. As a kid there were guys around the corner that had a club. They

Spade George in San Francisco, 1971

Spade George with crew, photo Ron Hardin

Spade George

Desperado, Spade George build

Spade George card

Spade George build

Spade George riding

Hole in the Wall tank

were always building hot rods and racing them down Bedford Avenue. They'd block off the street on both ends and then race.

In Brooklyn there were the Satellites and the New Breed. A girl up the street from me used to go out with a member of the Satellites so they would come by all the time and it was impressive. They liked the dresser style. Me, I never went for that style. I always liked things stripped down. I never went for baggers.

My ideas are very different than a lot of these guys that are building show bikes. That's not to say that I don't like show bikes, it's just coming from a different place. A lot of builders go for the rigid frame. I like to deal with the swing arm frame. They are a little harder to work with and they don't handle quite as good but if you know what you're doing they are good. I build swing arm bikes and a lot of people think they are rigid. From 1958 to 1986 Harley ran the swing arm frame.

Between 1929 and 1948 are my years. I am in that era. That's what I consider to be my time. You walk into my shop in Redwood City and you see that's where I'm coming from. I have been at this for a while and I respect a lot of people that I have been lucky to meet. I still think that the best information about building bikes travels by word of mouth.

In New York, we would pay attention to the looks of certain bikes and the way they had been built. Riding in that city demanded a certain way of making things. I'm sure it still does.

Spade George at bar in San Francisco

Hole in the Wall shop, San Francisco

Spade George riding

Spade George

Mel Bernstein

WE WANTED TO BE DIFFERENT AND THIS IS HOW WE WANTED TO DO IT

Brooklyn

Mel with flames on bicycle, c. 1960

I was brought up in Brooklyn. When I was fifteen years old my parents moved to Long Island. That's about the same time I got kicked out of school. I went to Roberts Technical Trade School on 59th Street. I don't know if it's there anymore. They couldn't really kick me out of school because I was under sixteen, so they transferred me to this trade school. That was a good thing. That's when I really started to learn something. I always liked motorcycles. This was '61-'62.

Mel's first hot rod: flames paint, 1964

Aliens bike at 9th Precinct

Mardo Bennett bike, c. 1967. Note Bronx handlebar webbing style. (Very rare photo. Very few photos exist of Bennett's work. Photo courtesy Bonge)

Outhouse car, picture frame window, bathtub knobs for light switch, 1967

As a young person I always liked the way a Harley sounded. I got into it just when people started to make choppers. Extend the front end, shorten the gas tank. This was long before the days of catalogs. What has been featured recently on TV really has nothing to do with people of my generation and what we had to deal with. For me, the guys that built choppers back in the '60s were really making motorcycles. You couldn't order stuff. There was very little if anything to look at. You had to think about it, conceptualize it in your mind, and then try to make it. This is a very different process from what exists now. There was very little information to go on. Bikers back then were dealing with a very different thing.

You have to remember that back then there was no information about bikes and building. The information and styles traveled with the guys and their bikes. Mardo was in the Bronx building bikes and he had a reputation. Guys would be coming into New York from places like San Francisco to visit with Mardo. I didn't have friends that rode out to San Francisco but this was definitely going on. Mardo worked on their bikes. The Aliens used to hang out at Nathan's in Oceanside every Tuesday night. So did I. Believe me, people saw those bikes

Mardo Bennett bike, c. 1967. Note Bronx handlebar webbing style. Note tank paint pattern. (Very rare photo of Bennett's work. Photo courtesy Bonge)

Sandblasting at Rockaway Beach

and were impressed with them. The long front end, high pipes, high handle bars, the high sissy bars. Ninety percent of the guy's bikes were rigid frames. These guys welded their bikes solid. They could handle the New York streets. That was the look back then.

There were not too many guys involved in this back then. You would have to think about the possibilities yourself. You would hear certain things, and then you would see certain bikes. You would sit down with a piece of paper and draw what you were thinking about. How you wanted it to look. These guys changed the tanks to a peanut type tank or they would narrow down a tank. They would split a tank and re-weld it.

The first *Easyriders* magazine came out in 1971. Before that there really weren't any magazines. There was no way to see what they were doing on the East or West Coast. A lot of the innovation had to come from your own ideas. My idea was the dragon motorcycle. People looked at the bike and called it all sorts of things. The crocodile. For me what's unique about it is that back then I didn't have any money. I was just a guy off the street. So all those original dragon bikes were welded together with coat hangers. I had to get the oxygen acetylene from a building site near me. I gave the night watchman a six pack and he'd let me borrow the tanks. I'd have to bring them back before the job site opened in the morning. Every night I could weld some of the dragon together and then the next night I'd weld some more. This went on until the bike was welded together.

I always liked flames. Ever since I was a kid I'd draw flames on cars. So I thought about doing this with a bike. I got some cardboard and I drew some flames and made a pattern. I thought this looked pretty good if I made a sissy bar like that. Then eight or ten years later I put a head on it and then I made flames come out of it. People saw this and started saying, "Hey, there goes that dragon man."

Early Bernstein bike, c. 1971

Early Bernstein bike, c. 1971

Early Bernstein bike, c. 1971

Early Bernstein bike, c. 1971

I still have the two original ones. One is from 1966 and one is from 1967. I used to go to Daytona Beach every year and there were a lot of guys there with a lot of money. So guys would say; I want to buy that bike. So, I told them to buy a Harley frame and I'd build them one. There are eighteen more of them around now. I made one for a topless dancer who worked in Port Washington that had three dragon heads on it.

Over the years I got into different things. I made four, double-engine bikes. I have the fastest speeding ticket on record in the state of Colorado—168 miles an hour. I had two Shovelheads with nitrous and an air shifter transmission. When you were in second gear doing about 95 miles an hour you'd hit the button and take off. The cop clocked me at 168. Out here the roads are really flat and really smooth. The cop came up to me holding his radar gun and yelled at me, "Who the hell do you think you are?" His face was all red.

I told him, "I'm dragon man; I live right down the road over there." I told him I just built this bike and it's all registered. I was just trying it out. He's waving his radar gun in my face and screaming at me, "Look at this! It reads 168 miles an hour!" I told him I was sorry but I didn't think I was going that fast. He said, "What are you, fucking crazy? You don't test it out on a public highway!" So I got the ticket.

I went to court but the cop didn't show up. The judge had never seen a ticket for that speed before. My lawyer told the judge that the cop must have had the radar gun pointed towards an airplane that was taking off from the airport that happened to be located next to where I was testing my bike. The judge shot my lawyer a look but he invalidated the ticket. He couldn't imagine somebody going that fast. It still cost me like three grand for the lawyer fee. I still got the ticket. That was 1991, I think. That same bike was in *Easyriders* magazine and was bought by Harley Davidson in Paris, France.

Early Bernstein bike, c. 1971

Early Bernstein sissy bar/ Dragon Bike form, c. 1973

Early Bernstein Dragon Bike form, c.1973

Early Bernstein Dragon Bike form, c.1973

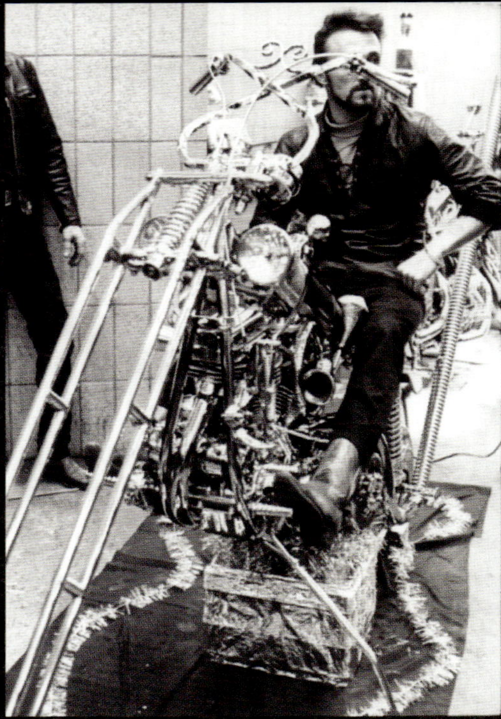

Handlebar webbing stylization as seen in the Bronx New York Coliseum Auto Show, c. 1966-67. Photo William Gedney, Duke University Library Collection

Early Bernstein Dragon Bike form, c. 1974

Bernstein drag bike style build, c. 1976

Bernstein handle bar webbing stylization. New York Coliseum Auto Show, c. 1966-67. Photo: William Gedney, Duke University Library Collection

It's on display in their show room.

The biggest thing with that bike was synchronizing the motors. After breaking three primary chains I figured out that the front motor had to be advanced ten degrees from the back motor. I had to do a lot of experimenting to figure that out.

Now I do around 90 to 100 motors a year. The main reason I could move to Colorado is that people can ship their motors to me. People and dealers send me stuff. I fix it and ship it back. Pretty good for a high school drop-out, right? When I was in school getting kicked out every other week, I remember when I was a kid I'd go with my parents to the principal's office and he'd tell them, "Your son is never going to amount to anything." I don't know what I'd do with a high school diploma. Hang it in the Bathroom? It's what you want to know, not what they want to make you know.

Mel Bernstein with chrome helmet, New York Coliseum Auto Show, c. 1966-67. Photo: William Gedney, Duke University Library Collection

Mel Bernstein bike at New York Coliseum Auto Show, c. 1966-67. Angel hair, fake smoke display stylization.

Bike build by Mel, c. 1973

Back in the mid-’60s I was really into the bike scene. I’d go to the New York Coliseum car show every year. It’s amazing that I never really got into a lot of trouble. You have to remember that there weren’t any bikers to speak of back then. There wasn’t much of anything said about the whole thing. It was strange behavior that had not been done yet. People didn’t know what to make of it. We were wearing chromed German helmets, sitting on choppers and we had tattoos. I don’t think it is possible to even imagine what people thought about it. It must have really twisted people around. There was no context for this; nothing to relate it to. Now, this has all been done. The movies about the lifestyle have educated people in some strange way.

We wanted to be different and this is how we wanted to do it. There was no information. Now, forget about it. Every other kid wants to be a biker. It has been reduced to a look and a stereotype.

It is very easy now to buy kit bikes. And a lot of the bikes all look the same. The whole thing has changed over the years. Back in the ’60s, none of this mindset existed. I remember in 1965 I decided I wanted to change the way handlebars looked. I added chromed metal webbing between the bars. I found a guy that did metal work for cemeteries and he chromed this webbing kind of thing I made. This is just something I wanted to try. This idea caught on with some guys up in the Bronx and some guys up there started running their bikes with this look. This is how things worked back then. Somebody would get an idea and make it. Other guys would see it and if they liked it they’d copy it. Back then guys would run into guys at Nathan’s or at a hamburger stand and they’d see something and it would influence them. A lot of motorcycling now has to do with the guys who do it on the weekend with their stick-on tattoos. These guys don’t get it.

We would go to Stanley and Walter Moskowitz to get tattooed. When I got all my tattoos in the early 1960s people literally thought this was completely nuts. I had 110 tattoos in the ’60s. My friends and I would stand with our motorcycles and we were heavily tattooed and people didn’t know whether to call the police or just run away from us as fast as they could. There was a reason those guys called themselves the Aliens. They were the Aliens. Those were the good old days. I miss all that. The whole thing changed. It will keep going but it will never be like that again. The sense of uniqueness and challenge. You know, back then you could actually go to school and beat somebody up and get away with it.

For myself, I like to work on the old stuff. The new stuff has really been influenced by the Japanese. Harley has been more and more influenced by the Japanese. No head bolts, no face bolts. For me, the real Harley Davidson period was 1969. That’s the stuff that I work on and other shops don’t even know about. I like carburetors. When I was young we didn’t have money to bring our bikes to a shop. We had to learn how to do it trial and error. We learned from our mistakes.

When I was young I had to start someplace so I went around and bought old milling machines in Brooklyn and the Bronx. I worked with them and figured it out. I made hundreds of mistakes but that’s how you learn.

As a kid we would ride down to Greenwich Village and hang around. We’d go out to the Conduit in Queens and race against each other. We’d use the tunnels as start and finish markers. On Friday nights. All the time it was late at night. It was really dangerous. The road where we would race was not level. It was on an angle going down. Sometimes we’d be getting up to 120 mph and then the road would start to dip down

Sissy bar swastika stylization by Mel, c. 1973

Dragon bike with girl, c. 1973

Popping a wheelie

from under you into the tunnel. It was really dangerous. Once in a while the cops would come and everyone would scramble. The cops would never catch the guys that were doing the racing. They were doing more than 100 mph. You aren't going to get anywhere near those guys. Everyone else was scrambling out of the way. It was fun.

One night some guys showed up with a fuel elimination dragster on a trailer. I don't remember where they came from. They off-loaded it and then some other guys showed up with a car. This is on the highway at like three o'clock in the morning! That's the kind of stuff that went on out there! These guys set up and they took off but the dragster went air born. We all stood there watching this car fly into the air and then crash into the wall at like 100 mph. The driver was killed instantly. The car was in pieces all over the highway.

We even made window stickers that read Conduit Killer. If you won the race you could put the sticker on your bike or on your butterfly window. Some of the races had printed flyers that told people when it would happen. A lot of guys used to race for a lot of money. But most of the kids just raced for the Killer stickers. That was a private thing. It meant a lot to certain people. You'd be at a light in Brooklyn or wherever and guys would notice the sticker. They knew you were the real thing.

Monticello run, c. 1973

Flame thrower, Colorado

Engine rebuilds at Colorado shop, 2010

Guns, Colorado

Bonge

I AM A TRADITIONALIST

Third Street, Manhattan

Early photo of Bonge with build, c. 1972

My family is from Bushwick, Brooklyn. I was born in Brooklyn and later I was raised out in Massapequa on the Island. When I got old enough in the '70s I started coming back to the city. I was out on The Island as a kid in the '60s. The early '60s with the Stingray bicycle explosion and all that. I wasn't into sports. Still, I don't know a baseball from a football or any of that crap. I never had any interest in it. My father was a carpenter and a cabinet maker—a craftsman with wood but not with metal stuff. We didn't get to do too much together as he worked a lot, but the one thing we did together was to go to the stock car races in Freeport. I was really into that. I loved the stock car racing. At that time in the '60s they were racing cars from the '40s and '50s. Fords with Flathead eights. Circle track racing. I loved that—all the action and noise. Then my brother used to take me to the New York Coliseum at Columbus Circle in the '60s for the custom car show. I was probably ten years old the first time. I would look at the cars and the bikes. Candy apple paint and chrome. Wow, man that was my world. It was a cool thing. I would think, *"Man when I get older can you imagine owning a fucking car like that? Look at that fucking shit."*

The custom bikes at the show always impressed me. I'd look at the guys standing next to the bikes and think that guy looks like a hooligan. Man, that's what I want to be like. Look at him—fucking cool looking bike and he can probably kick anyone's ass. That appealed to me. I didn't care about anything else really. That was my world. Now, you can pick up any magazine—Ed Roth, Ed Roth, Ed Roth. But I was around for the first round of Ed Roth in the early '60s. A lot of kids built models. But I was really into what he was about. His whole thing. Roth faded in the '70s. He became a sign painter at Knotts Berry Farm. A lot of people forgot about him but not me.

I found some old photos taken at the custom show of Mel Bernstein's bike and the handlebars he made. These photos were taken at the Coliseum. The New York custom car show that was every year, November 25th–28th (the weekend after Thanksgiving) the year was 1967 or 1968. I remember the show, it was the year before Mel built the Dragon Tail bike, and put that in the show, and before I started putting my custom bikes in the show. I worked for Mel from 1975–1983 a few years after that show.

The handlebars he made went out of style on a chopper, he took them off and they went from Johnny Pinstripe to Tony "Fat Boy" Carterelli to Alex in Wonderland, the pinstriper, who turned them over to me in 1977. I still have them. How could I get rid of something as creepy as them?

In one photo Mel is standing next to a guy who is sitting on the bike with the bars. It was when Mel was in the Mind Benders from Brooklyn (a loose-knit bunch from the Cross Bay Blvd. area). The sand-casted center piece of the bars was made by a guy who made shit for cemeteries. He casted it for Mel and Mel welded it into the bars. The chrome on them is still good to this day.

At that young age I was aware of this custom car world through making models.

Early photo of Bonge with build, c. 1972

Early photo of Bonge with coffin bike build, c. 1977

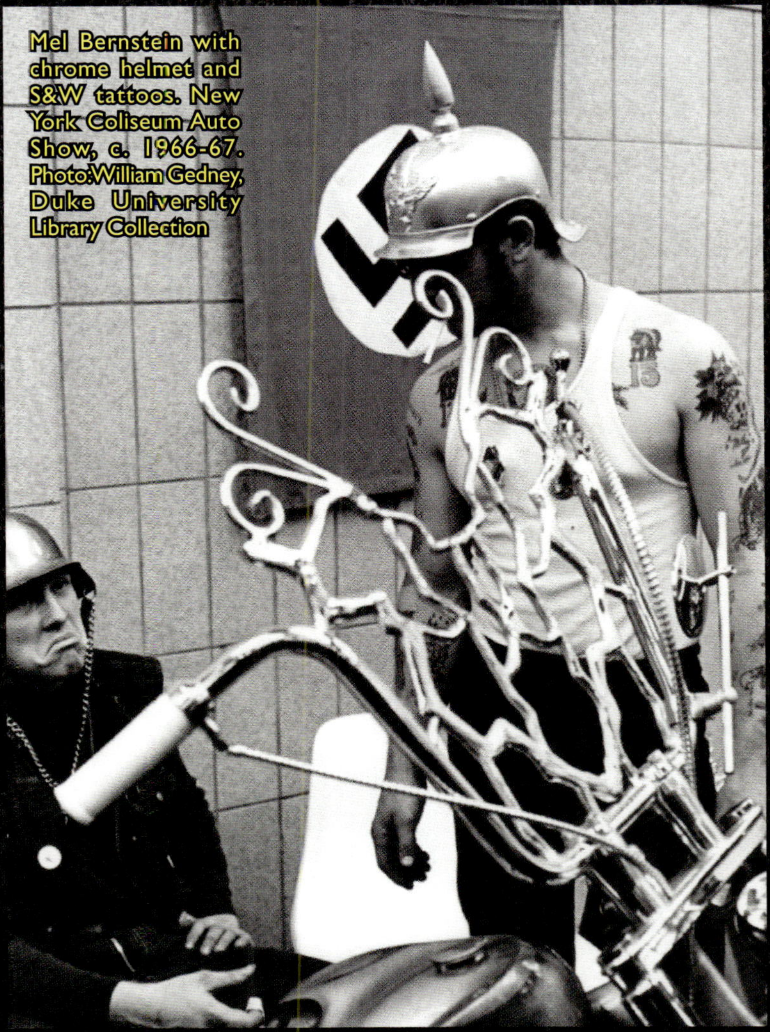

Mel Bernstein with chrome helmet and S&W tattoos. New York Coliseum Auto Show, c. 1966-67. Photo:William Gedney, Duke University Library Collection

Mel Bernstein in bath tub at show, c. 1967

Bonge with his first tattoo machines and tattoo artist certificate, c. 1970

Bonge with trike build, c. 1975

Handle bar web stylization, 1975

Bonge at Bernstein show presentation: Bar Hopper Chopper, c. 1976

Bonge with Dragon Bike build, 1976

Bonge with handlebar webbing, c. 1975.

I was very impressed with model kits. That's how I knew who Ed Roth was. I was just a kid but I'd see Ed Roth's cars and it was like, man look at that. I remember me and my friends called them future cars. These cars they made into models, everybody thought these were cars you were going to drive around in the future. Some crazy bubble top like Beatnik Bandit. Those were the really over-the-top cool cars. When the World's Fair was held in New York in 1964–65, they had an exhibit of custom futuristic cars like Ray Farner's "Little Coffin." I would have my parents take me back to that exhibit each time we would go. This is before they had Hot Wheels and any of that. This is just model kits. I became a big fan of Roth's work.

As a teenager, as I got a little older I got into the bike thing too. I went from peddling a Stingray bicycle to putting motors on them and building these really dangerous motorbikes with no brakes. Friction motorbikes. I had a whole bunch of them and then I got into mini bikes. My father bought me one because he thought I was going to kill myself on one of the Stingray bike contraptions I was building with high handlebars. One hand on the handlebars and one hand down on the throttle on the carburetor. It had a grooved metal pulley on the motor that would press against the rear tire, so I would wind up with shredded black rubber stuck all over the back of my white t-shirt. No brakes. It was dangerous as shit. There were a few kids in the neighborhood that had motorbikes. A few kids had mini bikes and go-karts but that was still pretty new. There weren't that many of them on Long Island.

So for me it was more like: Man, Mrs. Wanson just threw her lawn mower out, so I fucking went and got it and cleaned it out and got the motor running. I took the motor off and got a piece of angle iron and did what I seen the other guys do. You know, I built a motor bike and rode it.

Interest in this kind of thing was limited in those days. There was very little of this then. In the '50s there were a few car clubs out there but the only one that really survived out there was the Rod Snappers. Then that turned into the Long Island Street Rod Association. But, once you use the word street rod you are getting away from that aspect of hot rods and it's a whole different bag of shit. You know the cars change; it's a fat tired, modern looking version of a hot rod. That really doesn't do much for me. Now there is all sorts of new terminology, like Rat Rod. It's a thing that isn't painted but it's done up all traditional fifties style and now they are calling it a rat rod. Like it's a new craze. Guys say, "Hey, I want to build one of them, that looks like fun." Fuck, that's how we were building them fucking 25 years ago. And people were building them that style 25 years before I was able to do it. A lot of guys stand around and talk about making stuff like cars and bikes. It makes for conversation. But to actually build it is a different thing. I was lucky and I had guys that helped point me in the right direction.

I am more artistically inclined than mechanically. I don't rebuild motors completely. I can do pretty much anything building a hot rod or chopper, but everybody has stuff they farm out. When I get an old car or an old bike, the first thing I do is pull the motor apart, send it out and have stuff polished and plated and then I give it to one of my guys that does my motor rebuilding. You can't do everything and there are skilled guys that specialize in this work.

In high school I was my own animal. I graduated in 1976. I was different from everyone else in a lot of ways at that time. I am sure there are kids in high school now who are into the hot rod scene, but back then there wasn't a lot of people into this

Bonge with bike, c. 1986

Bonge with Panhead, c. 1986

Bonge with Ed "Big Daddy" Roth, c. late 1980s

kind of thing. There wasn't a lot of people into tattoos or people that had hot rods or were into bikes. Back then, out on Long Island, or in the city, if somebody rode a chopper you knew who he was. Or it would be, "What's up with that guy?" Pretty much everybody knew who was who. Everybody's bike looked different and you came from a circle of people that hung out in their own areas. There was a Coney Island crew, a Bay Ridge crew. The Long Island guys like Alex in Wonderland and his whole crew. But you could pretty much count them on one hand who was in your area. Anyone who was on a chopper you pretty much knew who he was. Or you knew somebody who knew who he was.

In the '70s there wasn't very many hot rod magazines that related to what I was into. There was *Street Rodder*—every once in a while you'd see a cool car in there that was done straight-up fifties traditional. But there were not many cars like that at the time. *Hot Rod* magazine was more geared towards muscle cars and all that shit, which wasn't my bag you know. There was a place called Farmer's Market on Long Island and as a kid I would go there. They had a magazine guy there and he used to get old magazines and sell them. So, I'd go there and buy old magazines from the fifties. The old 5x7 magazines. Any kind of bike magazines that were early. The early issues of *Easyriders* magazine. I was looking for traditional fifties-style bikes and cars. Then, through the model kits as a kid, I learned who the big wigs were: George Barris, Ed Roth; guys like that. This whole Kustom Kulture thing didn't exist. This rat rod thing is all very recent stuff from the 1990s.

Myself and the other guys I knew about, we were operating in a bit of a cultural vacuum. We did this because we wanted to do this. There were old guys out there and there were a few influential guys, but we had to pay attention. In the '70s I was building bikes that looked like straight-up old style '50s. Metal flake paint when people weren't into metal flake any more. Candy apple colors. I was into the traditional old style stuff. I am not the pioneer. It was done before me by craftsmen. I grew up knowing who Ed Roth was and seeing his stuff in magazines and going, "Oh man, this is the motherfucker I want to be like." You know? This influenced me a lot. I wanted to build things that style and that way. I have stacks of Roth's *Chopper* magazine.

There was somewhat of an East Coast style to making things. I am not going to say that everything cool came out of California. That would be very far-fetched. There were a lot more builders and a lot more action going on out there. That's where Roth and Barris were from and a lot of it originated there, but I gotta give credit to the East Coast, too, man. There were guys building customs here, too. You look at those old magazines that Roth and Barris were in and there were always East Coast customs in there that were done straight-up cool shit.

I was a part of the Baby Boomer thing. The first big wave of younger people. But in terms of some kind of cultural power? Let me tell you, in high school the chicks didn't want nothing to do with me [laughter]. They used to say, "Oh, he's a motor head." They were into jocks. People knew I was out there but I'd pull up to school on something like one of my bikes, like my dragon bike and people would look at this thing like, what the fuck is this guy up to?

I was a graphic arts major in high school. They had a print shop there and a dark room. I would print photos, silk screening, and all that shit. And I was into metal shop. I had what was called a co-op teacher, this guy Doc Watson. He was a funny guy and a wise-ass. He would talk about the other teachers like, oh, that guy's a jerk. He would come into class laughing and say, "I seen that contraption you got." He was talking about my dragon bike. He told me that all the teachers would be eating lunch in the teacher's room and I'd come roaring up to school on my dragon bike. They'd all jump up yelling about me, "Here he comes!" They'd all run to the window and pull the blinds apart and be yelling, "Jesus, look at that thing!" The teachers would flip out.

At that time I wore studded wrist bands. This is pre-punk rock. It wasn't big spikes but it was leather gauntlets with studs on it. The teachers would see me wear that and they'd go, "There's something really wrong with him." They all thought, "*What kind of lunatic would be riding around on a bike with flames over his head and studded wrist bands.*" I was in eleventh and twelfth grade and I was hanging out with guys who were 28...29 years old. I worked for Mel [Bernstein] and I was hanging out with a guy named Louie. You know, older biker guys. Sometimes Louie would come and pick me up after school to go to work on bikes at his shop or they'd come up and visit me at school. The teachers would be in the windows saying, "Oh, the Hells Angels are here." You know, not one of those guys ever became a Hell's Angel like I did.

You have to remember this is 1975. The teachers see me meeting with these older guys. You know, tattooed bikers with big long beards. They are like, "Whoa, what the fuck does this kid got going on?" I'm seventeen years old with tattoos all over me from S&W Tattoo and Richie Montgomery. I borrowed my friend's ID so I could fake my age. This is before photo ID. My friend's name was Jules. So I got an eagle with a banner from Stanley and Walter—the Bowery Boys. They knew the ID wasn't mine so they busted my balls asking, "What you want in the banner kid? How about your name; JULES? That would look nice." I'm like no, put USA in there. They said, "You sure, Jules? I think that would look good in there." I'm like, if this mother fucker writes my friend's name in there, Jules, I'll have to carve it out of my arm. Walter did the first one and Stanley did the Christ Head, and so on.

I really appreciated this world of bikes and cars. Like Alex in Wonderland always says, "We are only custodians to these things we build." You know, we build them and they're cool and they get passed on or sold to others. I can't say I am an originator because I'm doing stuff that was done in the '50s already. I didn't create this stuff. People did it before me but because guys like me got into the style and actually made these things, I did play a part in this. I got into it and this helped to bring it around during the '70s. There was old bike guys that were around years ago who would look at my stuff and they liked that I was doing it. They'd bring guys around and say, "Man, you gotta see what this kid is doing." They really appreciated it. I was a young kid and these older guys would see it and appreciate it. "Hey kid, that looks like something from the old days." I did my homework and these older guys could see it.

That's just the way I am. That's just what I am into, the way I build things. I was a younger guy hanging out with older guys who were into this stuff before and now they were building new style bikes. But I was going backwards. I was looking into old style stuff that had come up in a world way before catalog builds. Ok, I'll take this front end and that sissy bar. I wasn't into that. I was into making it myself. I learned how to do this shit, you know? I was into it. I made my stuff in high school in the metal shop. I was able to use their lathe and weld shit. I didn't have these kinds of tools at the time. I was able to use the equipment for a year after I got out of high school.

I worked with Mel and that was a very unique period of time. He started that whole thing with that dragon bike. That's when people were really into wild, over-the-top custom style. Because everybody built

Bonge, "You Loot We Shoot"

their own stuff. And everything was more different than the other. I remember seeing him and this was early '70s. I was a kid at the time. I was probably thirteen. I used to race dirt bikes. I would go to anything motorcycle related. I went to a custom bike show at the Long Island Arena in Commack. I seen Mel there completely covered with tattoos and this was very different for back then. He had full sleeves and on his hands and stuff. I seen him with his style bikes at that show and I was, "Hey, man, this is what the fuck I'm into." I wound up meeting the guy and working with him. I started building stuff with him. I was respectful about this. I looked to the older guys. I tried to ease my way in respectfully.

There were a few chopper magazines that were on the mark. There were very few car magazines that were about '50s style customs. There was very little to do with nostalgic stuff. Now there's a cross-over. You pick up any of these Kustom Kulture type magazines: I hate that term. But that's what's going on. There's a crossover. Back then it wasn't like that. There was the bike crowd and the car crowd. And in the '70s, the car crowd was mostly muscle cars and street rods.

My parents were somewhat supportive of my interests. My father tolerated me. I got arrested for assaults and stuff, but I was young. My father said, "Hey, look, he gets up out of bed every day. He's busy doing something. He's constructive and building things." He wasn't on my back too much.

I started with bikes first. I built two or three. The bike with the coffin. I got that in pieces. It was an old meter maid's trike. A 1946 Harley Davidson Servi-Car it was called. I did all the work to that bike. The paint job me and a guy Louie did. We laid on layers and layers of Jade Green metal flake. Louie gave me the paint gun and showed me how to do it. I was like, "Hey, this is pretty cool." That's where I started painting

Bonge with Bar Hopper bike build

Olds and Bar Hopper builds by Bonge, 1980s

Bar Hopper bike

from. Having an older guy say, "Here, you do it." Throw me in the middle of the ring. So I built that trike right around the end of high school and then later I got a stock '57 Ford and did it up as an old style, lead sled type of car. I welded things up as close as I could and then bondoed it.

I found a set of cruiser skirts, and then a Continental kit for it in Hemmings Motor News. I had Alex pinstripe "The Wild One" on the back. I put motorcycle fishtail exhaust pipes on it coming out of the bumper. I lowered it with spinner hubcaps and put teardrop spotlights on it. I'd drive it around. I'd go out with girls and they'd say; you're driving this car like it's something from *Rocky Horror Show*. They didn't know how to relate to it. Then old guys would see it and say, "Hey, wow, that looks like the car I had in high school 20 years ago."

At this time in the '70s everything became muscle cars. Jacked up with wide tires. If you notice the trends in the magazines: the '50s were custom cars and hot rods, early '60s custom show cars and some hot rods. Then in 1965 it started to get to be about performance; people going to drag strips. This is pre-funny car. Performance became the big thing. Every year motors got bigger. With Ford it went from the 292 to the 312, then the 390. With Chevy it was the 283 then the 327 then the 396 then the 427. They just got bigger. People wanted more horsepower During the 1950s the muscle cars were the big Oldsmobiles and the Chryslers with hemis. People would take those motors and put them in lighter cars. When Chevy had 283s and 327s in the early '60s. They didn't even call them small blocks at the time.

I tended to be interested in traditions. I liked the old Ford Flatheads. They are cool looking. You see an old one done up old style with aluminum heads, two or three Stromberg's on it, it's a beautiful thing. It's cool. You can do all sorts of race work to it, all sorts of horseshit to it, but at the end of the day a stock 350 will blow it off the road. It's not really a performance-minded motor but it's a really cool looking motor. But the overhead valve Olds motor in the '50s was more of a fast motor. Flathead motors can run hot and be more problematic. When I told Robert Williams I was dropping one in my '31 Ford Coupe, he asked me if I have Triple A [AAA] towing. That clown.

There were names I followed, Larry Watson the painter, Gene Winfield the customizer. He's probably in his seventies now. That guy just rocks and rolls. He is a powerhouse. He gets out of bed early and gets in the shop and works. To this day he is a builder and a craftsman. This kind of skill was more promoted out of the West Coast. People like George Barris. He built the Munster coach and the Dragula and the Batmobile. That's TV and you can't get any better publicity than that. A lot of the name builders were out west. When I was young this kind of thing was very influential. When I wanted to build something, these guys and their cars were on my mind. The way they made things; the forms they used and stylized. It was all in there. So first it was bikes and then cars.

I built a car for Brian Setzer of the Stray Cats. He was from Massapequa also and got a hot rod. When he just started to get into the old bike and car thing, I'd give him a stack of old magazines and showed him old car styles. I told Brian about Ed Roth and the cool shit he did so he got Ed to do some record sleeve art for one of the Stray Cat albums. Ed was big in the '50s and '60s but not many people after that really knew anything about him. He got into the bike thing and then Revell dropped him because they didn't want anything to do with bike clubs and crazy shit. People knew who he was but not like years before. Brian's label had to hunt Roth down. Nobody knew where he was then. I even remember *Hot Rod* magazine doing an article then called, "What Ever Happened to Ed Roth?"

I have been a member of a car club called the Beatniks for some time. A tattooer, Jack Rudy, and a few of us started the club. There was a bunch of guys that used to go to the Paso Robles custom event in California. So he thought about forming the club. He wanted to put Koolsville on the bottom rocker. So, you could be from anywhere. Because Koolsville is wherever we're at. Jack grabbed the bull by the horns and got shirts printed and went to Paso Robles and handed some out. It started out loose at the time and then we organized it more. So, we drafted up some rules and by-laws for the club. In the States there are fifty or so members and we don't just give things away. We don't just let people in that easy. Basically we are into traditional '50s hot rods and customs pre-1962 done in traditional '50s style only. That was the thing. We are basically guys that are into going to shows, traveling and living the beatnik lifestyle. Most of us are artists of some sort. Either painters, pinstripers, tattoo artists, or some kind of art related background. We are into the whole beatnik style thing. We don't go sittin' around reciting poetry or any of that horseshit, but we are non-conformists. Years ago we'd go to a car show and people would look at us. People thought we were scumbags with all these tattoos. They stayed away from us because they thought we were going to kick their fucking asses. A lot of people steered clear of us. And that's kind of what we wanted to be. Different from the Mom and Pop car club people; all tattooed up with cool-ass cars. Doing everything our way and our style.

Now the world has kind of caught up to us. As it happens with everything. Back in '84 I did an article with *Outlaw Biker* magazine and I remember saying that I saw the whole tattoo artist thing as changing. It became

MC
Est 1969
NEW YORK CITY
NO PARKING
EXCEPT
AUTHORIZED
HELLS
ANGELS
BIG VINNY
HELLS ANGELS
MC
NEW YORK CITY
HELLS ANGELS
NEW YORK C
7
7
Bonge

like being a shoemaker—nothing special. But, back in '76-'77 when I was tattooing, or the years before that, people would be so impressed. I remember they said, "How did you learn to do that?" That's like being a witch doctor or something. It was like a real weird carny type thing. But that's how things go. People are always going to get into things that are cool. Then you respect the people that did it before you. That's just the process when it gets bastardized, and too many squares get into it. Also, then it's time to abandon ship and move on.

But ever since I was a teenager I wanted to be a biker. I wanted to be a Hell's Angel. I'd seen the movies and I heard they were located in the city in the Village, so I was like, "Man, that's what the fuck I want to be. That's number one." So I first got into that maybe when I was fifteen or sixteen years old. To be a biker, to get into the bikes.

I have accumulated a lot of old motorcycle stuff. I'm a member of the Antique Motorcycle Association. I go to all the antique meets. Word of mouth about this and that. I am into old bikes and old stuff. Traditional '30s and '40s Knuckle and Panhead motors and Indians to build the choppers or whatever I do. I've got one traveling bike my FXR. They don't make them anymore. They made them up until the mid-nineties and then they started making Dyna glides or something. But it's a good handling bike and frame. That's why a lot of the guys in my club prefer old FXR frames. So I just keep updating that bike constantly instead of buying a new bike with a bigger faster motor and six speed transmission. That's my one traveling bike. I have spun the odometer twice on that bike. I have been to California numerous times. Up and down the United States on that bike. All over the place.

To do that on a bike day after day without ending up on the side of the road, you need a reliable bike. When my club rides, we pull out of a motel at maybe eight o'clock in the morning and we'll ride till seven or eight

Hubcap collection

Beatniks club plate

Bonge
(photo with permission)

o'clock at night. That's a good 6–700 mile day and to do that at 80MPH for 12 hours on a bike is brutal on the machine. It breaks down the oil; it wears on things the way we ride. You need a new bike for that. Antique bikes and old choppers are cool for around the city or local runs, but if you think you are going to get on that thing and go cross country? Yeah, I used to do it but I thought my teeth were going to vibrate out of my head. The old rigid frame bike riding to Colorado or Sturgis. You know? That's brutal. It depends what you are expecting your bike to do. You got to keep it in perspective. If I think I'm going to get in the middle of a pack of Hell's Angels with my '48 Indian Chief and keep up and not blow my motor to pieces it ain't happening. Yes, you can ride cross-country on a '48 Indian Chief, but not at 80 MPH for 12 hours at a clip with a bunch of members. That ain't happening. You know?

As far as the other stuff I build, I am a traditionalist. A lot of guys will build a car out of a '49 Merc and pull out the original motor and tranny and put in a Chevy engine. That's good for them. It's reliable. But for me, I am into leaving whatever came in that car and was in that car in the '50s. Or what guys would have done to make it a hot rod version in the '50s. That's what I am into. My '57 Olds has the original Rocket 88 motor with the factory tri-power done up with some hot rod stuff.

I built a '27 Roadster Pick-up and I got a '59 Rocket Olds motor in there. Most of the cars and bikes I build have the original old stuff that would have been in there as a cool thing in the '50s. To find the parts it's a word of mouth thing through people and to come across stuff. This has changed of course. There are a lot more events and things going on. Some of this is good and some of this sucks. You get some fucking poke-ass motherfucker that built a bike that gets in some magazine. Whatever. That's what it is. You can't walk around and complain too much about the new guys. Then you become a disgruntled old prick. Not that there's anything wrong with being a disgruntled old prick. It is what it is. If somebody's full of shit, I can smell it on him a mile away. This is something I do. If someone gets something out of it, cool.

I have been over to Japan to the Mooneyes show in Yokohama. This is interesting. These people are fascinated with American '50s. They always have been. They think that it was a perfect world then. Big luxury cars, a wife with big tits, and a beehive hair-do. You can't go wrong with that. These people do their home work, they know what's cool and they want it. In America this whole thing is a part of our past. We take it for granted. But in other parts of the world, 1950s America means something. For these people, what's cooler than having a 1950s American car all done up and restored? Nothing.

For me, it was always Ed Roth and what he was doing with cars. This was encouraging to me. In terms of motorcycles, it was the Hell's Angels. The style of their bikes was important. In California they were doing the really groundbreaking work with their bikes. The early choppers. The guys in the club had really cool stuff back then. This was very influential. The 1960s biker movies were important. The guys riding the bikes in a lot of those movies were in the club. All the styling in there, the bikes were really off the hook different. That really influenced me. In the '60s the chopper style in New York was cool. There were clubs like the Aliens and the Mind Benders and their bikes were choppers. These clubs were known for their bike styles. There were also chopper guys that weren't in clubs that were building really cool stuff.

Bonge's FXR, paint by Bonge (photo with permission)

The information about bikes traveled coast to coast with the bikes. In the '40s and early '50s it was the Bobber style. Taking stuff off the bikes. Stripping stuff off and maybe good paint jobs. Stripping stuff off to make the bike look faster, more outlaw looking. In the mid-'50s and '60s it was all about custom and chrome. Bikes were copying what was being done to cars. There were no magazines or books back then about bikes. When Roth put out the first *Chopper* magazine, that was the first of its kind. Until then all motorcycle magazine were square-assed and had nothing to do with choppers. Roth keyed in on this new style. Guys in New York and other places saw this and these new ideas changed the custom world.

Paint by Bonge (photo with permission)

Alex in Wonderland

IT WAS COOL AND THAT'S WHAT MATTERED

New York

Alex in his workshop in front of his '57 Panhead Hardtail

'66, '67, '68 we were riding all over the Island [Long Island, New York] and we would go into the city on Friday nights. We didn't know where we were going; we were just following the pack. We were riding the 20 miles in from what was mostly farmland. This is pre-suburbs. Back in those days it was really moody riding in the city. It would be late at night; there were not many traffic lights. If there were we'd ride through them anyways; there were no cops anywhere. We would be riding and the noise from our bikes was echoing off of the buildings. This was surreal to us. There were no helmet laws and no headlight laws. It was dark. Today everyone takes for granted that New York is what it is. Back in the '60s New York was a different place. I was a country boy and going to the city was a thrilling experience.

We would go there in the summer time mostly. It was hot out and it would be even hotter in the city. This wasn't so good for our motors and they didn't like it. We'd ride around the city all night. There wasn't any traffic; there wasn't anything going on. Maybe downtown in the Village there was something going on but we would ride around in a dream. We'd ride over the bridges and go to Brooklyn. We'd have the bridge all to ourselves. We'd ride around until four or five o'clock in the morning. We'd have the whole place to ourselves. We'd stop off and listen to bands playing in the parks in the middle of the night. It was a very different culture back then.

Alex in Wonderland build, '57 Panhead Hardtail

Alex's Panhead dresser

Alex's Panhead

Alex at 1966-67 New York Coliseum Show. (Note handlebar webbing style on bike behind Alex.)

Alex with dresser, c. 1968

Alex's Panhead, c. 1967

Al Zolo, 1968-69

1967-68 New York Panhead chopper style

Al Zolo, c. 1968

Hanging out in New York City, c. 1968

High pipes style, c.1968

Alex's brother Louie, 1968 (note headlights style). At this time there were no headlight laws in NYC for bikes which opened the door for stylization.

Alex's mother sitting on Elvis Presley's dresser, c. 1969

Choppers had been around since '48 and '49. Guys were modifying their Harleys. There were machines and styles coming out from California. We'd see these bikes and we'd copy them. East Coast guys were influenced by the music and the hot rods and we'd see the California movies like *The Born Losers*, *The Wild One*; when those movies came out this exploded the interest in this culture in New York. Everyone went nuts. We were all riding around with spiked German helmets on and all that.

This is the beginning of some sense of outlaw youth culture. We were looking for some way to express ourselves. And we were using these machines and this special way we wanted to dress as a way to personalize our dream. The Harley or Triumph or BSA choppers that we built and rode around on were our rolling pieces of art work. We had our own sense of taste about how we wanted to do this. Maybe we were successful or not. Some guys had more money to build their bikes but they might not have had good taste. It was all about taste and the style of the bike; did you pick good colors? What was the style of your bike?

I am not sure young people today can imagine how we felt riding around the city on our machines during that time. You have to remember that we are talking the 1950s. The culture was locked down and fearful. WWII had just ended. The world had just gone through a major economic and war disaster and our parents wanted safety. This is how we were brought up; play it safe, don't take chances. For me to build my machine and then to ride on it meant one thing: freedom. A way to get away from the crushing pressure of the culture.

For a young guy experiencing this in the '50s meant freedom and speed and testosterone. You're a young guy riding a bike like this and your testosterone is raging. It's the peacock effect and you are looking to score a girl. There is something about that

Don Meyer (Fuzzy) build, photo 1968

Alex's Panhead, c. 1968

Alex, c. 1968

Alex, c. 1968

Alex's Long Island crew on night ride to NYC, c.1968 (photo courtesy Bonge)

Alex's Long Island crew on night ride to NYC, c.1968 (photo courtesy Bonge)

New York Coliseum show, c. 1967
(note handlebar webbing by Mel Bernstein)

Alex's crew pipe styling, c. 1968
(photo courtesy Bonge)

Mind Benders, Brooklyn, c. 1968

Late 1960s back fender stylization by Alex

Jet fuselage in Alex's back yard

Alex's Long Island crew (photo courtesy Bonge)

Alex's Long Island crew, c. 1968
(photo courtesy Bonge)

Alex in Wonderland in his shop

Fender skirt paint by Alex

Alex's Long Island crew, c. 1968
(photo courtesy Bonge)

Alex's Long Island crew, c. 1968
(photo courtesy Bonge)

Alex's painting

frigging throttle; when you start cracking on that throttle and you got open pipes, it goes right to your head. It's a shot of adrenaline. It's youth, it's exhilarating and we had a lot of fun. I didn't know we were having a lot of fun but looking back on it we were having a lot of fun. We got carried away. Especially after all the biker movies came out. I could have rode into the city every night.

I was doing concrete work at the time and it was tough, but after work I'd jump on my bike and chase around and look for girls. Back then it was sweeter, and innocent, and much more open. We had less options; it was all Panheads and there were some Knuckleheads around and some Flatheads but there weren't any Shovelheads around. I always loved the look of a Panhead. There is a lot of intricate detail going on. A lot of jazz going on. Like the cam cover with the fins, the oil filter cover. You will never see anything like that again. The trumpet horn? You will never see anything like that again. Looking at my Panhead now; that thing is really a relic. Hard tail, drum brakes.

Our influences were very limited. We did not have much to go on. In my area there was a guy named Don Meyer—Fuzzy. He had a radical chopper that influenced us. He was an artist that went to the School of Visual Arts. Before him there were my mother's brothers. I was a young guy and young guys are very impressionable. My mother's brothers were always hep guys. I would visit them in their garages. These guy's garages were like a man cave. That's where they kept their toys. So as a kid I'd walk into a guy's man cave and see his nice car or bike and if he had a nice machine you'd say to yourself, "That's a better way to live." It was parts and pieces, a collage of things that influenced me as a kid. I kept this bike because it represents an important part of my past. It's a stock '57 rigid frame. You don't want to go over a pot hole with it. You'll take it right in the kidneys. Riding these bikes is for a 20-year-old. It's really cool but it's crazy. I look at this bike and I think about it. If it's just sitting and idling on the kick stand it makes this sound and it rocks back and forth. It is a kind of expression.

A bike like this was all handmade. You had to go through a lot to make a bike like this in the mid-'60s. I wanted to make a sissy bar that finished with a medieval type point. But in 1966 where do I find this? I found an abandoned Long Island mansion that had a thick iron fence that went around it. I wondered, how do I get one of those spiky points off that friggin' fence? If you ask permission they are just going to say no, so I went back in the middle of the night and took a hack saw and sawed the friggin' point off the fence. I welded that point on to the top of my sissy bar and ground it out nice, and chromed it and it looked perfect. It was cool and that's what mattered.

Alex's workshop

Alex's business card

Alex's car

Rufus "Brooklyn Heavy" Boyd

HEAD HUNTERS DRAG RACING CLUB COMMEMORATIVE SUMMER PICNIC

Bedford Stuyvesant, Brooklyn

Brooklyn Heavy (photo courtesy Brooklyn Heavy family)

I am Brooklyn Heavy's daughter. He lived in a small town in the Carolinas—born and raised. He moved to Connecticut in 1958–59 and then a couple years later he moved to New York. As a young man he always loved cars and he worked in a gas station back in the day when he was a young man. Cars had always been a passion of his. In New York he became very serious about this interest. He had a job in a gas station up here in New York and then he got real serious about it. In the early days he ran with Impalas and Camaros. He loved Camaros. Then he got into Dusters and Pontiacs. But Camaros were his passion. In the late '60s he started racing seriously on the street in New York. He raced on the Concourse [Grand Concourse].

Heavy had learned about engines from older experienced people he had worked for. He understood high performance engine making. He raced nationwide, and became really known starting in '71–'72. He'd race in Berlitz, North Carolina; Rockingham, North Carolina; Suffolk, Virginia; Englishtown, New Jersey; and other places. He always got geared-up and raced in style. He was known for having his cars, trailers, and race team all having color-coordinated colors and outfits. He always raced in style. That was his thing. Always show style. He raced from '69 to '76. He became ill and he passed away in 2010.

He had a wide reputation. Everybody knew him. I never raced myself but I followed Heavy and his racing all the years he did it. When he started racing his name was Brooklyn Wild Pumpkin. He always raced an orange car. Always an orange car. I don't know, he just liked the racing and he had a natural thing with it. Once he got into the racing he started to know the big guys at the tracks. This is how he got into the pro-stock. Bill "Grumpy" Jenkins with his '66 Nova then the Vega [Grumpy Toy], then the Camaros. There was Sox and Martin. Grumpy was tearin' them up with that Nova. He made a lot of money.

Back in the day it was all street racing. The big boys went to the track and into Pro-Stock. But my father started out on the street. When Heavy was around cars with big motors he was like a kid in a candy store. He had this passion about these kinds of cars. He would stand there and look at the cars. Just the sound of it brought the biggest smile to his face. To hear that engine roar. It was like some kind of medicine for him.

Brooklyn Heavy setting up at race (photo courtesy Brooklyn Heavy family)

Brooklyn Heavy family at 2010 picnic

Head Hunters picnic line up

Line up at picnic

Line up at picnic

Head Hunters picnic attendee

Brooklyn Attitude AC car

Picnic attendee

Brooklyn Attitude AC member

Kenny (aka Big Red)
Head Bangers Racing Club

Street scene at picnic

Street scene at picnic

Pete Ranko

RANK CYCLES

Ozone Park, Queens

Pete with his '66 Chevelle, 1979, corner of Ludlow Street and Stanton Street

Back when I first started to become interested in motorcycles, there weren't many magazines to look at. There was *Street Chopper* and *Iron Horse* and maybe one other one. In those days when you rode around, you wore your leather jacket and your boots. You knew that you could run into somebody along the way that was a club member or was in a bad mood that day. You were just an independent guy just trying to run around. Not that any of us were nice back then either. You know, everyone had their issues. Not that we were tough guys but everybody was, you know; didn't take much shit. So you could run into the wrong person any time of the day.

Now, these years you run into a lot of guys who wear $300 sneakers, and ride a brand new stretched out chopper. So people are more tolerant. This was when I was in my early twenties so this is the late '70s. I had grown up on the Lower East Side on Essex Street all my life. I hung out right around the corner from where I lived because that's what I did on Ludlow Street. I was only eight blocks from 3rd Street. Angles would come down Ludlow Street to go to Delancey Street to take the left and get on the bridge. That's basically how I got into it. I'd be there and watch those guys go by. I'd think, "*Damn those fucking guys are cool. Those guys are animals, man.*"

When I was 17 I was like six-three and 260 pounds. And that's how I kind of grew up. When I was young I always wanted a pair of colors. We had that whole street gang thing. In those days the two big gangs were the Dynamite Brothers and the Javelins. They might have had thirty of forty guys each.

Plus there were what they call off-shoot gangs like Baby Dynamites. Kids that were like 13...14. You know young kids. The other guys would be older guys, 18...20. These were the street gangs. They'd have a storefront and collect dues. They had meetings just like any club. You'd have a pair of colors. You'd have to have a jacket with your colors on it. If you walked in a different neighborhood you turned your jacket inside out. You had to know a handshake. If you didn't know the handshake or you only kind of knew the handshake, you might get your ass beat by one of your brothers 'cause you didn't get the handshake right. One of your brothers would come up, shake your hand and test you. One of the fingers is supposed to be bent, one is supposed to be straight. You'd get a bad beat down if you didn't know how to do it right. They'd tell you, "You screwed that up!" It was a club.

When I was young that was the thing; you wanted colors, you wanted to belong somewheres. I am a product of that typical story. My mom raised me since I was six years old; my dad disappeared when I was six. I had a brother and sister who were much older than me. My mom worked all day so I started hangin' around a club on Avenue B—The Newcomers. I started hanging out with a guy in that club and he hung out with a guy who was a Dirty White Boy member and there were other guys: Snoopy, Batman. He was the club leader for years. He had a big '82, '83 FLH. In those days the Hispanic guys had the big FLHs with the huge saddle bags and the big touring pack in the back with a stereo and they would put a million little lights all over their bike. We called them rolling juke boxes. I wouldn't say that to their face but that's basically what they looked like.

So I started hanging around with that Newcomers guy a little bit and things just got progressively worse. I bought one motorcycle and then I bought another motorcycle. Once you buy that first motorcycle it's all over. Until that time I was basically just a car guy. I was about 15 and I didn't want to go to school any more. My mom had to work all day. She would leave the house and I wouldn't go to school. After about a year I got caught. My mom comes home sick one day and I'm sitting in bed watching TV. She took my house keys away and I started hanging around the corner on Ludlow Street.

In those days there used to be a lot of street mechanics. I grew up in a basically Hispanic neighborhood, couple of Jews, couple of Chinese people. The Spanish guys would fix their cars in the street. Some of these guys were undesirable. They got parts from other people's cars. And they needed someone to remove them for them. That's how I fell into being a mechanic. I would hang out with this guy Hector and we would go and steal parts. He would take me in his car. He had a '56 Chevy wagon. To me this

Pete on his '73 FX Superglide, Essex Street and Rivington Street, photo taken by Pete's Mom, 1981. She worked at the pickle stand on the corner.

Pete's 1949 Dodge Coupe, c. 1988

Pete's 1949 Dodge Coupe, c. 1988

Pete's 1949 Dodge Coupe, c. 1988

Mechanics Alley, LES

Pete's off-road build, c. 1989

Pete's niece Jessica posed with 1993 Fat Boy, 2004

1969 Charger "Dukes of Hazard" car. Pete bought the original car from a Midwest dealer, restored the car, and sold it.

was a cool car. We would go around at night and sometimes we would see a junk car and Hector would say, "Oh, I know a guy who needs a part off that car." So we'd get the part. Take a couple of wrenches, go under the hood, take your part and get back in the car. A day or two later Hector would give me a few dollars and say, "Yeah, we sold that part." I did that for about a year or so.

One of the guys in the neighborhood, Jackie, he started saying, "Why the fuck you hang around with that guy? That guy's going to get your ass in trouble." Jackie was one of those guys who would go to Jersey to Rahway and he'd look through the junk yards and he would pick up cars that were damaged. Insurance jobs; whatever they were. He would buy them—title, legit, paperwork, everything. He would go through junk yards, find the parts and fix the car.

One day he tells me to stop hanging out with that guy Hector. I told him that I didn't go to school and my mom locked me out. I needed to do something to make some money. He said, "Come down tomorrow; don't hang around with Hector no more, hang out with me." So. Saturday morning we get in his car, go to Rahway, I see what he does. We get a car and bring it to Ludlow Street, park the car in the street. Of course it has a pair of crappy plates on it. In a couple of days we have fixed the car. We took one part off, put one part on. Basically, I became a parts changer. From stealing parts to parts changer. I still really didn't know what the part did or why I was changing it. I was just told, "Take those five bolts off, put these five bolts in. The part has to be in this position, that's the way it's supposed to look." I did that for about a year.

About a block away there's a guy named Raoul. He just did street mechanics. He didn't build anything or steal anything. Guys knew him from the neighborhood. They'd say, "Hey Raoul, can you change this? Hey Raoul, I got a noise under my hood, can you listen to it for me?" Raoul was a real mechanic—he knew his shit. He went to school, he was self taught; he used to race cars when he was younger. He was an all-around guy.

One day Raoul comes down the block and says, "Jackie, I need a hand with a car up the block." Jackie was busy, so he said take Peter. So I got introduced to Raoul who asked if I knew what I was doing. I go with Raoul back to his spot up the block. A guy comes over with his car and asks Raoul about an engine noise he is hearing. Raoul listens to the car and says, "Yeah, that's easy." Raoul looks at me and says, "Can you fix that?" I said, "I don't even know what the fuck's wrong with the car."

Raoul is like, "What do you mean you don't know what's wrong with the car? Don't you hear that?"

I say, "I hear a lot of things. I hear belts turning, I hear things grinding. Things turning around."

Raoul says, "No. Do you hear that *tap tap tap*? Listen to that." At the time I didn't get it. Raoul says, "OK, take this off, put this on." He says, "Do you hear the noise anymore?" I say, "No, the noise is gone." Raoul says, "Try to remember what you heard before and what you hear now. That noise means this."

I remember that I bought a car off the guy, a '66 Chevelle. Somebody had painted it turquoise with house paint. With a friggin' paint roller. Roller marks all over the car. A real Lower East Side classic paint job. Raoul took me under his wing and started explaining things. We'd go for test drives and he'd ask, did you hear that squeak? He'd say, "That squeak means that the bushing on the shock absorber is getting dry. We could change the shocks out or spray some WD-40 on it now, get some money and six months from now the guy will need new shocks and we get some more money."

I worked with him in the street for about two, three years until I was 18 or 19. We worked at Ludlow and Stanton.

Back then cops would kind of harass you about working on cars in the street, but they wouldn't really bother you if you kept your side of the street clean. It was frowned on back then but they didn't bust your balls too bad. Raoul knew people. He worked on some guys cars in the street and they wore a badge later on in the day.

I was living with some girl on Broome Street and I'd get up in the morning, get in my ratty little car with my greasy pants and my dirty shirt and my hoody if it was chilly out and go sit on Ludlow Street and wait. Raoul would say, "I got some business comin'. A guy needs his brakes changed."

After a while he kind of slacked off. Like everybody during the mid-'80s he was into some shit. He would be missing for days at a time. People would be looking for him. So I started doing the work. Then I became a street mechanic. I had worked with Raoul for a few years, so I knew all the shit.

Back then the area was all drugs. People would stream in from Jersey to get their drugs. On Eldridge Street between Rivington and Delancey—that was the street. You could walk along and any storefront there was selling the stuff. That was my neighborhood. If you needed a job that was your calling—selling. I knew how to fix a car so I didn't have to do that. I was lucky. At one point I needed money and I worked behind one of those doors for a couple months. People would pass their money through the door and we'd pass the coke and dope back. For me, life on the street was only good as long as somebody needed their car fixed. If I needed some money, I could go up the block and say listen, "I need a couple days work." They'd put me behind the door. They'd give me a bundle, 20...30 bags at a time. Ten dollars dope, nickel bags of coke. Through the peephole, "What do you want..?" I'd say.

They'd say, "One coke, one dope." I guess I was a renaissance man. That was the whole thing on the Lower East Side. If you didn't know how to fix cars you had to do something else.

I had a friend Bruno. He was into the drug money thing. It was constant and you didn't have to do much work. Walk five blocks down pick something up and walk back, drop it off and there's your whole day's pay. One day the cops come down the block on Ludlow Street. They put a bunch of guys against the wall. My boy Bruno was one of the guys. He was transporting serious weight. The cops yell, "Empty your pockets!" They come to Bruno and tell him to empty out. He would have been in serious fucking trouble with the cops and also with the connection for losing their dope.

The cop noticed him and said, "I know you. You hang out with that guy who fixes cars in the street."

Bruno says, "Yes sir."

The cop says "That guy's out there every day fixing cars and getting grease all over my street! That's your friend right?"

Bruno is like, "Yes sir."

The cop says, "You know what? Get the fuck out of here!" And he sends Bruno on his way. The cop saw me every day messing

Pete build, 1973 Harley Frankenbike, custom '69 Pan-Shovel

Pete build, 1983 FLH, Jeremy crouching with bike

Pete build, in memory of Indian Larry

Pete build, in memory of Indian Larry

up his street fixing cars so he knew I wasn't a drug guy. My street grease monkey shit saved Bruno's ass.

So, for me, the process was less cars and more motorcycles. They are easier to work on. I could bring a motorcycle into my living room. On Broome Street I lived six steps up so I could get one or two of the guys to give me a hand. In the winter time I could bring my bike in the house. One summer I really pissed my ex-wife off. She came home and there was a motorcycle in the bedroom. There was a motorcycle on my side of the bed. Grease on the bedroom floor. That wasn't good. I told her, "Baby, I got to fix it and its cold outside." I fixed it, got a couple guys and got it back out down the six steps. It's only like 300 pounds. Put it down on the street, you're on your way. It's fixed.

I was mechanically inclined as a kid but when I worked with Raoul he actually taught me stuff. Hector didn't teach me anything except how to get a part off a car. It's this size wrench to do this. Go get it! Fetch, boy. That's what I was. I fetched parts. A dumb white kid. I thought I was going to learn something. I learned how to steal parts off a car. Luckily I met Jackie who introduced me to Raoul. Jackie was a good guy. He pointed me in the right direction. Later, he got shot by somebody in Santo Domingo. He gave me a 1968 Toronado. It was like a luxury car. An Eldorado with bubbled-out fenders and a big performance engine. It was a quick car. It should have been a hot rod but they made it front wheel drive and luxury. He gave me one because we were fixing somebody's car and something happened to the deal and Jackie couldn't pay me. Then I had a Toronado.

I really didn't like the car. I was already into hot rods and stuff but I drove it around for a few months. No insurance, bullshit license plates. In those days you put down $50.00 and get a set of plates. Somebody would use their license and they'd put your name on the registration as an owner. They would be the driver. You would pay $50.00 to the person behind the window and they'd give you a pair of license plates legal. You were supposed to pay your insurance by the following month. You'd do that, get your sticker and then file for a refund. But you still had the registration sticker good for a year. Unless you got pulled over, it was all good.

Pete build

Pete's bench

But it was downhill after you owned a bike. It's just money hand over fist. Like the boat guys say, "Owning a boat is like throwing the money into the water." You never see it back. These days I sell stuff on e-Bay, we have a blog where we sell parts. My garage is like a parts store exploded.

In the beginning I had a Honda 450 chopped out with a hard tail and ape hangers. The whole bit. I had a 750 Honda chopper, straight bars with a long Springer front end. I always liked choppers. Late '70s early '80s that's all I saw as a kid. Choppers were a California thing but there was an important 1970s New York chopper scene. West Coast guys had taller bikes. They had what they called a Swedish frame. The frame was up in the front. The bikes had long forks but they were kind of straight. Here in the city guys did that, too, but it was like the car thing. On the West Coast the guys dropped the back of their cars; here guys were lifting the back of their cars. It's always been: whatever they're doing we're doing the opposite.

I was only a young kid and I only knew what I saw. Later on in life I started buying magazines. There would be a few photos from different places. That's where you learned from. In my teens I didn't know too many motorcycle guys. I would see bikes passing by in the street. Then after I started hanging out with guys I could see what they were doing. Still a lot of guys in New York don't go for that ape hangers look with the big tank. That's a West Coast thing. Sitting back on your bike stretched out. Ape Hangers. That's a West Coast thing. The drag bike stance is the East Coast thing. Fast and low. Like you're getting shot out of a rocket.

Here in New York there are strict traffic laws about where you can go on your bike. No lane splitting, no shoulder or break down lane to prevent your bike from overheating. In New York the law don't care how hot it is. You gotta stay in your lane. But if you are stuck in traffic you can do what you gotta do. A cop is going to be stuck in the traffic when you pull out between the lanes. I'll basically stay in my lane. But if the traffic is stopped, there is no reason why I should be sitting here.

Riding in New York is trouble. It is a challenge. People in cars are not aware of the bikes. I have been in accidents. A serious one recently. I don't remember what happened. I woke up in the hospital. After I got out of the hospital I was working with my brother-in-law at a little place in Brooklyn—Sunset Cycles. I had to walk around with a cane and crutches but I was sitting in a chair working on a bike. After a couple weeks I am feeling pretty good. I had a doctor's appointment so I pull my bike out. I ride to the hospital, hobble across the street, have my check-up. I get back on my bike to go home. Now, most guys on bikes in the city don't stop at the white line. We pull up into the crosswalk. You want to be as close to that turn as possible to keep away from anybody. So, right in front of the hospital I am at the light and for whatever reason I do not pull up into the crosswalk. I stand up on my bike looking for something. All of a sudden I hear BAM! This fucking car slams through the light, hits the back of a pick-up truck and that fucking truck comes flying towards me through the crosswalk. Goes right in front of my bike at like 100 and misses me by an inch. It bounces off a tree and slams into the side of the hospital. I get off my bike like, "Shit!" If I had been in that crosswalk like I

Recent build by Pete

Recent build by Pete

Outside Pete's shop

Pete Ranko outside his shop

usually am I'd be a dead man. Killed going home from my check-up at the hospital. Damn. This is the shit bike riders deal with every day in the city. It's intense.

I got into working on bikes because by that time it had become a little easier. I had learned about the noises. An engine is an engine. The lifter always makes that ticking sound, that sucking sound on a carburetor when it is bogging down. It always makes that same sound which means it's too lean or too rich. The transition to bikes was easier. They are smaller. I didn't have to jack it up. I didn't have to put a block of wood under the tire. I could get a couple guys to pick it up.

Harley Davidson is not necessarily too excited about people working on and changing their bikes. They don't like this whole chopper thing. They want you to buy a new bike from them. Harley has changed around a lot of the frames. You cannot take one part out of this one and put it on another one anymore. They got rules. If a guy brings in an old Harley to trade it in, they scrap the old one. Scrap it. Garbage. They don't want guys building choppers out of their old stuff. They want their new product out there. Guys are riding around with chopped off fenders. Bobbers. Harley doesn't like that shit. You got no rear fender; no place to run your tail light? Then put it on the side. That's how this stuff goes. Somebody just didn't buy a brand new bike and chop it all up. It was a reaction to a need. People might do it now but I'm sure in the '60s that guy might have tipped his bike over a few times. The floor boards got bent. So maybe he thought about mounting some foot pegs. It is just a functional thing.

Bikes are just like everything else. It's a cycle. In New York during the '50s and '60s, guys were running around on their motorcycles. You really didn't hear anything during the '70s and '80s. Guys like me were still riding our bikes, people were still fixing their bikes and customizing their bikes but you didn't hear about it. Then in the '90s with that whole biker build-off there was a big craze again. For the past 10...12 years it's been a big thing again. Guys building bikes with a big tire, guys with a nice paint job. Now, everything is quieting down again. So of course everything goes back to the older guys. Back to that same chopper/bobber. Basically we are stuck in our ways. We go back to what we know.

The market has changed a lot. There are many influences today—aftermarket products. It probably drives Harley crazy. Back in the '60s Harley was changing things. They were switching from Panheads to Shovelheads. Instead of changing the whole motor they just changed the top half. Maybe Larry [Indian Larry] got the idea from this process. It was not easy when he did that. It's easy now because the different heads are made aftermarket to fit correctly. I did one and it was straight forward. It was not straight forward for Larry. He had to figure everything out. Believe me that wasn't easy. This kind of process shows you how things change.

Inside Pete's shop

Pete's card

Inside Pete's shop

Frank Voto in his Staten Island Wolf's Pond shop

Frank Voto

AT FRANK'S SHOP

Staten Island

For me there is a history to these machines. There are reasons why they look like they do and I know something about these reasons. Then a guy comes in here and wants me to put some new grips on his bike—I don't do work like that. I don't care about grips and I don't want someone coming in here and see me doing grips. I work on engines and motorcycles.

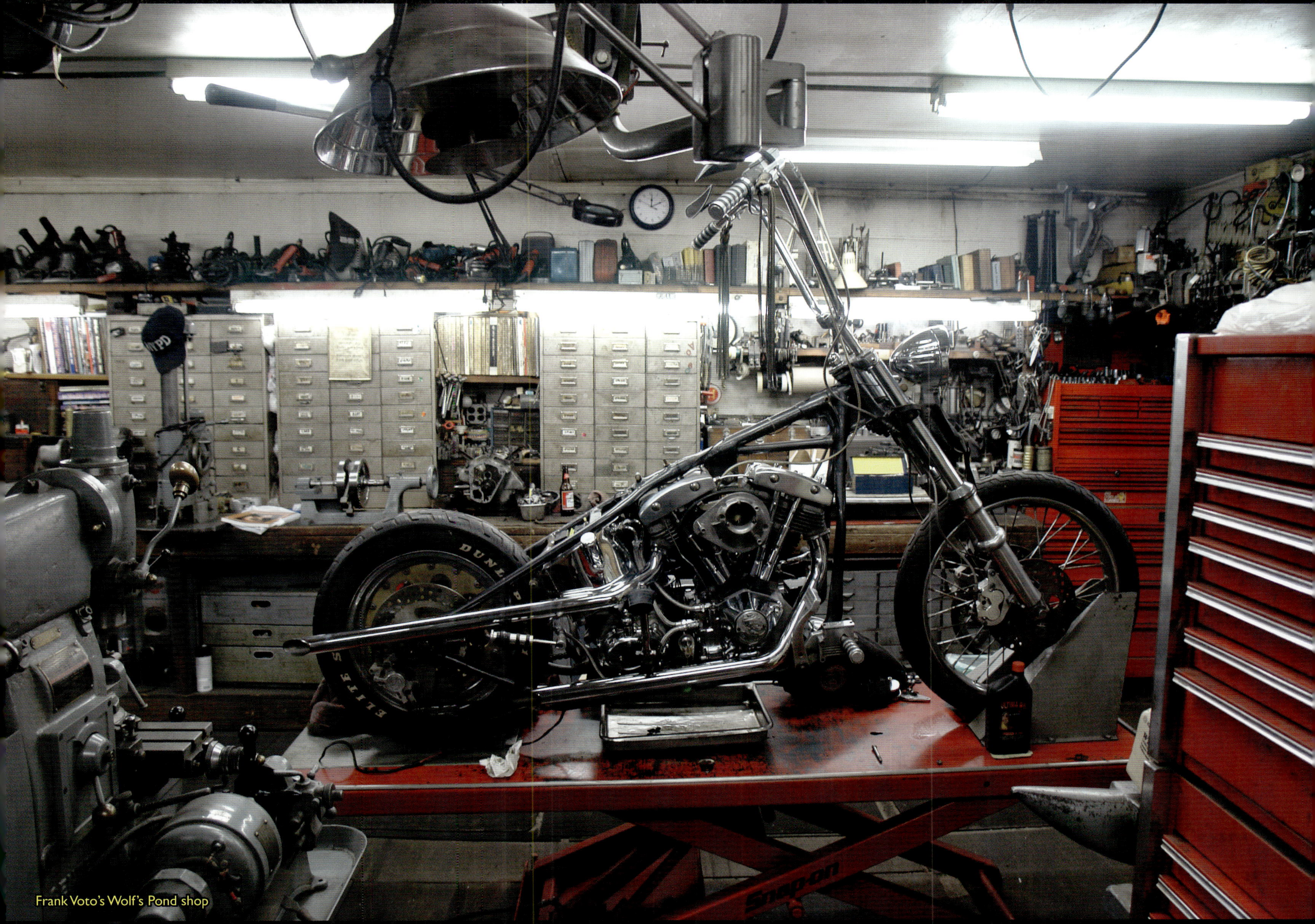

Frank Voto's Wolf's Pond shop

I work a lot on older style bikes. Rigid frame, small tank, some people might say it comes from the San Francisco outlaw style. This style traveled across the country from San Francisco to New York City. The style traveled with members of a few clubs.

The small tanks were popular because you have to remember, gas was plentiful in the 1960s. Guys were riding choppers with peanut tanks. Gas was cheap. Twenty-five cents a gallon. Then, when the gas crunch days hit, everyone wanted a bigger tank. These clubs really rode and if you were really riding across the country that was a problem. In the '50s guys rode dressers, then the style changed in the '60s and outlaw guys started riding rigids with peanut tanks, then it started to change again in the '80s back to dressers.

I love the rigid. It's lower to the ground and more stable. The swing arm started in '58. Before that you had the rigid. But think of how the roads were back then. You still had cobblestone roads and bad roads. The rigid is lower to the ground and more stable. I have an old swing arm but I put stabilizers on it. They sway around on the highway. As old as I am I still like a rigid.

I first started getting into motorcycles in 1967. I was 17. I was always involved in engines. As a kid in the neighborhood I was always working on lawn mowers and outboard motors over by Great Kills. Small motors. Then some guy come by with his Harley and asked if I could fix it. He gave me the manual and I gave it a shot. Then a friend of his showed up with his Indian. I studied the engines and I liked the way they were designed. Now, I think that I am the oldest engine guy in New York City. I have lasted the longest.

Things about working on these old engines have changed very much now. No Harley dealer wants to work on these old engines any more. They don't know nothin' about them and they don't want to

Frank Voto's Wolf's Pond shop

Frank Voto, c. mid-'70s

Voto custom build, c. mid-'70s

Frank Voto riding his custom build, c. mid-'70s

Voto at Daytona, c. mid-'70s

know nothin' about them. There is no real knowledge anymore about these engines. The dealers just want to do warrantee work. They came out with the Evolution and that was a drastic improvement. That was a smooth motor. I don't like the way they look but quality-wise they are a big improvement. The design of the top end is better.

Indians are funny. They look like something out of the Flintstone age. They are so primitive you can just look at it and know what to do. Take the motor out, take it apart, look at the rockers; it's so simple to work on. Now they are collectible but they are crude. No matter what anyone says, they don't run smooth. I still work on them and I have all the specialty tools. Guys ship me their engines from all over. I have worked on guys' motors from Australia, from Germany, from England. These guys crate up their engines and send them to me in Staten Island. This all from word of mouth.

I feel an attachment to something like a Shovelhead engine. It goes back to where I started from. After-market companies still sell parts for these old engines, but they don't know nothin' about them. They don't know how to make them run. I like to change the parts around to make them run better. I put the whole valve train from an Evolution on a Shovelhead. They told me I was dreaming. It couldn't be done. Oh yeah? In that case I am going to make a stroker to boot. So I made a 92 incher out of a 74. It was a challenge. I'm dreaming? Don't think so. Fucking thing purrs like a kitten.

There are valves and there are lifters. If you put a stroker kit on these, they'll collapse. You got to use solid lifters. With a stroker, the motor gets hot and everything stretches out. You get a twenty percent loss of power. There's a lot of pressure. Things are going to keep rising and rising until they hit the top of the piston. Well, these people didn't do their homework. If they had they would have changed the springs to tri-springs. And that will make up the difference in stiffness. They use the wrong cam and there is a difference in degree. It's only four degrees but it makes a difference.

Engines are all about the angles of things. A Shovelhead and a Panhead have different angles of the cylinders. The Shovelhead motor produces more torque than the Panhead. Harley developed a different geometry with the Shovelhead to produce more torque. Some guys switch the Pan and the Shovel around on the same bottom end and they get more power that way. It all comes down to whether the engine can breathe right. What kind of ports you use.

We have moved into a different era. There has been a shift in ideas about working on engines. It has happened to me on more than one occasion that a young guy will walk into my shop and then he gets a look on his face. I can see him looking around the shop but he looks lost. He doesn't know where he

Voto custom build, c. mid-'70s

Voto engine display

Voto engine display

Voto engine display

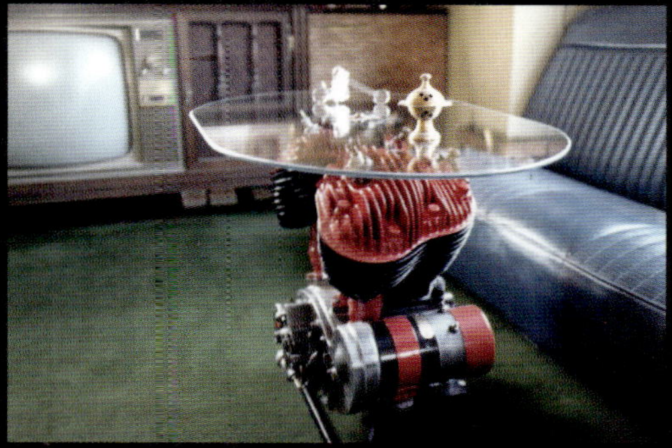

Voto engine coffee table

is and he doesn't feel comfortable. One guy walked in here recently and he asked me, "What do they call this place? They call this a machine shop?" He had no knowledge of a screwdriver. He's pointing at this and that and he's asking, "What is that?" He was pointing at the lathe and asking what does this thing do. I said to myself, "Holy shit."

He's been riding on a motorcycle and he's the member of a big club and he doesn't even know that the tools are. For the young, they are not being taught this in school any more. It has become a lost art. They do not teach machine shop in high school any more. I went to McKee Technical High School on Staten Island. They had machine shop; they had electrical shop, woodworking shop. Now that is all gone. I see myself as a dinosaur. There's nothing I can do about it. But there are dinosaur hunters out there looking for people like me. This shop represents a completely different world. Now, a shop like mine is bid on and sold to salvage brokers that buy it and send it all to South America. Mexico and overseas. It's all gone. Harley is designing bikes so you can't work on them.

Back when I got into this in the '60s, people told me I rode an old man's bike because I was riding a Harley. Young guys rode BSAs and Triumphs. Then, in the '70s the motorcycle movies made the Harleys popular. In my time nobody wanted these things. You could buy them a dime a dozen. Then that movie *Easy Rider* came out. In '67 I had bought a full dress Panhead for $300. Nobody else wanted it.

I do look at myself as someone who is holding onto the history. That's all I got. These engines and these old bikes are my life. I started off doing this work as favors and it kept going. I spent three years accumulating the machines I needed to work on these engines. I bought these old machines all beat up as scrap and I put them back together. The guy delivered them one by one. They

Matty's '50s style chopper

Matty, Brooklyn tattoo, and bike

Matty on his chopper, mid-'70s

Matty riding his chopper, mid-'70s

Mark Kmiotek's '48 Pan

Mark Kmiotek's '63 Plymouth Belvedere

were so heavy that they destroyed his truck. He was like, what the fuck are these old machines made out of? I remember when my whole shop floor was covered in parts. I took them apart piece by piece. I paid less for these machines then you would pay today for a Black and Decker drill. My machines are cast iron solid. Cincinnati. There is no aluminum in my shop. No vibration. Every vibration shows up on the tooling. Believe me. But my machines go back to the last generation. I do not tolerate vibration. All this new machinery is inferior but now they are stuck with it. All the old cast iron companies are gone. Any vibration in the machine will show up in the milling. But now there's nothing you can do about it.

The quality of my work and my reputation has to do with the fact that I found these old cast iron machines and brought them back. I am self sufficient. I have made the decision to do it this way. I was not going to give this machining work

Mark Kniotek, 22 years old in 1976, Living End club jacket, 11 club members, disbanded 1980

to some shop that uses bad tools This only creates problems. I wouldn't do it. There are roller bearings and there are shims and there is a flywheel. All of this has to be perfectly centered. There is a clearance of only four-thousandths. You have an old Panhead and these things have to be tightened up but it has to be done correctly. I learned all of this by trial and error.

I have a set of standards that I work by that is based on old heavy cast iron technology. I don't need to work with a Bridgeport. It does not meet with the standards that I am interested in. They don't make nothin' like that no more. Today

Frank Voto-style bike, 2010

Frank Voto sitting with his bikes, 2010

Frank Voto engine rebuild style

people just go out and buy something. That's a consumer world. I don't live in that world. I live in a producer world. All this aftermarket stuff is made now but it doesn't fit. It isn't made correctly. What are you going to do? Do you know how to use a reamer? No, you are going to have to bring it to a machine shop for them to fix it. Why should I have to bring something to a machine shop that is supposed to work in the first place? Because the bushings were not correctly made? All this aftermarket is shit. How do you sell something to somebody that doesn't fit?

There has been a shift in values. It doesn't piss me off but today people just think everything is going to work no problem. Well, it's not going to work. There is no such thing as a "no problem" on these old engines, but that's why it's interesting.

A guy come in here with an old Harley that he said didn't sound right. I took a look at the motor. The carburetor and exhaust were totally detached from the engine manifold. You could see daylight through the connections. I looked at the guy and thought, "*The motor doesn't sound right? The whole thing is disconnected. Can't you turn a wrench?*" But it still runs. These old motors are like that. You could spit on the peddle and they'd start up. They were designed during a different time when guys could turn a wrench.

You have to be mechanically inclined. If somebody tells me, "Well, I want to be a mechanic." I ask them to let me see their shop. First thing I am going to do is look to see if they have any gizmos. Stuff that you save from old motors. Little pieces of things, old odd-ball bolts. If you've been saving that stuff that means you are really into it. If you go into some guy's shop and he has three screwdrivers and a couple wrenches its like, "No, no, no." This guy doesn't get it. You gotta be a pack rat and save stuff you can use. I got drawers with labels that read

Gizmos drawers

"gizmos." There ain't no name for them but you need them. I save stuff because somewhere, someday that thing is going to look cool on something. It's going to look funky on something. The only guy I ever heard use that term was Indian Larry. We were looking at a bike and he said, "That bike don't have no gizmos on it." I nearly fell back in my chair. What did he just say? I couldn't believe he just said that. I thought I was the only guy that said that.

I do wonder if these kinds of things are going to pass on to the next generation. I'm not sure, but I hope so. It's the way these things go. A lot of this has become a dying art. I work on guys' bikes and these guys own a motorcycle shop. They'll mess around on yours but they don't want to take a chance on their own. These old engines will last forever but I wonder if the knowledge to really work on them will last that long.

Frank Voto shop machine

Voto shop

Frank Voto shop machine

Frank Voto shop machine

Frank Voto

Voto card

Krazy Kevin

THE FLOW OF INFORMATION

New York

Krazy Kevin, 17 years old

I had two older brothers that were hot rodders. I got into motorcycles around the age of fourteen. In 1967 I got my driver's license and in those days you didn't need an endorsement for motorcycles. If you had a license to drive in New York it was good for everything. At the time I had a 1941 big twin Flathead that was considered a chopper back in those days. My interest in all this kind of went forward from there.

Krazy Kevin, c. early 1980s

There were numerous builder icons that started here in New York during the 1950s. There were plenty of kustom cars and hot rods. I was attracted more to the motorcycles. My brothers would discuss certain metal flake or candy apple paint jobs. We'd look at the interior of this or that coupe to see what they had. There was Herb Gary up in Sea Cliff, New York, who was a big customizer at the time. Johnny Pinstripe and Frankie Wheelchair with their crazy bikes out of Brooklyn. You had Mardo Bennett and Eddie Reed, who are my heroes, doing things with Harley that nobody had ever seen before in the New York area. These were the innovators. These were the guys that had done all this kind of work.

You know, we had three or four drag strips in the area at one time. They have all gone by the wayside. They used to have the Freeport stock car races; there were drive-in theaters all over the place. During the '50s and '60s the public felt differently about cars and motorcycles.

There were little cliques in Brooklyn and in the Bronx and in Queens. My brother was a member of the Dragmates. My cousin was in the Four Aces. These were established car clubs. There were motorcycle clubs in the city. Each sector had their crew. But everybody knew everybody. Back then it was a tight knit thing. There were guys all the way out in Coney Island and there were guys in Belrose Queens but everybody knew where Connecting Highways was if you wanted to go drag racing. People always hung out in Coney Island with cars and bikes. That's just the way the scene has always been in New York.

Guys like Mardo Bennett, Harry Lang, and Eddie Reed did it all. If you didn't have the tools or the knowledge you could go in and pencil sketch a sissy bar or an exhaust system and they would fabricate it for you. Mardo and Eddie were always tinkering with motors, making big cubic inch motors with dual carbs. Back then all the speed tricks were trial and error because there were very few people making Harley accessory parts. In those days guys were trying to figure out the stats of the weight to horsepower ratio. They'd strip everything off the bike so they could make it as light as possible and then they'd go from there. Now, you can call up S&S and order a 114-inch motor, dump it into a frame and have a hot rod bike. But back in the early days, you had to grind your own cams and mill your own heads. These were the guys that were doing it and doing it successfully.

These guys were from the Bronx. Eddie's shop was on the border of the Bronx and Mount Vernon. Mardo and Harry Lang seemed to always have store fronts without the correct permits. So the fire marshal would come around and there would be acetylene bottles all over the place so they'd get closed. They would re-open two blocks away and change the name from Cycle Circus to World Cycles or something. The story that I have always been told about Mardo was that around 1958 he pulled into a gas station in the Bronx in a Chevy panel truck with California plates on it. He had the goatee and collar length hair and the two gas station attendants were playing hand ball with the buzz-cut hair-doo of the day. And out comes Mardo and he asked the kids, "Hey can you give me a hand getting my bike out of the back of the truck?" So, the kids are thinking like it's going to be a Triumph or something like that. Mardo opens up the back door of his truck and pulls out a wooden plank and starts rolling out this radical, green metal flake extended Springer Harley Davidson and the kids' jaws dropped. They had never seen anything like this. It was shocking to these gas station kids to see this kind of machine.

If you look back at what we were doing then of course it was not a product of trend or fashion. This has all become trendy very recently. We did what we did out of necessity.

Krazy Kevin trike build, c. 1970

Krazy Kevin, c. late 1980s

Krazy Kevin and his wife Sue, c. early 2000s

Krazy Kevin riding his build for his wife Sue, c. 2007-8

As an example, there were only two ways to get a pair of bell bottom pants. One was you had to go to the Army-Navy surplus and get a pair or you'd have to get a pair of Levy's and split them down the leg from the knee, add a piece of V shaped fabric and sew it together. Was it a fashion statement? No, we wanted a pair of bell bottoms and that's what we had to do to get them.

When the first one or two bike shops opened that sold aftermarket stuff it was all too expensive. It was just cheaper to go home and cobble out your own sissy bar or gas tank or whatever. But prior to these shops being open, you didn't have a choice. There was no way to get a custom anything. If you wanted a custom tank you'd have to change out your Sportster tank and remake it. Or maybe you could get a peanut or banana tank from England onto your Harley chopper.

Back then, you made your own seat pan because each bike had its own little

Krazy Kevin with bike, winter 2010

Krazy Kevin, c. 2009

Krazy Kevin in his office with 1st Brooklyn Invitational poster, 2010

glorification. I might want a solo seat and the next guy might want a spoon style seat because he rides with his old lady. You look back at it now and I don't think we had any preconceptions like we were setting a trend. I certainly never thought I was. I was building my next bike so I could ride it around until I sold it.

Information flowed very differently back in the '50s and '60s. Most of our knowledge was influenced in part by the early magazines we could get our hands on. And most of those magazines came from California. You had the Bay Area Frisco-style bikes. They were set up for that part of California. You had longer stretched bikes in Los Angeles and San Bernardino Counties. The next traffic light was 20 miles down the street. If I could take a pie and cut it into many slices I could talk about how the Bronx was doing certain things and Brooklyn was doing certain things. How guys out on the Island in Nassau were doing certain things.

Early Krazy Kevin frame build and paint, c. 1970s-early 1980s: brushed green metal flake paint, hand-rendered dragon

Early Krazy Kevin tank design and paint, c. 1970s-early 1980s: hand lettered

Krazy Kevin in his office, 2010

It was all about customizing or personalizing your own individual style and flair.

In New York there were definitely differences in style between say Brooklyn or the Bronx, but I don't think it was as dramatic a shift in style as you might see in a California bike. In other words, here in New York if you extended your front end or if you ran ape hangers or drag bars that was a personal choice. It wasn't like you were going to see ten bikes in Bay Ridge that were all kind of the same except they had different color paint. But every year things might change. You might see the gangster white walls or the drilled out Swiss cheese back rims and you knew where the bike originated from. That's not to say that guys from the Bronx didn't run white walls, but it was primarily a Brooklyn thing and a little more flamboyant.

You gotta remember that everybody knew everybody in the old days. But if you lived in Brooklyn, why would you pay a dollar to go over the Throgs Neck Bridge to a painter in the Bronx when you had Johnny Pinstripe right there in Brooklyn at his shop House of Color? He was shooting metal flake and candies as good as anyone. If you were from a certain area you would use the pinstriper in your area. I kind of think that most people stayed neighborhood when they got work done on their bikes and cars. New York was grounded in the cultures of the neighborhoods. It was like a concentrated form of regionalization. In the early days work got traded off between people you knew in your area. One guy would paint your bike and you'd make a sissy bar for him. This process of trading work kept the whole thing neighborhood oriented. There might have been a better painter out there but you were trading for the work so this kept it in the neighborhood.

You have to remember that the technology of all this has changed a lot in recent years. When I was young there was no such thing as an airbrush. There was no such thing as all these diverse paint finishes. Guys really had to sit down and figure out what they wanted and what was possible. In the '60s nobody knew what was possible. These innovations are the part of a long process of experimentation, trial and error. During the very late '50s and early '60s, flake appeared. But then somebody had to figure out how to put it down correctly. That's a whole different thing. You have to remember guys were shooting enamel paints or lacquers. These paint jobs moved. They cracked on a surface level and they got dull and this is what gave them this interesting patina. From bouncing around on the street. You cannot duplicate that surface.

Regionalization in the city tended to be expressed through the different looks of motorcycles. New York has always had a number of clubs that were defined by the different races or ethnicities of the members. This is how different clubs define themselves. Different ways they want to look and/or behave. Some clubs had full dress Harleys with full accessories. As much stuff as they could put on their bikes. Two-hundred little tail lights around the back. Continental kits on the back of a motorcycle. The outlaw type clubs were more interested in choppers and going fast. They were taking as much stuff off their bikes as possible. It was a question of style.

I think the chopper style would have materialized even if there had been no association with the outlaw style mystique. The image of the rebellious guy that had a bike rather than having a car was there. And then if you have a number of these guys in the same area the whole question of one-upmanship would come into play. One guy is going to go for the metal flake paint job, one guy is going to go for the higher handlebars; a little bit longer front end. The clubs that were here are a part of New York history. But as I remember, there were plenty of bikes in the New York shows that had been built by guys that had no desire to be in a club. And also the guys that had these bikes did not own a motorcycle shop. They just wanted a custom bike whether it be a Triumph, a BSA, or a Harley Davidson. Yes, during different eras there were clubs that had their bikes displayed, but I think that the custom bikes would have been here regardless.

People forget that the whole issue of cars and bikes as something that can empower you as a person is a part of American history. It has grown and gained significance and this significance is taken for granted by young people today. Until relatively recently, there were not nearly as many cars on the road. In terms of self preservation and riding a bike: In the past in New York we could behave differently. We used to run our bikes with no front brakes. We ran bikes with longer front ends that may not have been put together correctly.

As time progresses, you start to get a little older and a little more savvy. You say to yourself, "OK, let's run a front brake." My road bike is dual disk front brakes, single disk rear brake. It's got some motor work done to it so if I have to pass a line of tractor trailers I can get past them. It also has the shutdown power that I can stop just as good from 80 as I can from 10 miles an hour. Today, there's a million more cars and a million more people driving right next to you that don't pay any attention to you and have no respect for bike riders.

If you look at any 1950s picture of Manhattan, the cars back in the '50s were these big flamboyant boats. We're talking 1960s Buicks and 1958 Pontiacs. The sides of New York streets were lined up with these kinds of cars. Take a '60 Chevy and try to park it today in New York. In that same spot where that '60 would fit you could probably squeeze two Mitsubishis in there today. So the same New York block today has twice as many cars as there were sitting there in the '50s. We always built our bikes on a nickel instead of a dime. We used what we had. Our bikes went up and down the road and that's what we cared about at 18 years old.

I see the Brooklyn Invitation show partly as a message. I see the bikes in the show as messages. They are built by young people for the most part and I think they have the same feelings as me—why buy it if you can build it? Yeah, maybe sometimes it's cheaper to buy it than to put your time into it. Cut it with a torch and then file it until it's smooth. Yeah, you can buy the same bracket for $79, but it just seems to me that if you don't show your own personality in your project, no matter what type of project it is, what's the point? Anybody can go down to the local chopper builder and plunk down $80,000, but why? You can build your own bike your own way and have something that you can stand back and be really proud of.

To me there is a difference between being a bike assembler and a bike builder. All this stuff on TV is showing guys that are taking pre-made frames, pre-made front ends and they bolt it together. They send their paint job out, they send their seat out. So I ask, what did they actually build? And they are expecting $80,000 or better for a cookie cutter looking bike. It makes no sense to me.

As a young person I experienced the early days of the kustom movement. As young people we were reacting to the first days of widespread manufacturing in America. Of course the automobile was a big part of that. But we were young people and we didn't have a lot of money. Most of the stuff I had were 1929...1930 model A Fords. Or I was a big 1959–60 Chevy guy. El Caminos. To buy a brand new car was definitely out of the picture. I could go down the street and pick up a car for 100 bucks. Throw a quick flamed paint job on it, cut the coil springs and drop the car on the ground where it belonged, or so we thought, and still do, and you have a cool car.

Krazy Kevin's bike at 2nd Brooklyn Invitational, 2010

Kevin's bike's back fender at 2nd Brooklyn Invitational show

Kevin's tank at 2nd Brooklyn Invitational show

I never made it to high school but all the rich kid's parents bought them 1964 GTOs or stuff like that and all the middle class kids had the '55 Chevy with the radius wheel wells, primer black or grey. Quite honestly, they couldn't afford to pay anybody to paint their car. If you were mechanically inclined and you got your hands on something that would run, you'd change it around and you'd have your own little thing. It's true to this day with this rat rod movement.

You can go to some upscale car show with $200,000 cars and also some so-called rat rods, and which car has the cool crowd around it? The rat rod. Why? Because the builder used his own ingenuity, his own ideas and he didn't buy some cookie cutter '32 Ford roadster high boy. This was just the way it was. I had two older brothers that were into it and I got sucked into the garage when I was ten years old as the gofer. I learned how to wrench at an early age. I was lucky to have these influences at an early age. I was lucky to be around the cool things to have. You can't buy cool.

There are a few different things going on here in terms of people and cars and America. Some people are just content having a car that will take them from point A to point B. And there definitely is a class statement as well about running a car or bike that does not conform to accepted forms of transportation. So, let's say you went to high school and went to high school shop class and there's ten other kids that also can turn wrenches so it's that common bond between these guys. Like my brothers and their friends that formed drag racing car clubs. They all had a similar interest in the combustion engine. One of them had a Vette; one of them had a '55 Chevy. My brother had the roadsters and stuff like that. It was an allegiance of guys that had the same common interests and I think this is the same reason bike clubs started. That mutual bond of the motorcycle. That openness of riding. The rebelliousness against certain things. There definitely was that sense of class separation.

Kids that came from well-off families, their parents bought them a new car for graduation. The guys I knew got the hand-me-down '49 Plymouth and the old man got his new '56 Dodge. There definitely was a sense of class separation there and cars helped us to articulate this and feel good about what we wanted to talk about.

Today you have mainstream car companies that have studied what car customizers like Gene Winfield have innovated and then integrate it into their design decisions. It's a part of the process and it's always been a part of the process. If I had the money I could go to Harley right now and buy a 2010 full dresser, go back and forth across the country and have fun with it but when I stop in Kansas City to get gas and the guy rolls in with the exact same bike I have with the exact same tires—that bugs me. That's why I was always into customization. Everything I've ever had I put a blow torch to and changed it to be my own personal statement.

My old man was like a walking muscle. He only went as far as like the fourth grade in school during the Depression. He worked for Carvelle Ice Cream. He drove milk tankers upstate to get the milk from dairy farms. So, it was a rare weekend that he was actually off. But one weekend he was working on his Ford Coupe and my friend was working on his '55 Chevy and I was working on a chopped three-wheeler. The old man is in the garage doing something and a highway patrol motorcycle cop comes by and stops. The old man comes out and asks the cop, "What's the problem?" My old man didn't take guff from anybody. The cop says, "I can't believe you're letting these kids fuck up all these cars and motorcycles. They should be putting them back together the right way." My dad was ready to knock that

Passing the torch: recent builds by John Copeland and Jeffrey Schad in front of Johnson Street garage, 2010.

John Copeland, Johnson Street garage, 2010

AJ's Shovelhead parked in front of Johnson Street garage, 2010.

cop off his motorcycle. He told the cop to get the fuck out of his driveway. He yelled at the cop that his kids had paid for their cars and bikes and can do whatever the hell they want to them. I guess it's just a certain way of looking at things.

Back in the early '70s I rode across the country three times. It was not an easy feat. When you think about it now, the trip wears you out. You are in the elements. I remember getting caught in a hail storm in the Dakotas and there were no overpasses. I was concerned about protecting my gas tank. I was getting pelted with this giant hail but it was a part of the journey. I stayed off the interstates. I wasn't interested in that. The back roads of America, the unexplored roads are what I am interested in. You see people and houses and farms and it is impressive. It is not the things you will see on television. I've been up and down the interstates. There's not too much to see from that perspective. Another Denny's? Another Comfort Inn?

That's why I admire these young kids from Brooklyn and their Brooklyn Invitational Show. They are making it themselves. This is refreshing for me to see this. You are always going to have a certain amount of talent. There is always going to be someone out there that is better than you are. But you try to excel at what your do. For me, I know these old bikes and methods of working on them. I am going to take that to the grave with me. I want a one-off machine when my project is done. I want it to look correct and feel correct to me. That's not to say that there are a hundred builders all across America that are doing the same thing and maybe doing it better and maybe not but they are doing it. That's what's important.

Meeting at Johnson Street garage to discuss 2nd Brooklyn Invitational Motorcycle Show, 2010 (L-R): Wes Lang, John Copeland, Vince Szarek, Neil Fenton, Jeffrey Schad, AJ, Keino, Andy Camay

Hugh Mackie

SIXTH STREET SPECIALS —GO FAST TURN LEFT

Manhattan

Hugh Mackie with his bike

I got to New York in July of '81. First three weeks I spent at my girlfriend's sister's apartment on 56th Street, but the smell got bad so it was time to go. I landed in the East Village and I had an apartment at 2nd Avenue and 4th Street. There was a coffee place on the corner called Binibon. The old Norman Mailer spot. He interviewed a guy named Jack Abbott who then stabbed a waiter to death in the place. Quentin Quisp, the naked civil servant, lived right around the corner. That was an amazing place. That was my introduction to the area.

Sixth Street Specials store front

'82 I moved to Avenue B and 10th Street. The park was a little rough then, it was just too dangerous. It was a tent city. Unbelievable. I've been around the park ever since. I have always lived right here in this little section.

Initially I did construction. Apartment renovations. It's New York; you have to make money. I met an English guy, Dave Adams, and we started working together renovating apartments. We worked together in a little company, Abel and Cain, so we could get under the A's in the phone book. I did construction for about ten years. I worked on a lot of the renovations in this neighborhood. At that point in the early '80s, this neighborhood was being turned around. All the bombed-out buildings were being renovated. I became a layout guy because I could read the plans. Maybe my background in art school helped me with that. I did that right up to about 1990. This all overlapped with the motorcycle thing. I got my first bike here in '82.

I bought a 500 Yamaha and had it for a few months. The guy next door had a store front. He kept pulling his Triumph in and out of his storefront. To me, that was the most amazing bike I ever saw. He gave me a ride on it one day and that was it. OK, I want a Triumph. I don't know why but we ended up going down to Philadelphia and picked up an old BSA. So my first Brit bike was a BSA.

I had that for a while but I kept blowing up the motor. I didn't really know anything about it so I kept finding other motors and changing motors and blowing them up. I got sick of that shit and finally got a Triumph but it was in pieces. So I learned how to put it together and that started the whole interest in wrenching them. Funny thing is, the guy who's Triumph I first rode on—it's now my bike. So the first Triumph I was ever interested in became my regular ride. That '70 Tiger is now the bike I run all the time. I remember when he called, "Remember

Fumi working out front

Hugh and Fumi out front

Fumi working out front

that old Triumph? You want it?" That's a nice connection.

With Brit bikes there's every kind of engine configuration possible. The parallel twin was the biggest selling bike coming out of Britain. It was the popular design after WWII. So, late '40s, '50s, '60s, and '70s, the parallel twin was it. Because of that, these engines went all around the world. These bikes were exported to the USA, Asia, everywhere. They took over and they won all the racing everywhere. They were just the best bike going around. Triumphs, BSA, Norton and others. When I got into it, those are the bikes that you found.

The English did not only make parallel twins. They have made every single kind of motorcycle engine imaginable. They invented the Boxer—a company called Douglas invented it and sold it to the Germans. BMW didn't invent that engine. Go figure. A Scotsman invented the In-Line four. A guy called Henderson. Indian made that engine but they were all copies of the Henderson. It was originally made by a Scotsman. BSA made V-twins. All the English companies made V-twins. You're talking last century. The V-twin was very popular. The engine just sat there and followed the line of the frame front tube. They wanted more power so they added the second cylinder at the back tube of the frame and that was the start of the V- twin. The engine didn't stick out because one cylinder was in line with the other. It made sense for the vehicle. That's why every company picked up on it. The early Harleys looked pretty much like bicycles. And then the whole thing grew into what it is. Engines represent systems; a system of mechanics. A good mechanic can work with any system. First you learn it, then you work with it. All these engines have a history and the British have had a lot to do with developing this history.

My history of it...I would say when I was here back in the early '80s there were very few people riding British motorbikes around. There were one or two people who could work on them. As a group we just kind of came together because of the familiarity and we started learning it. And the group grew a bit. We were also at that young trendy age. We spent our whole time running around the night club scene. There was a huge after-hours and underground nightclub scene in the '80s. So the whole East Village was full of these clubs. Every block had an illegal after-hours place. Save the Robots—I did a lot of the construction on Save the Robots. It started underneath my apartment on Avenue B and 11th Street. Dominic Blondo lived up on the top floor. He did all the artwork in there. The club was in the basement. The bigger it got, the more legal it had to become. The fire department was shutting them down; they had to do a bunch of construction like fire exits. I did a lot of that work. The guy who owned it Denis Pruvot started it in a storefront on Avenue B; he was a big French guy. He had a '50s style store in the day time and at night time the gate went down and they moved all the furniture out of the way and everyone snuck in there after hours and partied. It got so popular he renamed it Save the Robots and he was successful and moved down to B and 2nd.

Basically there were a bunch of trendy kids running around that whole scene. There were bigger clubs: Palladium, Area, Danceteria. All these places were huge at that time. We would pull up on these bikes and we got really well known. There were maybe a dozen of us doing this whole club scene. We were fixing our own bikes and people were seeing them everywhere. Over at Avenue A—the restaurant 7A. We hung out there the whole time. Then Sidewalk Café opened at 6th Street and a little bit later we all moved over there and that

Hugh working in his shop

Fumi in the shop

Hugh Mackie working in the shop

Side Walk Café building photo

Dimitri Turin riding with pumpkin, c. 1989

became our hangout. There are still photos of us up there outside on the wall. The numbers of Brit bike owners just grew and grew. Eventually we turned our home into a shop. That's kind of what happened. We were doing the construction business and the bike thing at the same time and then eventually it flipped over and we just did the bike thing full time.

The whole business about the bike thing took off and we were doing more and more bike stuff, so we started going out and buying them. This is obviously pre-computer so we had to search around in classified ads. We placed ads in *Bike Journal*, *Special Interest Vehicles*, *Want AD Press*. All the papers that were within a 100-mile radius of New York City. People would answer the ads, "Oh, I have a Triumph and I have a BSA sitting in my shed." There was something about this country during the '50s and '60s when these bikes were new: The minute they broke down or reached 10,000 miles or the points went out or something happened, people would just shove them in the back of the garage and buy a Harley. It was like the Triumph was a stepping stone to the Harley. In England you'd have to sell that bike. There was no not selling your bike and then getting a new bike. People couldn't afford just rolling the old bike into the back of the garage and forgetting about it. In the USA people had more money and they could do this.

So what we found out was there were thousands of these bikes sitting in people's garages all over the place. So we started getting them, buying them, bringing them here and fixing them up. Of course tons of them had been chopperized. That movie *Easy Rider* influenced people. I found more than 400 of these chopped Brit bikes. At that time we spent our entire time shortening the front forks, taking off the sissy bars and the king/queen seats. We had to get rid of the Harley bike wheels and convert them back into stock-looking Triumphs. That's what

Neil Fenton visiting Hugh and talking shop

Day to day at the shop

Sixth Street Specials shop floor

Hugh at his desk

people wanted in the '80s and '90s. Standard street bikes. This whole shop grew out of doing that. When you concentrate on one thing you just get better and better.

Dimitri Turin was my partner in construction and in the shop. He'd be coming down into this area all the time from Boston. One day he saw my BSA and parked next to it and one day I saw his Triumph and we became friends. My BSA was the only one sitting in the neighborhood, so he immediately parked next to it. I was a part of the British bike interest in New York. People were getting the bikes from us and maybe also fixing them on their own. People came by with their bikes. We had a shop and we were into it big time and all the time. So, if you were into bikes and you saw us running around on these British machines, this influenced people. You know, a lot of people just liked that image of riding a British bike. If you are standing in line at the Palladium on 14th Street waiting to get in and a bunch of hooligans pull up and park right on the fucking sidewalk, right at the door and then they walk right into the club for free? You look at that and go damn, what is that? You know, that was the scene and I was in it. I knew all the club owners and I knew all the door people.

In those days being a door person was like being God. People would stand outside and look bored and the door guys would say, OK, you and you can come in and you go fuck off. It was horrible but that's what was happening. So if you would just pull up and make a bunch of noise with your straight pipes it got people's attention and the door guys remembered us. We'd leave one club and then go down to the Milk Bar on 7th Avenue—straight in there. Go down to Area—straight in there. It was a part of the scene.

Now at the shop, for the most part we do stock stuff. We don't build motorcycles necessarily. I have made some racing bikes. Usually I am repairing and putting back together stock stuff. As far as I'm concerned, as close as you can get to original factory stuff, the better your bike's going to be. Because it was tried and tested out at the factory and it's about as good as you're going to get. The closer you can make your bike to an original: Original motor, original set up; the motor is going to last better, the bike's going to be better. That's what I'm really into for the most part. You can put high performance in a Triumph motor but it makes it more fragile. Most of the time a stock motor is plenty powerful enough for any kind of situation riding in New York. It's really a question about how you are willing to ride it. You are going to be going plenty fast enough. All the talk about racing cams and pistons and all the rest of it, is really just for talk.

The stock 650 Triumph produces 49 horsepower. The 750 only puts out about 52. But that's a lot of horsepower when you're telling the truth. People who are talking about 75, 80, and 85 horsepower are just lying. They really are. In an old bike like that it's just not going to happen. If you put a real race motor together in a Triumph 750, you are lucky to get 65 horsepower out of it. People who are talking about getting more are either really, really talented or they're just lying.

I always say, if you have a well put together stock motor on a stock Triumph 650 or 750, that's fast enough. It really is. You can do high performance shit; and I've done tons of it but it really makes your bike harder to live with, harder to start; it don't idle so good. High performance cams, magnetos, all that kind of shit, it's really all for racing. In terms of New York City streets, the closer you are to stock the better it's going to be.

My ride is a 1970 Tiger. It's pretty much a stock bike. There's a couple things that have been changed on it but it's still just a single

Hugh's bike

Brit bike fix in process

Hugh's bike

Racing photos on shop wall

Sixth Street racing photo

Photos on wall at Sixth Street

Hugh racing:
Go fast turn left

carb. And it does everything I could possibly need. I've ridden tons of bikes. I've ridden all different kinds of bikes. But I still boil it down to a single carb. It's all you ever need.

I've ported and gas flowed heads for people—I've done all that shit for people. People talk about the Triton with a Triumph motor and a Norton Featherbed frame. It's a style from the old London Ton-Up days. I have done one or two of those. The guys in London—a guy named Dave Degens started with these in the 1960s and has been building them ever since. He knows all about it. That's motorcycle history. I have been involved in building one or two. If you want a good solid bike built, I can do that for you. I'm into that. All the bells and whistles and the custom this and that. I have no real interest in any of that.

I am involved in flat track racing, Middletown, Schenectady. My partner and I used to go to watch the races in a town called Weedsport, New York. Every year they have this race called Days of Glory. We went up there to watch these guys running vintage dirt track and boy, it was just so impressive! And we said, damn we could do that! So, the years went by and we never did it and then eventually the time was right. It wasn't until I was forty-five when I started racing. That gave me a whole new interest in the Triumph thing. I was getting tired of the same old same old. So I started to make a few racing bikes and that really turned the whole thing around and got me interested again. I do a lot of motor work for the racing bikes because they need it. Those are the bikes I build if I ever build a bike. 703, that's my number, that's my race bike. The season goes for about eight or nine months a year. They run right up until November. I try to go at least once a month. If I'm lucky I go twice a month. On the race track it's not the bike that makes me go fast; it's me that makes the bike go fast. Go fast, turn left. That's racing. It's good. Yeah, man.

When I was younger I studied printmaking. I went to art school in Glasgow. I know how to talk about things like this. I have always appreciated the beauty of a motorcycle. I would say that the Triumph engine is the most aesthetically pleasing and beautiful engine ever designed. And a lot of people would agree with that. Personally, it's a balance between function and the form. First there's the function and then the form. One is a product of the other. It's a parallel twin and that is unique because it's symmetrical. Most engines are not.

The original design of a Triumph with two pistons side by side going up and down. It's not a V, it's not a flat. It's two pistons side by side. A Triumph is unique because it has two cams in it. It has an intake cam and an exhaust cam. So if you look at the bike from the timing side, the timing cover is particularly pleasing because it's symmetrical. The design makes it very small and it's very capable for the size of

Shop floor at Sixth Street

it. The Bonneville puts out 49 horse power; maybe 50 on a good day. But, for example, the Vincent Rapid, which has a huge monstrosity of a V-twin and is a gigantic motor, only puts out 45 horsepower. The Black Shadow version puts out 50 horse power. And people would give you their back teeth to own one of them. Because of all the folk lore and all the rest of it. But it's not a very pretty engine and it doesn't do very well in comparison, in terms of the scale of the thing. It's 1,000 CCs but it only produces as much as a Triumph 650.

The Triumph is a unique design—it's very efficient and it's very compact. The Harley Sportster motor is a huge 1,000 motor, but your average one only puts out 50 horsepower. That's brand new. 883s don't even make 50, I think. Look at the Norton Commando 750. That engine produces maybe 54–55 horsepower but they have tremendous torque. They have a top speed of about 115 mph. That's pretty good for a 750. It would take a hell of a Sportster to keep up with that bike. Engines all have different bore and stroke. The size of the pistons and how far the pistons move. They all have different valve designs, intake designs, carb designs. It depends a lot on what you are trying to achieve.

Some bikes are built more for top-end power, some for general run around. Even though they all have a very similar design, they are all affected one way or another by how you employ the design. When the Commando first came out, it won best bike for five years in a row in *Cycle World Magazine* 1969–1974. No other bike has ever come close to that. Originally, the K model (1956) Sportster, was a response to the European invasion. But the Japanese undermined everybody in that market. They produced all those little bikes and they got people who were 15...16 years old and they just took over the world. If they can get you as a teenager, you are more likely to stay with them. That's really the case. It used to be that England made the best, but because of bad management and all the rest of it, by the '70s it was over.

My shop and interest in English bikes is more a coincidence than anything. I never had a motorcycle when I was a kid. I got into it when I was here in New York. I'm not really exactly sure why the Triumph motor ended up being my favorite. Maybe because it is such a good machine and I like the looks of it.

I've had a lot of different bikes and I've boiled it down to where I live and what I do. The best bike for me is a 650 Triumph. For all the categories—aesthetics, performance, function, everything. It's just the all around best user-friendly bike. It's the same engine on the street or going racing. That's me. You meet a V-twin guy and he feels the same about his V-twin. They got their place in this world as well. It's just that they are not quite as high on my table of contents. You know?

Basement threshold at Sixth Street

Basement at Sixth Street

Basement at Sixth Street

Charlie Krause

STREET SMART

Brooklyn

Charlie Krause at his shop

I was brought up in East Flatbush, Brooklyn. My home is still basically a stone's throw from where my shop is now. I went to Grady; it's a vocational technical high school. I can't actually say that I learned how to work on cars in Grady, but believe it or not I got one of my first jobs from one of the teachers, Eddie Milazzo, and I learned so much working at his shop. He had a regular automotive gas station. He was a hot rodder but he was also that TV-story type school teacher. He took a few kids under his wing and kept us on the straight and narrow. Saturday afternoon he'd pull a car into his garage. He was a Chrysler Mopar guy [Chrysler high-performance division]. He'd be doing headers and high-performance stuff and we watched.

I had a lot of young friends who were street racers. My sister's crowd was a little older than me and they'd drag me along to some of the races. This was late '70s, early '80s. Four-hundred horsepower was probably a lot back in those days. A drive-around car had maybe three if you were lucky. You didn't have the tire technology like you have today. There was no availability of aftermarket parts. Basically you were hunting down certain year, make, and model engine parts. It was like treasure hunting to find the parts you needed to make your car go fast.

I was lucky to know an older gentleman who was an old school hot rodder. When I first went into business I started buying parts from him. He was one of those guys you could just call with a question. Every Monday morning I would call him and talk on the phone about what races went down over the weekend. He knew it all and we'd talk every Monday for 15 or 20 minutes until his boss would yell at him to get off the phone and go to work.

He was just such a warehouse of knowledge. What U joints fit what car, what part you needed for this and that. He had been into this for his whole life. He wasn't the healthiest guy and he passed away. Now, every Monday morning when I walk into my shop I think about him. That was my Monday morning call for the last 10...12 years. The knowledge this man had was incredible. Now with the Internet you type in a few words and you get a billion things to look at, but you know, in the old days you didn't have all that. You'd go hang out on a Friday and talk with a few people. Listen to somebody who was better than you.

I couldn't really say for sure when I made the jump from being interested in cars to actually making a high performance car but I was working on mini bikes and go-karts and bicycles since I was young. My dad was a truck driver so he was a wrench and a shade tree mechanic. He was into bikes. He had a lot of old Indian bikes back in the '60s, before the whole thing became popular and vintage. He always had two or three motorcycles in the garage, we always had a boat, we always had two or three cars. There was always some old '30s or '40s car in the front yard.

My dad was a Ford guy. I'm definitely not a Ford guy. During the '60s and '70s he always had Ford cars. My dad actually raced tractor trailers. Just the cabs. They used to race them on a track out in Freeport [Long Island]. So I was around this my whole life. Just like my kids are now. My oldest son races now more than I do. And he's a real good wrench. He's a kid still so he don't come to work on time and things like that. But let me tell you, when you are into cars like we are, there isn't any time to go out and get high and get drunk.

I always hot rodded. I always had a garage somewhere. A little place where I'd keep my tools. I did work on the weekends to my own motors from when I was a kid. I'm not going to lie—in the big scheme of things I'm a Chevy guy. Which is probably the easier road to follow. People talk small blocks but my first fast car was a big block Chevelle. You know, you get a taste of that big block and that's it. A lot of times your first love is what you go with for the rest of your life.

I was a Chevy guy because it's easy to make them go fast and it's easy to make power with them. It's easy to find parts. I love GM cars. Don't get me wrong, I love all cars but as far as things go, I have only owned GM cars. Guys will tell you about their Buicks and their Oldsmobile's and the angle of the pistons and the increased torque. Getting thrown back against the seat. Yeah, I guess in theory this all means something, but you know, build a 600-cubic-inch big block Chevy and forget about that Oldsmobile and the angle of the pistons. You know, bigger is better no matter how you look at it with street racing.

Even before I owned a car I would ride out on my bicycle and watch the races on a Friday night. Fountain Avenue was the hot scene back in the late '70s. I was really into it even before the time I was 14 or 15 years old. The races went on over by the landfill. It was deserted. Actually, it was a big thing back in the '70s because it was a Mafia burial ground. There are tons of stories about the old Fountain Avenue landfill. Back when organized crime ran private sanitation and they could pretty much do whatever they wanted—it was a great spot for dumping bodies and racing.

There was Columbia Street which was a dead end down by the piers in Red Hook. First and 3rd Avenues were racing hot spots. Down by the 20s—all those avenues down there. This is long before beepers and long before cell phone calls. Basically, everybody would just go to the parking lot—the Fountain Avenue and South Conduit Avenue spot on Linden Boulevard. You'd go there on a Friday or Saturday night; you'd tow your car or drive your car. We would tow our car a block away and then drive it in. Let everyone think that we drove it there. Try to psyche out the competition. Eventually they would get to know who's who and you'd have to change cars.

Nowadays the world is so small and everybody knows everybody. That whole sleeper thing, that's cool to read about in magazines but those days are over. Guys would be real secretive. These guys were racing from behind tinted windows. No one knew who the hell they were. They never gave up anything. Now, those days are over.

As a mechanic, the thing I was really famous for was hidden nitrous kits. I have done so many of them. I won't even do them anymore. It's so dangerous now. People

Krause shop front area

Krause garage bay

1985 Monte Carlo SS: Chevy small block, money car, no information about car available for publication

1985 Monte Carlo SS front end with good luck Batman. No information about car available for publication.

Charlie Krause in garage

Mid-1980s Monte Carlo, Bill Mitchell 454 Chevy small block

Charlie Krause working

Garage tool area

are getting hurt. Basically you are stealing somebody's money when you have a hidden nitrous kit. In the old days, people didn't know. I could probably spend four days telling you some of the ways we hid these kits. You weren't killin' it with the stuff but you'd hit the switch and add 50, 80, a 100 horsepower. Or just pumpin' it at the end if you needed it. It was all hidden.

People say they can smell it but that's a wife's tale. You can't smell nitrous. Trust me, you can't. Between unburned fuel and camshaft overlap, exhaust fumes, people might want to say, "Oh yeah, I can smell the nitrous." But believe me, you can't smell it. You can see nitrous; the way the car explodes with power if they're hitting it with a big shot. But typically you are trying to sneak it on somebody so you are not hitting it with a lot. You are hitting it with a little because you need it to be subtle. You know, if you have a 500 horsepower motor and you're hitting it with a 100, that's not super noticeable. But if you have a 250 horsepower motor and you hit it with nitrous, that's a little more noticeable. These are little hustle races here and there. Beer money races. You race four, five times. Make $100 here and there. People raced with the family in the car. They tied the kids down in the baby seats.

What, you don't think I raced with my kids in the baby seat in my car? The whole family in the car? Full out racing for some money, then take the family home. This was pretty much a form of Brooklyn family entertainment. After you'd beat everybody you'd take the engine out and put it into a different car. Make some more money. I have an engine now that's been in six different cars. The trick to make money racing is to start out with a car that is fast at one speed and then every week or two just keep working on the engine and keep making the car faster. You can't have a car at the same speed and make money.

You get to a point where it's pretty much as fast as you can make that car go without going crazy, and then you start with another car. Or, then you start with a different person. We have a car we call "The Company Car." Basically it's a car that we pooled all the parts together. One guy's motor, one guy's transmission, another guy contributed the body. I did the work. Then you bring in a driver nobody knows, or an owner nobody knows. You get somebody interested in a race. You do your negotiation. Hopefully your guy can drive. If not, you put in a stipulation to bring in somebody new to drive. You smoke them. You move on.

I got locked up. The police were getting nervous about all this. Ten years ago the police did some homework. They figured out who everybody was. One morning at like five o'clock they banged on our doors and arrested everybody. The cops had been secretly video-taping everybody all summer. The cops would get the fire department to open up the fire hydrants on the streets. Wet down all the racing streets. You cannot race on a wet street. You'll kill everybody.

At the track

Duster at track

The whole thing with street racing in New York had different things going on for different age groups. When I was really young there were certain cruise spots. 86th Street under the EL [elevated subway tracks] that was a Friday, Saturday night thing. You could cruise there beeping your horn, talking with girls. You know, a girl would jump in and you'd drive a few blocks, make a U-turn, and come back. Like you see in the old-school movies; it was a lot of fun. There was a whole line of cars doing the same thing. You'd cruise along and then when you'd get to the end, the spot where the junk yard was, you'd go down and turn around and race on the way back. Sometimes it was a macho thing. You'd do it for free, no money involved. Sometimes you'd try your driving skills out or try out the car or just to brag.

I knew guys who drove Chevy's and whenever they'd see a Ford they'd have to race and beat it just to make a point. I'm not like that. I love cars. What made me love the cars I like was not the engineering behind it. It was the cosmetic thing. I'm really into certain cars because of their body shapes. My first fast car was that big block Chevelle. It was just a hot looking car. That car was all muscle. For me, Chryslers were nice cars but they were always a little goofy looking. I always looked at cars and was attracted to the sexy looking one. Today, I think the Challenger is dead-on the hottest car out there. It blows away the way the Mustang looks; it blows away the way the Camaro looks. I work on all the cars. The engineering overlaps on all the cars. It's not like the old days when car engineering was different.

I started with all this when I was a kid. It's easier when you are a kid. You make the cars go faster and faster. You grow with the car. Some people are really good drivers, some people are not. Some people develop

1973 Plymouth Duster, 340 Chevy small block: 430hp, Nitrous kit adds 120hp, all-Krause build

skills for what to look for. Put me in any car and let me make two, three runs and I'll let you know that at the top of one gear I felt something and we have to pull the timing or do something with the carburetor. I go down the track and feel like everything is in slow motion—I'm feeling, seeing, experiencing what is going on with the car. It can get complex. There are atmospheric things. An engine is basically an air pump. The more air you can get into it the more power you can get out of it.

When the air is very hot and nasty the air is thick. You are not getting as much air into the engine. Nitrous cars aren't as susceptible to atmosphere, but, you get a turbo-charger car or a normally aspirated car and you will lose a lot of power when the weather is up or down. During the summer in New York it is very humid. You definitely have to know how to make certain adjustments to your engine to deal with the atmospheric conditions in New York.

Some people talk about the difference or quality of speed. Different kinds of speed, torque versus horsepower. I'm not so sure about that. For me, power is power. You are looking for E.T. (Elapsed Time. The time measured between when a car first responds to the green light and when the car crosses the finish line). It's about the first one to get to the finish line. Seat-of-the-pants torque is one thing, horsepower is another if you build a car to have fun and beat up with on the street. The big motors always feel like they are more fun but big block or small block, when it comes to street racing if they both go 12, 0s then it's the same thing. Torque is definitely seat-of-the-pants and feels like a lot more fun, but in street racing, horse versus torque isn't going to make you any more money. It's all about getting to the finish line first.

Today tire technology is ridiculous. Back in the day everyone had their trick—little street tires you could buy and drive around with. Compared to today's tires you can't even imagine how this has changed. It's like the difference between the Wright Brothers and the space shuttle. The compounds and designs. The engineering of the tire. You have drag radial tires now where guys are going deep into the sixes with cars way over 3,000 pounds. You couldn't have done that on a slick 20 years ago. Back then slicks weren't as good as the street tires are today. Rubber compounds have changed a lot. You watch old movies of guys in the '40s and '50s smoking tires down the street. Back then, making horsepower was hard, but getting it to the ground was harder.

You still got to heat your tires up. Do a couple burn-outs to make them sticky. Back in the day all the old guys had secret recipes for various stuff to pour on the street to make your tires stickier. It was similar to guys who made moonshine. In the old days guys would concoct all sorts of stuff to pour on the street so their car would grab it better. Fifteen years ago you couldn't buy any of this manufactured stuff. You used your secret recipe. Originally it was a personal mix of water and bleach. Now they have stuff called Track Bite. There is more exotic stuff. Now the big stuff on the street out in the Midwest is called Pimp Juice. I've used it. It has a different smell but I don't notice that much of a difference. It looks like contact cement. It gets stringy when the tire rolls over it.

The whole thing can get pretty deep. I'm not into it as much as I used to be. It's hard to run a business 70...80 hours a week and then still hang out until two or three in the morning. I pick and choose the races. It's not uncommon to go out and street race and stay out all night and the race doesn't come off. Either the car breaks or the streets are hot with police or there's an argument or there are issues. Certain crews I don't even bother going because there is a good chance they are not going to race. They are into the drama and I don't really need all that.

The Internet has really killed street racing. Now everyone knows what everyone else has. There is no more of that closed hood or looks-can-be-deceiving type of thing. The sleeper type of thing. What degree head, what size carburetor, what size tire. In the old days it was basically you had two or three different things to worry about: with juice, without juice. Big block, small block. Race car, street car. In the old days it was a psyche—you would draw them out. The car that I have today isn't much faster than it was back in the day, but then everything was hidden and concealed. The car had a quiet exhaust, no fancy switches, no twenty gauges on the dashboard, no fuel system hanging underneath the car. Back in the day, when I pulled up in my car, people probably never thought it was as fast as it was. In its day we raced a lot of people with that car. We made a lot of money.

Back then the whole thing stayed pretty regional. We weren't getting called out by guys from the Midwest or California. Word didn't travel like that back then. Nowadays the big thing is the North versus the South. There are a lot of guys down South that race and there are a lot guys up here. They have these North versus South races all the time. But there are guys that come up to the city looking for money and they make things dangerous. They don't know what they are doing with horsepower. We deal with it our way. We isolate these guys. We let it be known that we don't want to race that guy. Or we set up a race in such a way that there is pacing between the cars. If he gets out of control and is going to crash I stay away from him then smoke past him.

Where is that line in terms of safety? Maybe as you get older you might draw that line closer and closer. But if you are younger and a little more wild, the line is further out, the car is out of control and unsafe. Those are the other issues with street racing. Am I a horsepower junkie? Yes, but I am not careless.

I have friends with cars that do like 200 mph but you are talking about guys with a lot of money and big operations. These are good guys, not spoiled rich kids. They work hard for their money and they have very fast cars. These are still stock-style cars: stock doors, the windows go up and down. They are not funny cars or dragsters. They are street cars and they go very, very fast. They would race on the south conduit. That was a big happening spot. People came from all over because that street was good concrete and good material to race on. Guys would come from Connecticut to race on that street. In the Bronx there is a place up on the Hutchinson Parkway by exit seven where they race. Personally I don't really care for the Hutch because the whole thing has a little curve. I am not comfortable going over 130 on a road like that. The little 11-, 12-, 13-second cars like the Hutch.

The city has different spots that are used for different kinds of horsepower. The streets have reputations and legends about them. The cops chase you around and try to break it up but guys still race. Back in the day we would take a car out and do a couple half-passes so people could see what we were dealing with. Then, we would do a full pass. People would see we were talking about a completely different kind of speed. There was no way the car was legal at those speeds. If people had the balls they would call us out, step up and we'd have a street race. It was like, "Alright, you want some? You got some. Now I can make some money."

Thank you note to Krause shop about build

Krause shop from across the street

Recently deceased friend of shop's Chevelle SS at the track

Paul Cox

THERE IS A PATH TO MY MECHANICAL SENSIBILITIES

Brooklyn

Shop floor

Of course things have changed in the city. Life here moves quickly. It's not that long ago that we had our little scene in the East Village. Before that there was a shop in Soho, American Dream Machine, that catered to a whole different group of people. Even within Manhattan there were sort of diverse regional differences going on. Different styles from other boroughs like the Bronx and Staten Island. A thing going on in Long Island which is a whole universe unto itself. I really miss those days when we had a Lower East Side, East Village niche. You know, by the same token it was also very international. Almost like coming out of this little pinpoint of a geographic location—literally within just a handful of square blocks. I feel in a way we sort of had this small influence internationally with the kind of response we were getting from the stuff we were doing. It was so purpose oriented and so kind of edgy and so from the gut. People were noticing it from around the world. We had a constant flow of visitors coming from Japan, from Europe. That kind of blew us

Shop floor

Paul Cox Industries, Brooklyn shop front

Paul's childhood go-kart

Shop anvil and hammers

At the time there was a good balance and a fortunate balance for us. It sort of comes back full circle to how Larry [Indian Larry] and I were talking about how we put ourselves in a place like New York City. *Iron Horse* magazine was based out of Manhattan. They were noticing what we were doing; they were noticing what Hugh and Dimitri were doing over at Sixth Street Specials. That was interesting to the guys working at *Iron Horse*. One of the early editors was Larry's roommate years and years ago. At this point they were in Manhattan and they were catching on to what we were doing and it was a good international outlet. We were all in New York City for a reason, whether it was me or Larry or Steg or Frank. We put ourselves there because of the stimulus, the excitement, the energy, and the access to the world. We were living this crazy lifestyle, pushing things to the limit and people were noticing. It was kind of beyond our control.

Such a big part of doing our craft or craft in general today is visibility and exposure. Today, anybody who creates anything feels very matter of factly it has to be attached to a website or a blog or a MySpace page. It has to be attached to the whole social networking aspect as opposed to just something that you do locked away in a cavernous warehouse someplace. That's the nature of things today; the nature of being an artist to some degree. But when you go back to say 15...20 years ago when I was doing this with Larry, the unique thing about that situation was that Larry wanted the visibility and the exposure because of the sort of carnival twist to him as a person. That feedback and the colorful lifestyle and the really in-your-face mentality of it all was a big part of this whole opportunity we created for ourselves. The interesting thing about the balance of his personality was that he would walk both sides of that line. He wasn't just a bullshitter. He locked the door and built what he needed to build—create, live, dream, do what was inside him. That needed to get out. Then, he could still put on the outfits and clown face and get out there and put on a show at the same time. And this gave people the opportunity to see what he was doing. And it gave us all the opportunity for people to

Shop front door

Indian Larry (photo courtesy Tom Zimberoff).
Photo available: Tom Zimberoff, 1364 45th Ave.,
San Francisco, CA 94122, (415) 246-2417

Larry's and Paul's builds on shop floor

see what we were doing. He was really the motivation behind a lot of that exposure. He knew that the business needed it and he wasn't afraid to do it.

I was more the reclusive hermit in the basement that was happy creating. I had the luxury to sort of sit second fiddle in Larry's shadow but sort of be by his side when he was doing the showman thing. I could be there without putting myself way out there because it wasn't my bag.

Larry had his own ideas about what was expected from the people who worked with him. He would throw a concept out and watch it bounce off you. One of the reasons that we worked together so well for so many years was that we could bounce loose concepts off each other and then just make it happen. We trusted in each other to know that it was pretty much going to be what we expected. Whether it was something he was doing for me or it was something I was doing for him. There was this one particular time when I was working on something and I wasn't happy with it. I brought and showed it to him and instead of saying, "Do it over!" his response was that he was fine with it. He would look at certain things and yes, some things had to be perfect, but other things were just more conceptual. He would explain to me that he looked at the process more in the way that Native Americans would. He would say that Native Americans would look at things and create things with more of a realistic eye that only God can create something perfect. A lot of times in their bead work and weaving they would make an intentional misstep in their layouts, use a wrong color bead or miss a stitch to represent the fact that only God can create something perfect. They allowed themselves to make a mistake and be conscious of that. He would point this out from time to time to say, "Give yourself a little slack to be okay with a mistake from time to time."

George Sedlak tribute paint. "I wanted this bike to have an American racing focus. By chance I met George Sedlak at Daytona. He was the person who painted all of Evel Knievel's motorcycles. I wanted to do something that had more of an antique look to it. Warm up the colors a little bit. It's kind of a reference to the Harley factory racers in the '70s—the XR 750s, the old Sportsters they used to use for racing. They had dual front heads. We run a magneto—that's something we have developed. We run a generator left side case. It reflects back to the early racing technology. You can run the dual carbs and it's a lot more tunable and you have a lot more options."

Paul Cox build, Sedlak-inspired paint

Sedlak-inspired paint

Bikes on shop floor

I do have certain ways that I think about the process of making a motorcycle. When I look at the issue of balance and design, I can walk through my workshop and look at the machines that I am working on. They can push that level of excess where you really have to look at what the concept is, what you are looking to create visually, conceptually, and then whittle that down with the practical concept of it still being a machine functioning as a motorcycle.

It is probably one of the easiest things to just do wacky mechanical art on this type of platform for the sake of visual impact or shock effect, absurdity, uniqueness. You can sit and do that all day long. But, once you get so far into that, the whole thing forgets what the initial purpose is. The project just becomes pure art as opposed to high-performance industrial art or high-performance mechanical art, which I think is the ultimate achievement here with these machines. When it leaves that practical realm and becomes just insanity, you have lost that balance. That's when I think it has to be whittled down with the "Scalpel of Practicality" back to still being a motorcycle. And that's what makes it challenging. A lot of people that "Get it" feel the same way. And then it becomes, what do you do with that functional platform.

For example, I don't typically run turn signals or horns or a lot of that excessive stuff that you will see on standard type bikes. If somebody says I really need to have turn signals or I really want to have a type of shifting system, I tend to look at that as a challenge to still create the way I want to create and still be comfortable with the end result. For example, to do some sort of electrical system that I have to engineer or a mechanical gear-driven concept that makes one thing work differently than it normally would. Whatever the technical aspect or answer is, things like this are a challenge because they are different from what I would normally do. By the same token it is important for me to make a properly functioning balanced motorcycle and this is the biggest challenge of all. That is the ultimate to me.

There is a path to my mechanical sensibilities. A lot of my design sense and original mechanical sensibilities are from my dad. Even though we didn't really communicate all that much or connect verbally that much, there is some sort of gut feeling I have in me. I have a go-kart up on a shelf in my shop. I had it my whole life growing up. It was the connection to my father. He had built it when he was 16 or 17, just a couple years before I was born. He was basically still a kid. He was still finishing it when I was born and growing up. So the connection between me and him was that go-kart. We'd take it to the drag strip and run it and take it to the airport and run it. Wherever we could fire it up and try to keep it away from the cops. When my grandfather passed away in Virginia my father said I should take it with me and have it. Then, six months later my dad died. Probably one of the most important connections to my childhood is that go-kart. It's still exactly the way he built it fifty years ago. He had hand formed and bent the chassis from scratch. He welded on certain parts. That go-kart is a big part of my past and sensibility.

I don't see my work as necessarily being too lost in refinement. I am certainly detail-oriented but I see it as only one element of my end result. In the end, yes, it tends to be complicated with an element of tedium like a braided down tube; I do enjoy getting lost in the details but still I remind myself to step back and check the balance and not get too lost in that. I am really inspired by turn-of-the-century design elements, Victorian concepts, things being elaborate. Three or 400-year-old armor and weaponry like the armor exhibit at the Metropolitan Museum. That blows my mind. So bringing some of those elements into these machines and then

Paul working

Bridgeport milling machine

still tempering it with a certain amount of practicality. And then finding that balance.

There are certain builders out there that really go super sanitary, very refined, absolute minimalistic. That's not me; I tend to bring out complicated elements and try to refine those to fit into the total package. I am always looking creatively ahead, desperate for the next project and level of inspiration and creative excitement, but I always feel that I'm never going to achieve it because I am behind in my actual schedule of making things. Physically I have been in that state forever it seems. Sometimes I feel that I'll never catch up. But that's okay because once you do, you die.

One thing I enjoy is the crossover of different circles of people. The connection to the art world. I have always been a fine artist with paintings and sculptures and galleries and shows and I enjoy that part of it, too. And it's an element that I bring into the machines. Those circles of people and that world in and of itself over the years has become more aware of motorcycles as mechanical art again. I say again because it has been here, maybe as a part of hippie culture, part of Low Brow before it was called the Low Brow art scene back in the late 1950s, '60s, early '70s. Bike culture was more connected to the art world and then sort of split off. Counter culture became tattoos, bikes, art. I think it was a big creative swirling pool. And now I almost see it coming full circle. For me personally to have some background in that makes it more fun for me.

Today, things have moved into a different territory with all of the personal, hand-held technology. It's funny because you start feeling like an old man. You say, "Things are just moving too fast." That's really the way I feel. Give me a minute already! It's like people are trying to get ten steps ahead conceptually whether it's even appropriate or not. People say the new ideas are so mind blowing—it's more, faster, sooner. Oh I see

Engines: Knucklehead (L), Panhead (R)

Paul setting up and adjusting machine

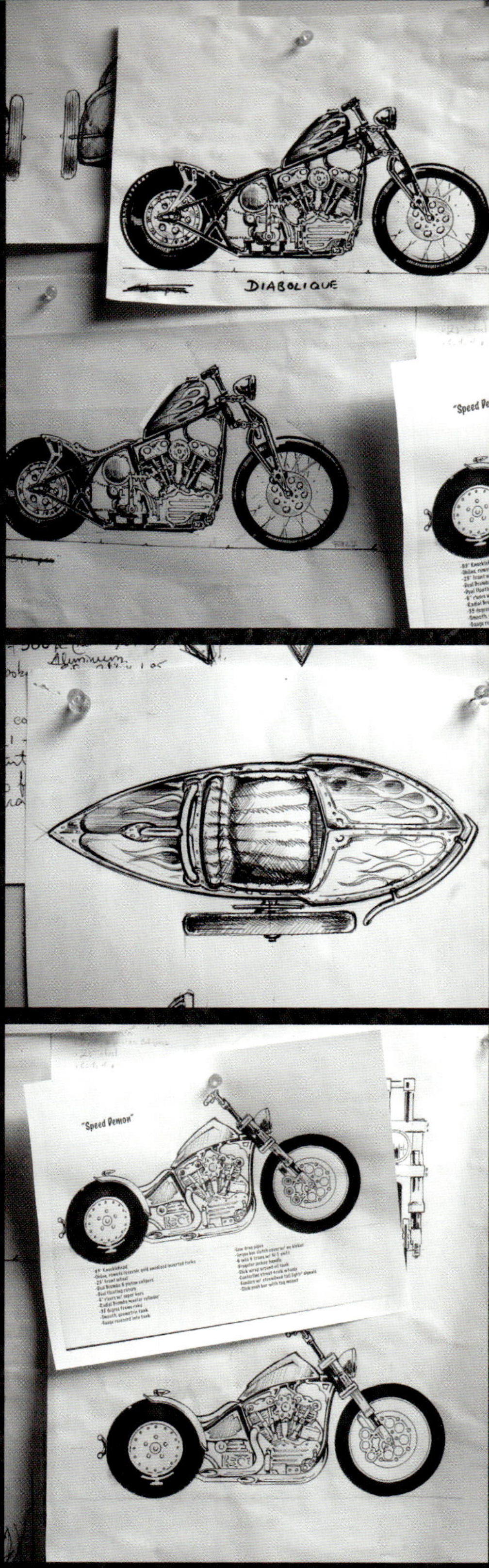

Paul Cox drawings

Shop floor

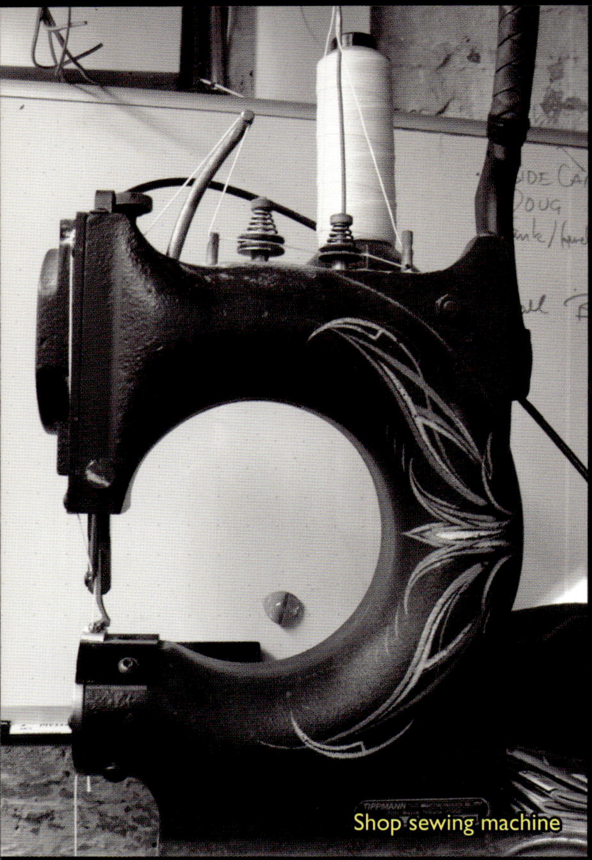
Shop sewing machine

that, let me copy it and make it like this. Well? Hang on for a minute. Enjoy the moment. Soak in what's in front of you for a minute and kind of live it instead of trying to "be" the lifestyle. Just live for a minute. At times the whole thing is so much so fast.

A lot of these creative worlds have grown together—motorcycles, cars, fabricating things. I don't see it as a counter statement to the process of technology. I don't see what I do as some kind of counter culture as it used to be perceived to be. Now, I see this creative process as a part of a new norm. I think it's actually become a little bit more valid. Five, ten years ago a lot of the really hard core stuff was starting to get noticed; people were getting turned on by it, but people were also keeping a safe distance from it. Now, I see people getting closer to the whole thing. The exchange of ideas on the Internet and sharing through electronic media has become a part of our reality. I think it has become real again and people who are doing this stuff now are really about making a real connection. Five, ten years ago it was a look. A weekend warrior mentality. But today I don't see that as much. I think it is kind of real again. That late '90s early 2000s thing has faded.

Paul Cox build

Metal etching detail

Metal etching detail

Metal etching detail

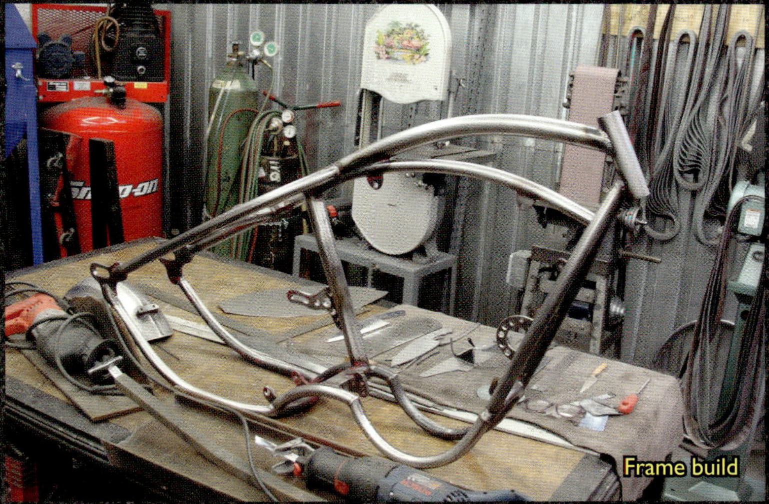

Frame build

Paul setting up machine

Knife blades and templates

That's what I see in the younger people around here in Brooklyn with all the little shops and garages opening up. The guys who are into the arts in this neighborhood are into mechanical forms of art. Even if they're fine artists who do painting or sculptures, there is some kind of mechanical or hot rod influence in their art. You see a lot of guys genuinely putting together underground bike shops and garages, car shops and bringing groups together and this is very important. In the past couple years, remembering and reacquainting myself with what's going on right around me has been very cool from a personal standpoint.

There is absolutely something really New York about what is going on right now. Maybe not as much as 20 years ago with the regional issue, but the kind of thing that's happening in our immediate environment is definitely very New York and it will continue to have a New York flavor. It relates to the streets we ride on, the buildings and garages and basements we work in. That definitely has its own flavor. The environment will continue to lend itself to the things that we do creatively. There is now a crossover going on between styles: West Coast, Frisco-style gang bikes from the '60s and the East Coast and New York that has its own style and mentality. People are having fun with it. This is a sign of the times. People are exposed to everything everybody does, anywhere in the world at any moment.

The builders and creative people in this area will never lose that New York City flavor because you just can't. Crime goes up, crime goes down but New York will never lose its edge. As much as people get pushed out of their little spots by rising rents, there's always going to be someplace to go. That's New York. For example, when Brad [Pitt] comes in here to check on his bike, he walks into this obscure little side street, into a little door—he walks in and the place opens up—the brick and the history. He looks and says, "I love Brooklyn." It's the first things out of his mouth every time.

The shop we had, Psycho Cycles on Rivington Street, even the physical layout of the place that opened up on Rivington and then had this half-a-city-block basement, it was just such a cool place to work. That sort of thing means a lot to me creatively. My shop area around my machines and the old walls, that really turns me on and it excites me creatively. When we came into this space the wall on one side was just raw cinderblock and the original brick was all exposed but I really wanted to keep it with the chipped paint plaster falling off because that is inspiring to me. My fabrication area back there with the Bridgeport and the lathe and some of that machinery positioned in front of that aged brick? That is the ultimate vision to me.

The fact that there is an immediacy of information that we have access to these days—I don't think it's all necessarily all good from a creative standpoint. I think that it blurs the lines between regional styles as they relate to something like hot rods and bikes. In the past, before all this, this regionalism is what made the stuff more special. Those lines have gotten so blurred over the past ten years. For example, whether

Shop floor

Shop floor

NYC floor board

Brooklyn floor board

Engine rebuild

you are in Boston or you are in Florida or Los Angeles or anywhere on the West Coast or across the Midwest, you are going to see the same style over and over again. Everyone is just doing whatever they see or hear on the same chat room or somebody's website or the latest magazine.

It used to be a lot cooler to have to travel to see the different stuff. If you didn't get to the West Coast, you didn't get to see the West Coast style. Maybe every now and then you'd see a good spread in a magazine. But the experience was more tactile and it was still a little more special. It was real; it was in your hands. Now every style is immediately accessible and everyone has the opportunity to knock off the same stuff. Now it doesn't matter where you ride or how you ride, it all boils down to what's the flavor of the month. It's the nature of what is going on now. It can't piss you off because then you just focus on the something that is negative. But it's not something that I ignore. It's something that I have noticed over time. And at times I find it disappointing. I think because of this new process, people relate to the hot ticket and the hot set up—as opposed to what they grew up with that might be more personal and they relate to on the inside.

For whatever reason I may see another person's workshop in a different place across the country and I am reminded about my place in Brooklyn. It is so different and I am reminded about how lucky I am to work in a place like this.

Keino

THE MOTORCYCLE IS WHAT I USE TO EXPRESS MYSELF. SOMETIMES IT IS ME, OR SOMETIMES IT IS WHAT I WANT TO BE, OR TRY TO BE.

Brooklyn

Keino in his shop, 2010

I was brought up in Fukuoka, Kyushu, Japan. My first experience dealing with motors and motorbikes was when I was young. My dad found a scooter on the street that was all beat up and we just started taking it apart like a Saturday-Sunday project. He had a little garage workshop so that's where we took the scooter apart. When my dad and I went through the process of taking that motorbike apart and then putting it together, I had a feeling of accomplishment. My dad was a chef and for a hobby he liked to make jewelry, stained glass, and wood carving. He was a renaissance man. Whenever we moved he had to have a garage where he could do all his stuff. I always had a craft orientation since I was young.

Keino build at Ist Brooklyn Invitational, 2009

Keino's shop

Keino build: High and Tite lacework paint, Shovel-Pan motor

When I was growing up, and then when I went to college, my parents wanted me to get into teaching. A degree and a secure good job. As a kid I listened to my parents and in college my major was history. I was going to do the whole thing—Masters, Doctorate—but at the same time I had these other interests—motorcycles. I kind of dropped that idea of being a teacher. I liked mechanics, I liked to create something. I wanted to learn to build motorcycles. At that time in Japan there was a phenomenon of the chopper going on. Nearly 20 years ago a builder named Shinya Kimura founded Zero Chopper. This inspired me very much. I followed Shinya's work and the progress of his creativity. Six or seven years ago a friend of Shinya made a book titled, *Zero Chopper Spirit*. This book helped Shinya and the Zero Chopper style to get worldwide recognition.

I talked to my parents and told them I wanted to drop college. I wanted to study motorcycles at the MMI (Motorcycle Mechanics Institute) school in Arizona. My English was not good enough at that time and it was also a question of money. So my plan was to finish school, get a job, save money. I waited four years to get to the point when I could go to America. At MMI you can focus on all the different motorcycle brands. I just focused on Harley Davidson. This was around 1998. I focused on Harley for reasons that are hard to explain—the sound, the feeling, the history. The engine design behind them. It has a bigger platform as far as customizing is concerned. More opportunity, a bigger market; the custom motorcycle magazine world focuses on Harleys.

When I got out of school I sent out some resumes. Mostly to California dealerships but nobody wrote back. A dealership in Brooklyn got back to me. The name Brooklyn popped up and caught my eye. I had never been to Brooklyn but I thought it was close to New York City and that sounded really good.

I worked for ten months at that dealership but it was not as interesting as I had thought. It was motorcycle service. Good to learn but it got to be too much. I went to two bike shops in the city to introduce myself. Both of them offered me a job but I took the job at American Dream Machine in Soho, Manhattan. First day I went I met Larry [Indian Larry].

At the time Paul [Paul Cox] was working out of his house with his leather work. First time I met him he came in on his Triumph and passed me his flyer for his art opening. That was around 2000.

Larry was a good person to work for. He would show you what he wanted and then he would let you do it. He would come back around and check it out but it wasn't his style to take your hand and walk you through it. It was up to you. When Larry was working he was very focused and he did not want to be bothered. This was a very important experience.

I have developed a sensibility about motorcycles from different places. Bottom line, a motorcycle is a machine. It has to function. A motorcycle has a parameter that includes many different things. I don't necessarily see a motorcycle as a part of an art form. To me, Art is Art.

There are things called art objects: A sculpture, a painting, it doesn't have to do anything. They have to be there and give people an impression. A sense of calmness or anxiety. But a machine has the same qualities—it can initiate excitement and an aesthetic function but also it has to run. Paintings and sculptures do not have to run. They are idle. So, you can call me an artist but I am also a mechanic. That combination has always stuck in my head.

The mechanics of a machine have to work. It's a machine. It's not going to last long; there is longevity. Something will eventually break down. It has to have reliability. So that is also a key element of

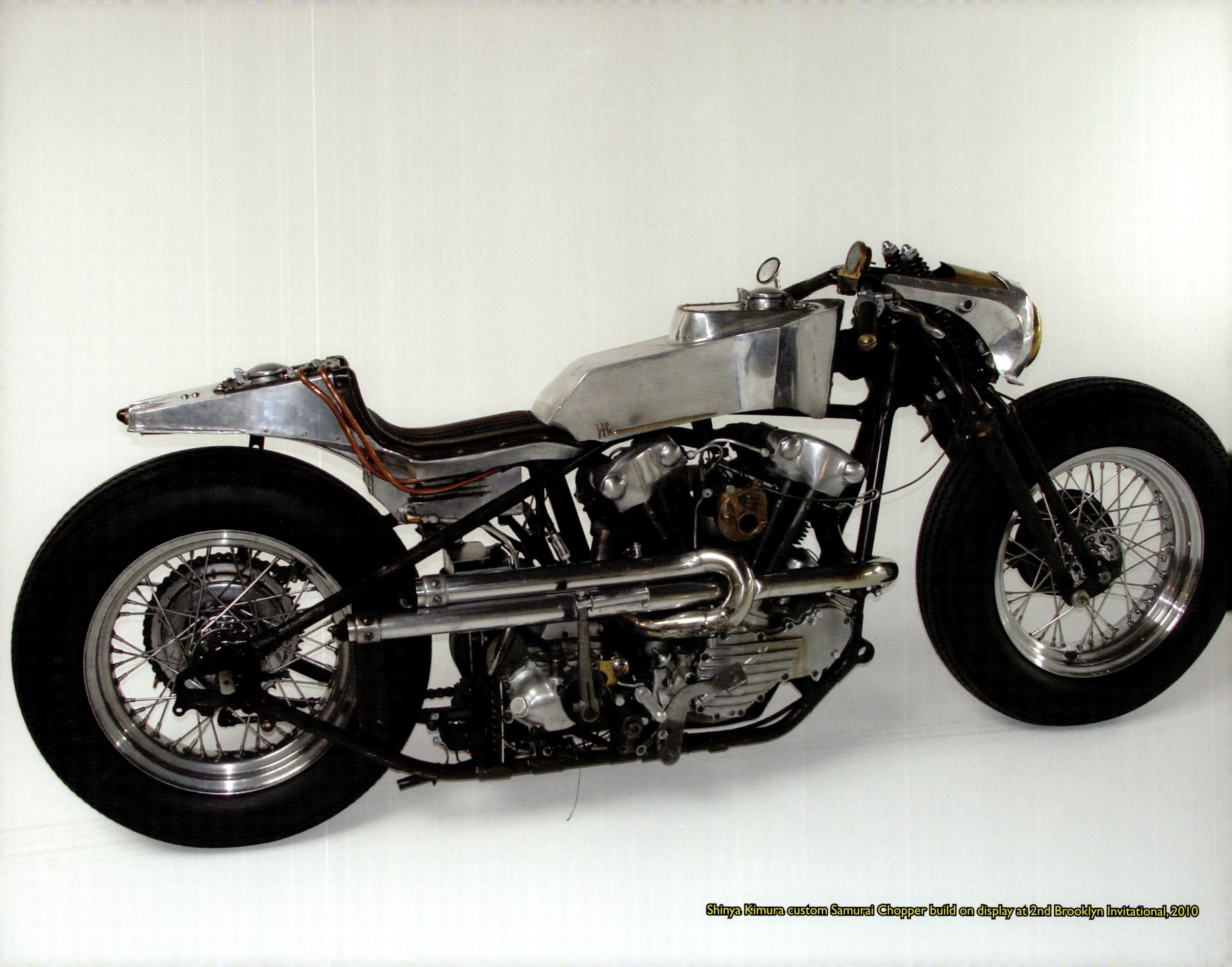

Shinya Kimura custom Samurai Chopper build on display at 2nd Brooklyn Invitational, 2010

Shinya Kimura custom Samurai Chopper build at 2nd Brooklyn Invitational, 2010

Shinya Kimura Knucklhead build

my work. In terms of design, how unique do you want to go? Do you want to have a long, long front end just to be unique? It'll work; it'll turn, but will it be easy to turn? No. Is it safe? No. So I must operate within certain parameters of this art form. How far can you go? Do you take it to the extreme just to be unique or just to catch someone's attention? I see some bikes and they look very interesting. I just wouldn't want to be the guy who has to ride it.

It's like an experiment. I push the variables. It has to run but it also has to be beautiful. I change the frame design, I lay out the components. There are little things that I am sensitive to and push to the next level. I think about it, design it, make it. If it doesn't work out, that is a part of a process. It's a challenge. I might be the only one who understands and gets it, but obviously that's why I do it. Other material like sheet metal is a key element in motorcycle design and fabrication. Tanks and fenders are another

Keino

AJ visiting Keino's shop

Noel visiting Keino's shop

key element of a motorcycle that I can make sculpture out of. I can change flat sheet metal and do something with it to make it my own. I can create with sheet metal.

Motorcycle manufacturers have philosophies behind their machines. The way they construct the engines, the frames, the sheet metal forms. BMW has the boxer twin and their philosophy; Harley has the V-twin and their philosophy. That is something I like to take and twist it up in my own way. Panhead and Knucklehead, Panhead and Shovelhead. This is an ongoing thing and I'll find out what happens. I'm not saying that I know everything about a Harley engine, but I know a little bit about them. I can do stuff—make a few modifications to make it work. So this is my approach and my process; to modify the engine in this way. I have been doing this Pan-Shovel combination for a while. So at this point I know it works. And I know how I can make it work.

There are different ways to look at engines. They are machines so you can be very practical about it—horsepower. I have worked with combining new elements. Larry worked on combining a Panhead and a Shovelhead. I thought about taking it to the next level—the Pan-Knuckle-Shovel combination. It would be great if the combination increased horsepower but I am not really after that. I am not looking at horsepower numbers. This is just an idea and I just wanted to make it happen. I want to hear it and make it run right. Then I want to say, "Yeah, I built this engine." I am dealing with a concept about engines. I have a bunch of old magazines and you see a lot of old crazy engines from back in the day. Harley started out 100 years ago. I have seen old magazines where people are doing weird combinations. Strange factory prototype engines and bikes. I am not saying that I am the first person to want to change things.

The V-twin is from '36 to '99. It's basically the same geometry. They share the same backbone geometry. You can tweak it and modify it. Make it fit. Sportster, Evo, Ironhead, Flathead. These engines have different camshaft arrangements. I have a project I want to try. I have to do some research, but I have this 1977 Ducati 900SS head. It has all the classic features that Ducati is known for—bevel geared, desmodromic valved—I want to put this head onto a Harley. I just want to make it work. Eventually I want to combine BMW and Harley. Anything to do with overhead valve engines, I want to put it on a Harley. To make it work to see what it sounds like.

In a place like New York or America there is an issue about space. Compared to Japan, America is a big place with a lot of room to move around. When I design and then build a motorcycle, I absolutely consider the space it will be used in. That's like a mentality. Before I came to America I grew

Keino building frame for Wes Lang's custom bike build

Keino working on Wes' frame

Keino working on Wes' frame

Keino working on Wes' frame

Keino's Bridgeport

Keino front end fabrication

Keino's shop mechanic's box

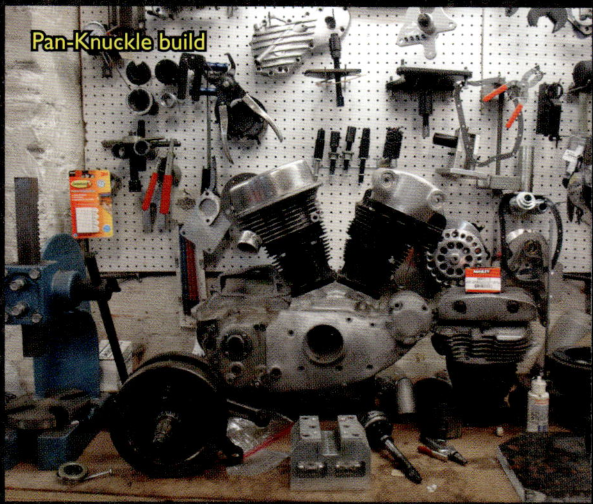
Pan-Knuckle build

up in an urban environment. I grew up in a place that is very similar to the situation in Brooklyn and its relationship to Manhattan. My neighborhood was 10...15 minutes from the downtown area. That's one reason why I feel very comfortable in Brooklyn.

I ride here the same way I did back home. Always splitting lanes through traffic, then if I ride out for a half hour I am in the countryside. Things open up and it's much easier. There are mountains, a shoreline, the sea. This reality has always influenced my riding style and the elements I put into building a bike. Not too low, not too wide, stop and go, turn. People come to me because they like my bikes but really, I just do what I feel, what comes into my mind. What I want to try next? I am not sure I have established my style yet; it's just an ongoing process. I am not necessarily married to this current style or design or whatever you call it. I am still learning and want to try new things and experiment.

My thing is engine and sheet metal work and front end. Three things. Mainly I do engine work but I am also interested in the handling of the motorcycle—the rake and trail of the bike. There are equations that make more sense than others in terms of riding and safety. These are elements I can play with in design. It is a style consideration. I might like looking at a bike where the equation has been exaggerated but I don't think I would enjoy riding it.

I don't want to limit myself to certain visual aesthetic things. I definitely have codes, rules, philosophy, guidelines; whatever you call it. There are some lines that I would not feel comfortable crossing. It comes down to personal preference. These kinds of things come out of my hand and the way I push myself. I try to break out of my shell and get into something different. I see this kind of process in my work.

I think a few years back to certain things I didn't want to do or I didn't think that I could do. Now, a few years later, it's not bad at all. The motorcycle is the thing that I use to express myself. A writer has language, a painter has a brush, the sculptor has a tool, the musician has an instrument, and a singer has a voice to express themselves. To live their life doing things. So, the motorcycle is what I use to express myself. Sometimes it is me, or sometimes it is what I want to be, or try to be.

When I worked for Larry I learned a lot about the correct way to approach this question. Something like the Pan-Shovel combination. I have thought about where that could go. In the end I would learn something, discover something. In the end I might try but I couldn't do it. I like to see people trying to do things. It's all challenging. I feel more comfortable working like this.

Motorcycles are aesthetic objects. Of course I am influenced by some builders in Japan and I admire them. This kind of work has been going on in Japan for 30 or more years. Before computers and the Internet, builders in Japan were very isolated. Maybe they would see a magazine but they were operating in a vacuum. They had to come up with their own alternatives, their own

Keino working on a fender

Keino working on a gas tank

Keino

Keino front end build for Wes Lang's bike

approach in their own environment. As time went on Japanese builders developed their own approach and they felt comfortable doing it because they had no other choice. Of course it was based on their nationality and culture. It was a process that took time because of the issue of isolation. I can't really pick out a time or an event when Japanese motorcycle or hot rod culture happened. It is a process that is definitely influenced by a unique sense of isolation.

In Japan a notion of Shinto or Buddhism is built into the daily basis of life. People take it for granted, but these things are built into daily ritual. There is also a sense of discipline—what your parents taught you.

Shinto believes that inanimate objects have their own sense or spirit or personality or power. I definitely think about motorcycles in this way. Absolutely. Motorcycles have a power and personality. Some guys definitely get superstitious about their motorcycles. I can't explain it. The other day a friend was in here with his bike. He was talking about selling it. The bike is a two-kick bike when he starts it. But after we had this conversation about him selling this bike he went to kick start it and the bike didn't respond. He just kept kicking it and kicking it. It wouldn't start. Finally he kicked it and it started. I said, "Maybe if you hadn't been talking about selling it, it would have started."

All guys who own kick-only bikes know that there is a funny weird jinx. If somebody is trying to kick start a bike, don't stare at him. If the staring factor gets involved you will never kick-start that bike. Like if you are in front a bar and there are people standing around and you want to start the bike, people should not look at you or the bike. The bike might feel the pressure that it has to start. You want to be bad-ass and kick that bike and have it start first kick but you think down deep what if it doesn't? Six times out of ten the bike will not start. The bike feels the pressure that you are looking at it and that you doubt it. The bike doesn't like this. A lot of guys are like this, they think, "*Oh, he's kicking, don't look at him.*" We joke about this all the time.

A bike is the sum total of all the parts that have been put together. Things are measurable and known about this machine. But even though it is all supposed to be measurable, two engines of the same type and exact same specs are two different engines. They feel different, they start different, and they sound different. The engines will have a different routine they need: One of the engines will want to be primed in a certain way before you kick it. The other engine will want something completely different: Same engines but totally different personalities. I don't know why, nobody does.

Motorcycle culture is strong now. There is a different sense of credibility now. You go to a motorcycle show in America and it's huge. People make plans and travel to go to some of these shows. In Japan this happens, too. The motorcycle market is smaller there but it is more concentrated. In Japanese culture the feeling about motorcycles is a little more idealistic.

In America the market is so big that even if you design and build something that is really unique even if it's out of stupidity and it's really not so interesting, somebody will want to have it. The market is that big. Just think of the used motorcycle market in America: There are literally tens of thousands of motorcycles just sitting on the used market.

I am custom designing and building unique motorcycles. This is a different sensibility from a mass-produced situation. And at times this becomes a dilemma for me. A customer goes to my website and sees something they like. But they only have a certain budget to use. They then become

Keino working on Wes' bike

Shovelhead build for Wes' bike

High and Tite studio, Brooklyn

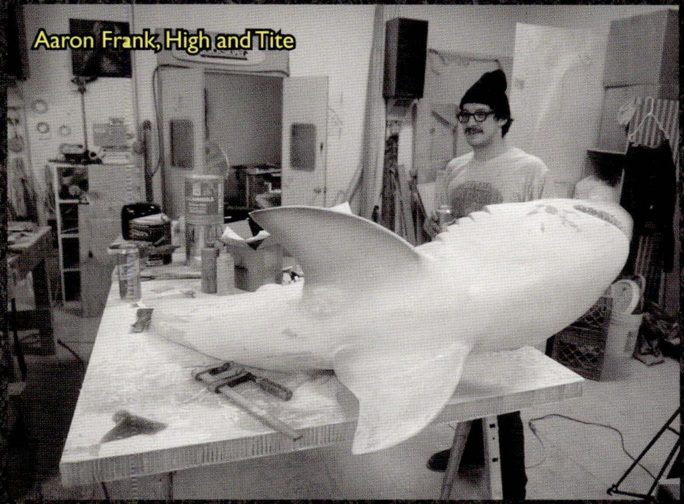

Aaron Frank, High and Tite

Vince Szarek painting tank for Wes Lang's bike

Vince painting Wes' tank

Vince painting Wes' tank

Wes' tank in progress

Wes' tank in progress

Wes Lang visiting the High and Tite studio

involved in a situation where they want something for a certain price but I can't give them what they want for that price. I end up pushing them away. They try to haggle over the price. It is a business and this type of negotiating is a nature of business, but I don't like to go there. I want to keep my dignity and my reputation. I don't want to be like a McDonald's builder. I'd rather just struggle to get a customer. I work small scale and provide custom quality for my customers. If people don't see that, they can just go away.

Sometimes people ask why I wanted to open my own shop. Personally speaking, I see my life as a process. I was brought up in Japan and I was influenced by my dad and then by Shinya and his Zero Chopper style. This planted seeds in my head. Then I worked with Larry and Paul and this experience reinforced my approach towards motorcycles. I have always seen this as a natural progression to pursue this on my own. That's a challenge, too. For me that's a perfect way to have respect for these machines. To remember what I have learned and bring it with me into my future. I see this as an opportunity to be more creative and try to make things for my customers within their budgets in a realistic way. Where everyone is comfortable and the creative process produces a unique motorcycle.

Keino

Wes' completed bike at 2nd Brooklyn Invitational

Keino at White Knight's garage, Brooklyn

Alex in garage

My approach to making a motorcycle is two things. I live in New York City and I ride in New York City. The bike should be strong. I don't want it to fall apart and all of a sudden something happens. The handling of the bike is very important here in New York. There is not a lot of room. The surface of the streets is very unpredictable. As far as my aesthetic goes? I like my bike to be very compact. It doesn't look sloppy. The bike looks together; it looks composed. This is important to me. The space between the front head and the frame neck, rear head, and the seat post. In my opinion, if you have a lot of room there the bike looks sloppy. It doesn't look like the builder has taken time to figure things out.

Window in garage

Alex with tool chest

I use red lock tight on everything. Larry [Indian Larry] used to say he used red lock tight on everything and, "I deal with it when I have to take the bolts out." On top of this I drill all the bolts and I safety wire all the major components. This way the bike will not fall apart. The vibration of the motor, the pot holes. This makes me a little bit more safe. How many times you see bikes on the road and the whole thing is falling apart. I try to eliminate the possibility of an accident because of a loose part. I do service religiously every 1500 miles. I put it on a lift and go over the bike. My CCCP bike with the Pan-Evo motor—that thing is engineered tight. I have titanium axles. This is how I make things.

I got a lot of my machine sensibility from my father. He worked for Fiat. He built regular and rally motors for that company. Also the Russian car company Lada (AvtoVAZ, a Russian car manufacturer in Togliatti. The car design is based on the

Alex's tight engine design

Alex's CCCP build

1966 Fiat 124 sedan). I grew up with this kind of thing. I would go with my father to his work and watch the making of cars. I spent time in the military and I was exposed to mechanics. Military trucks. Big stuff.

I came to America in 1990 and I wanted to get into motorcycles. But I had no way to become a part of this. I didn't know anybody. I did not have the opportunity to go to school—MMI and all that. I didn't know anybody in this business. The first job I landed in New York was a busboy in a restaurant. Across the street from this restaurant was a biker bar. It was used in many movies during the 1980s. This place was no joke. You could really get your ass fucking handed to you. This was real bikers, not what is going on here today. Guys would go into that bar after work and start drinking and fighting. They would come flying back out the door on their fucking heads. I was 20 years old and I'd look across the street at what was happening at this bar and it was like watching a movie. I had just come from Russia and I was amazed by this place.

One of the guys hanging out there worked at a Harley dealership. I would talk with him but he was like, who is this fucking kid? I gave up on the motorcycle thing and went to college for computers. I needed a job and I was walking past a Harley dealership and noticed a help wanted sign. A guy named Bogey came out, "You wanna wash bikes?" he said. "Five bucks an hour." I said OK. He was like, "Yeah?" I did that for probably two months and then something happened—one of the mechanics fucked something up so I told them I'll bring my tools and fix it. I was driving a real nice car, an El Camino. So, the guy at the dealership looked at my car and he looked at me and said, "Bring your tools and try it out." I'm still trying it out.

I started working on bikes at the dealership and realized—wow, I can do a lot of different things. With the cars I could do some things, but I discovered there is more freedom with a bike. One day Larry passed by the shop and dropped off some flyers for something. He was riding Grease Monkey and I saw this bike for the first time. Wow—Seeing this bike changed things for me.

It is true that Grease Monkey is a New York City bike. He rode this thing every day. I used to see this bike all the time in the Village. At the time I knew it was an influential machine. To me what is important is that Larry rode that bike every day. It was not built just to look pretty in the corner. Every day that bike was ridden.

Indian Larry engine build on display at annual Rumblers Brooklyn event

Alex's every day bike

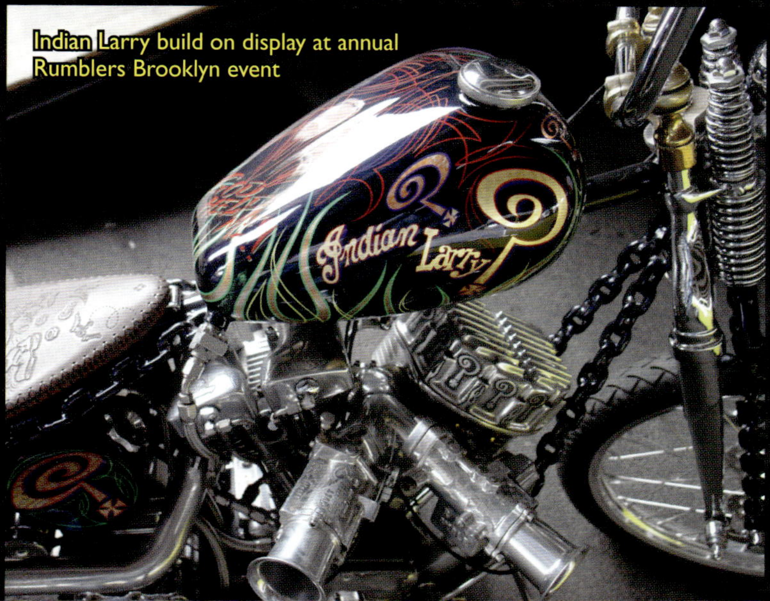

Indian Larry build on display at annual Rumblers Brooklyn event

First time I met Larry he was working with Steg at a shop, Steinway studios in Astoria, Queens. I used to go there if I had a couple questions. Larry was always cool. I didn't even know him. He was always in the back working on something. Then, when I had my Queens County Cycles shop, I think this is the first time I actually met him. Gasoline Alley opened up after Dream Machine and they needed a couple extra hands so I worked there for a couple months.

At that time I was developing my own style but it was early. Certain things that Larry was doing were very impressive to me. I remember thinking that nothing could

Alex Lerner build in Indian Larry Legacy garage

Alex Lerner engine build

be done better. These were aesthetically functional and beautiful machines. Larry's work was always a very unique balance of function and beauty. Pure machine. His idea about using an external oil filter is very functional. In New York you go from light to light to light and it raises your engine temperature. Larry's external oil filter is very New York and it just looks good. This influenced me and this is how I wanted to make a motorcycle. It could be a 550 Honda—I didn't care. This is how I would approach building or working on a motorcycle. I was serious about educating my customers. What would Larry do? How would he do it? This is key on my mind and always will be. He has been dead for seven years and I am still thinking, "*What would he do? How would be approach this?*"

I build a bike a year. I have my own style. This is how I work. I am building non-stop. I do not discriminate—Harley, Japanese, Kawasaki, Yamaha. I have gone through periods when I am questioning motorcycle tastes. Harley is obviously very important but there are different kinds of motorcycles. Of course there is a trendiness to motorcycles but this has good and bad sides. For example, a lot of people riding Hondas come here and say, "Yeah, I am riding a Honda now but someday I will ride a real motorcycle—a Harley Davidson." I thought about this and decided I wanted to spend time building a Japanese bike. A Kawasaki. I took an engine out of a dirt bike and put it in a different chopper frame. Now, that bike has more than 30,000 miles on it—all New York. It has never given me any trouble. I rode it from New York to Lake George and back in one day. No problems. Five-hundred miles. That bike took me to Canada, to New Hampshire. I never go to Bear Mountain and all that. It's not my ride.

I see myself as a mechanic. I like to work on things and change them and make them better. Sometimes I dream about the customer who walks in and wants to spend $100,000. An opportunity to build whatever I want. The guy says, "I saw your stuff. Here's the money. Do whatever you want." You never know, but chances are, this isn't going to happen. If it did, I wouldn't build something wild. I'd build the most reliable bike. If he said, "I want a vintage Knucklehead," I'd tell him, "Look, yeah, the Knucklehead is the best looking motor, but you aren't going to get out of New York."

I have ideas to combine different types of motors. Part motorcycle, part aircraft. Just to do it. When I built my Pan-Evo motor it was just the challenge to do it. I didn't want to be distracted. I built that motor in my bedroom. I wanted to be completely isolated. I built a special table to work on it. It was an interesting project. All the things that I didn't think would give me a problem became a problem. Other things that I figured would be no problem became big trouble. I was using a Panhead aftermarket case with an Evolution lifter block that wouldn't fit, so I had to change things. The flywheels wouldn't fit properly in the case so I changed things. At the end of the day things worked out well.

I am not necessarily fixated on horsepower. The way I see it: If I can get on I-95 and comfortably keep up with the traffic, that's my issue. That is a for-real road. Seventy-five is not a speed there. At seventy-five you are going to get run over by a tractor trailer. If I go to Connecticut and I get on I-95 and I go into the middle lane and I can keep up with the traffic without people honking at me or running me over then that's good.

If I have 30 horsepower and the bike can do this then I have no problem. I have this Evo right now. It's a 120-inch motor and all its capable to do is from one shop to another. You cannot handle this thing. For me, if you want horsepower go buy a Japanese bike. A Ninja. Make 100 horsepower on one of these dinosaurs? It will only hurt you. They don't handle like that. A lot of guys get crazy with big motors. They burn nitrous, but you can't. It won't handle. It's for show only. By the time you get to this peak horsepower, your hands will not grip anything from the vibration. So, if I get 55 or 60 horsepower so I can keep up with the traffic on I-95, I am very happy.

There is something called the power band. This is the balance of torque and RPM and horsepower. If you have this huge motor, by the time you get to the power band, when the engine makes peak horsepower, there is so much vibration you hands will go numb and you can't hold on any more. So what is this? Do you need 120 horsepower?

Alex on his every day bike

Alex's every day bike

Alex's every day bike

I am a loner. This is how I like to work. This is a conversation I am having with myself. This all goes back to the way I have always done it. I have always built a bike a year for a customer. Since the beginning I have been serious about this process. I never felt too serious about sending photos of my work to a magazine. Look at the work in a lot of these magazines. Guys are using electrical tape. Electrical tape? Zip tights? What? And these bikes are in a magazine? What the fuck? You know what? I don't want to have anything to do with a magazine like that. I don't want to be there.

My standards came from when I was young. My dad was a fanatic. Everything was done the Old Russian way. Whatever he did was coming out of this old European craft sense of making things. Look at the way I organize my tool boxes. This is how you do it. Everything in the right place. Then in New York I was lucky enough to meet this guy John Bruzzo [Bruzzo Family Racing]. He was a great car mechanic. He was racing cars, dragsters. Somehow I got introduced to him and I was lucky enough to see him work. He just blew my mind. This guy is so focused and serious about making things. The color of the wire in his wiring harnesses had to be perfect. The wire lengths had to be perfect. If a hole had to be drilled there was always a pilot hole drilled first. Little things like this on and on and on. If he was doing wiring, everything was measured perfectly. No bullshit. Everything was done like this. His work looked like a 1930s circuit breaker board. I watched John a few times and it reminded about the way my father did things. This is how I learned to do things. I was building a bike and Bruzzo saw the bike and he liked it. He invited me to his house. He showed me his dragster. That was a state-of-the-art dragster. A 30-foot-long dragster. This has stayed with me.

I see these flashy bikes on the street. The work is not good. Nobody is paying attention to the way wiring is supposed to be done. You look up close and somebody has screwed in threads and the measurement is off. The threads are just hanging there. Why? Cut the fucking bolt. It's not a question of these people being lazy; it's more than that. They don't know any better. The correct way of doing things is not in their mind. For guys who do work like this, what's on their mind is lots of chrome and a flashy paint job. Ninety-eight percent of the people do not get past the chrome. That's what they want. All this deep knowledge and sensibility and standards get lost somewhere along with zip tights and electrician tape. It is not even a question of caring or craftsmanship. This is just the way it's supposed to be done. Whatever I am going to do, this is how it's going to be done.

I was brought up in Russia. There was not too much emphasis on pretty. The culture was like this. The emphasis was on function. I see bikes with a very long extension and it doesn't make sense to me. Maybe to someone else, but not to me. That's just the way I am. I can't go back too far with all this history. What it comes down to is that I have some influences and these give me a sensibility and I have my own style. It's like this. When I build a bike I usually re-do everything three times. At least. I make it, I don't like it. I make it, I don't like it. It gets to the point where I get a little obsessive. People don't know about this. People look at my CCCP bike that was in the 2009 Brooklyn Invitational. If they know anything they usually say, "Man, that bike is built. It could be thrown off a fucking bridge and it will just stand up."

When I first came to this Indian Larry shop I had to deal with a very serious set of standards. Larry and then Paul and Keino, who worked with Larry, are very talented. They raised the bar to a whole new level. They raised it so high that when I first started working here this issue was very serious for me to deal with. At first I thought, "*OK, how am I going to deal with this?*" Then I thought, "*You know what? Just do what you have always done.*" So that's what I do. Bobby and Elisa asked me four times about working here. There was such a history here. Those guys do very important work. It was hard for me to imagine. Keino talked with me about it. He said, OK, no worries, now it's up to you. This definitely gave me something to think about.

New York City is an endless carnival. Larry understood this. The motorcycle scene in New York is also a carnival with many kinds of people. I had been working here for a while and one day I hear a Harley pulling up. I am inside but it sounds like a Shovelhead. I take a look. I look out the door and there is a six foot seven transvestite with a really short skirt, big boots, and tits like you wouldn't believe. He is speaking with a deep, deep voice. He is riding a real cool Shovelhead that Larry had something to do with at some point. Maybe from the old Psycho Cycles days. This guy wanted his bike totally re-done, so of course I rebuilt his bike for him. He was pretty crazy. He was riding this kick start only Shovelhead. I was like, "Man, this is fucking New York City." I had to change the belt on his bike but I kept the old one. He had painted all these designs and artwork on the belt. I thought about this. It was something to remind me about the way it is. Everywhere I go this belt travels with me. It reminds me of what goes on here in New York. Like I said, this town is endless.

Annual Indian Larry Brooklyn event

Fallen heroes tribute motorcycle on view at annual Indian Larry event

Bikes at Indian Larry event

Fallen heroes tribute motorcycle on view at annual Indian Larry event

Craig Hoffman in his garage

Craig Hoffman

TORQUE AND HORSEPOWER

Brooklyn, Queens, Long Island

I was born in Brooklyn and I lived in Queens as a kid. I must have been about five, and we lived on Grant Avenue in Brooklyn. I used to sit on the stoop with my father and name all the cars going down the street. He taught me how to identify the cars. When I got older I used to hot rod around. Something happened recently that brought me back to those days. Years ago when I was a kid, I had a Camaro. I had worked on it to make it go faster. I hot rodded that car and then I sold it and lost track of it for many years. It was one of those things that I always regretted doing. Then recently the car turned up and I bought it again. I got to look at the car and see what I had done to it years ago. I'd look and say, "Wow, I really fucked that up." It's funny, you see how you evolve. I straightened out the whole car and now it's really nice.

Friend's GTO—classic NYC muscle

One-Eye Jay's '66 Chevelle SS. "We brought that car back from a basket case. It has a 427 big block with a Muncie 4-speed. Jay had the car painted and I assembled the rest of the car."

Craig with his 1973 Camaro, photo 1987: "I owned that car for about 10 years, sold it back to my friend that I bought it from who then had it for several years before he sold it again. He recently bought it for the 3rd time and I just completed a total rebuild on it. It's funny, we talk about cars that we owned when we were kids and it was cool to work on one that I actually owned."

When I was straightening that car out I could see all the stuff I had used like blue hose fittings. This is stuff I would consider gaudy now. This car was a mess when it came back to me. I took the whole thing apart and replaced everything. Made it look brand new under the hood. All of the details, down to replacing all the nuts and bolts. When I do a rebuild I don't like to let anything out of here without a new front end suspension, control arm bushings, steering, and brakes. Everything is updated. The car is going to stop and steer, get up, and run. Right down to the wiper motor; I straighten out the wires. I like to do the details. To make the car look like it's been here. It's like my signature to do work like this.

I went to Brooklyn High School of Automotive Training. I got a little bored with it. I had been working on cars since I was a kid so I knew a lot of the stuff the guys were teaching me. I used to work in gas stations in my teens. I picked up a lot of knowledge just from practical experience. This was probably '78–'79. At a couple stations where I worked, I started to develop a reputation. When a car would come in and nobody knew where to start, I became the go-to guy; they'd say, "Ask Craig." My wife makes fun of me—she says I must have had my crib up on jack stands when I was a kid. At some point, if all this means something to you, then you understand what all the engine noises mean. You take a heavy gauge screwdriver and put it against the manifold and put your ear to it. You listen. It's your stethoscope.

A lot of the oil they use today is not friendly to the flat tappet cams. Today, most of the cars use roller cams. These hot rods have a flat tappet that rides on the lifter to actuate the cams. The old oil had a high level of zinc that would adhere to the metal to make it easier for the cams. The EPA mandated that the zinc was bad and they took it out of all modern oils. If

Craig in his garage

John Delaney

you use modern oil in one of these high performance motors, you're going to ruin the cams. If you wipe out the cam, all that metal has to go somewhere and it gets into the oil. It will wipe out your crank shaft bearings and that's the end of that. This stuff is as fine as talcum powder but it's still going somewhere. If you really want to look for engine wear the only way to really tell is to take the motor apart and mic [micrometer] it up. Measure the OD [outside diameter] of the crank and the ID [inside diameter] of the bearing.

When I was younger and I got deeper into this, there was a specialized knowledge some people had. Secrets. The motor I am putting into this car now [sitting in his shop at the time of the interview] was built by a guy who is not a throw together guy. He is known for high horsepower motors. His name is Lee at Lab Precision. Ever since I was young I always understood there were levels of knowledge with some guys.

I was always into anything mechanical. I'll take anything apart. Some guys are afraid to take something apart because they won't be able to get it back together. I'll take anything apart. I'm a GM guy—I don't know, I was always into Chevys. Now I have an Oldsmobile. Everyone dropped Chevy

Craig sitting with friend John Delaney

John Delaney's Chevelle rebuild in progress

John Delaney's Chevelle rebuild in progress

Engine about to be put into John Delaney's Chevelle rebuild

John Delaney's 1965 Chevelle rebuild in progress: "It had a 6 cylinder and automatic transmission when he bought it. We did a lot of work to this car. We rebuilt the suspension, steering, and brakes...upgrading to disc in the front. It had a 350 small block that we installed to get him running until we found a big block. It now has the motor that was sitting on the floor. It is a 454 LS6 spec big block. We also converted the car to stick shift and changed the rear end. It has a super T-10, 4-speed and a 12-bolt rear with 4.10 gears."

motors in their Oldsmobile's; it's easier and cheaper. The parts are more plentiful. But I wanted to build an Oldsmobile motor. So I spent the extra time, money, and effort to build an Oldsmobile. The bore is different and the stroke is different with an Oldsmobile. The angle of the cylinders is different. If you look at a Chevy motor it's a narrower angle on the intake manifold. With an Oldsmobile it's different. The pistons are at a wider angle. Oldsmobile's have a longer stroke which creates more torque. Think of it as leverage. A longer stroke gives you a longer lever so you are getting more twisting force. Torque is what's fun about driving around in the street. Torque is what pins you back in your seat and what gets your heart pounding. Torque is what gets the car moving; horsepower is what keeps it moving.

The Olds motors are known for low RPM torque, the Chevy motor is known for higher RPM horsepower. The Olds and Buicks make a lot of low RPM torque. The Chevy is better for racing around a track because they have that high horsepower. But beating it from light to light you want that Olds motor. You gotta know what you're doing to build an Olds motor because they don't hold together as good as a Chevy. You can wind a Chevy up to seven grand and beat on it and it will hold together.

Chevy spent a lot of time and money making four-bolt main blocks and steel cranks. Oldsmobile didn't go for a lot of that. But if you know what you're doing and put the Oldsmobile parts together right, you'll have a real steamroller. It'll just get up and run.

There's a lot of brand loyalty. There are guys who are like purists. If it didn't come from the factory, they wouldn't have it. We're more like hot rodders. If it don't make it go fast we don't want it. If it's not GM we don't deal with it much, but if it is GM then we can make it go faster and that's the idea. I was never an Oldsmobile guy, but I found this '65 442. I got a good deal; there was no rust and it was a nice car. Now I'm an Olds guy. This Chevelle [car sitting in the garage during the interview], my friend John [Delaney] didn't have a dime, but the boys in the garage loaned him the money until his tax return came in. We dragged the car here with a rope. He couldn't get the smile off his face for two hours. Now we are working to make this car fast.

It had a six cylinder with a power glide automatic that had sat down on its rims in a plumber's garage for five years. We brought it home, got a battery, fooled around with it for 20 minutes and I got that six cylinder going. We drove it around the street five times and then we took the motor out and threw it in the junkyard and put in a big block motor. We put in new headers, and a new intake cam. We all just do this kind of stuff for shits and giggles.

We all pitch in together here. I have a good reputation. I try to do things right. It usually works out that the cars I work on are friend's cars. If they weren't friends they wouldn't be in here. I wouldn't work on their cars. There are some people out there who have asked me to do work, but no, I really don't know them. People have come in and they say, "I just want you to do this." I tell them, "No, I do it my way. The car ain't leaving here unless I say it's ready to leave." My garage is almost a clubhouse. I have always thought that some of the best ideas and work gets done in a place like this. John here and the other guys, sometimes we just sit here on a rainy night. Talkin' and dreamin'.

I am working on this '65 Chevelle now. It's not a high-end car. But I tell you, especially during the '60s, for me the cars from that period are definitely a work of art. I see a car from the '60s and it brings me back. Like that Camaro I was talking about. I drove that particular car when I was in high school. I could have bought any Camaro, but I didn't. I found that car, that actual car. Having that car back with me was pretty cool. We lowered the stance, redid the rear end, and the steering linkage. There was some rot in the back end that you could stick your fist in. I welded that up. It was looking cool but then I always ask myself, "What if I did *this* to the car?"

In terms of working on motors, recently I needed to rebuild a transmission. There's a lot of parts in there. I had the transmission apart and there must have been fifty million parts all over the floor. John walked into the shop and he looked like he was going to have a heart attack. He was like, "Holy shit! How are you going to deal with this?" But I looked at the manual and I figured it out. There's always the first time you do something. It can be intimidating, but that doesn't mean you don't do it. Like I said, I'll take anything apart. You just gotta do it.

Hoffs Garage stamp that Craig puts on all his engine rebuilds. Stamp reads, "Johnny D."

Chris' 2004 Harley Springer Softail, rebuild by Craig

1965 Olds 442, 650hp, Craig build

1972 Nova 350, Craig build

1934 Ford, supercharged, partial build by Craig

Dick Zigun

Dick Zigun

SIDESHOWS BY THE SEASHORE, CONEY ISLAND - HOT RODS, CUSTOM MOTORCYCLES, AND A PROCESS OF POPULAR CULTURE IN NEW YORK CITY

Brooklyn

I was born 1953. As a kid I was exposed to the first real decade when the automobile became powerful in American culture for everyone and not just for a select few. In terms of this automobile culture there were differences between East and West Coast. LA was a twentieth-century city. It had a newer tone than cities on the East Coast. LA has always been about car culture. The older cities on the East Coast like New York predate this.

Coney Island beach scene

Cyclone roller coaster

Banner at Sideshow by the Seashore

Banner at Sideshow by the Seashore

Strongman getting run over by pick-up truck

The history of the twentieth century has a lot to do with the broadening of identities. The options of personal identity became more complex. The twentieth century was the century of hipsters, bohemians, beatniks, even hippies; whatever you want to call them. The century was always framed by various counter cultures. And the options of personal identity were expressed visually through the use of style. What you wore and what your drove.

There were counter cultures of one kind or another and the way you identified with one counter culture over another was, of course, what your wore, the way you cut your hair, what kind of tattoos you had. Also, where you lived and how the stylistic particulars of your area influenced you. For example, from the nineteenth to the early twentieth century Greenwich Village in New York City was a neighborhood that promoted and reinforced alternative sensibilities.

Later on, the Lower East Side and the East Village, even late-'70s SoHo, became centers of counterculture behavior and aesthetics. For the people who lived in these areas, part of their identities came from the neighborhoods where they lived. In the early eighties I moved to Coney Island and at that time it was a counterculture area but in a working class way. People here were involved in an alternative life based on a rare, personal, and unique version of an entertainment economy.

During the past decade in New York, this sense of neighborhood and particular identities has changed. There has been a renewed interest in the cities and there has been a gentrification process that has accompanied this. Now, the days of cheaper, outsider arts neighborhoods are no more. In New York City, there are no more bad neighborhoods. Coney Island is being re-built by the city. Cheap and marginal is either being renovated and rehabbed or it's being torn down. New York is all about real estate speculation.

So, this movement that developed during the twentieth century, where you could get your identity by living weirdly but cheaply with a group of other artists or musicians is now a memory. Williamsburg was probably the last place in New York where you could do that, but now it's totally unaffordable. This sense of outsider sensibility just ain't happening in New York City any more. So, if you are in New York and you still have that kind of outsider attitude what do you fall back on? Getting tattoos? Well every high school girl now has tattoos and a pierced tongue. Wearing a Mohawk and coloring your hair a punky color? So the fuck what? Nobody cares. Outsider dress and tattoos are now tolerated in mainstream jobs in suburbia. So the sense of neighborhood is gone, different styles of dress are gone. So where do you find this kind of alternative now in New York City? I think a lot of these impulses and energy are going into customizing motorcycles and cars.

Rumblers member at Coney Island hot rod event

Rumblers member Lil' Chris at Coney Island hot rod event

Rumblers member at Coney Island hot rod event

Anthony White pinstriping a Rumblers car

Customizing a large machine is not something that you can casually do. If you are picking up a cheap old car, number one: You have to put a lot of effort into searching for it and then you have to garage it and then you are either going to restore it yourself which means you have to have blue collar mechanical skills or if you don't, you are dropping a lot of money. This kind of thing isn't common, it isn't easy. It takes focus and dedication of your time or your money.

So, to have this type of alternative community you have to have something that you can do that a select number of other people can do but it's not easy to figure out. You really have to have the dedication. I became cognizant of this process because I was really good friends with Indian Larry. I had the privilege of being the pastor at his wedding. I married Larry and Bambi the Mermaid. They got married right here at Sideshows by the Seashore. Larry was prominent in our annual tattoo and motorcycle show. I have organized and ran the show since 1986. I started with the Mermaid Parade in 1983 and we always have had antique cars. I have been the go-to guy in Coney Island when it comes to cars.

I got shocked and kicked in the ass a couple years ago after Larry died. Suddenly, not through me, there's this club called the Rumblers that I had never heard of that's doing a car show on Stillwell Avenue. They didn't come to me first asking advice about dealing with the community board and the cops and I thought, "*What the fuck?*" This is going to be terrible. But it wasn't terrible and these guys had the most amazing cars I've seen this side of Ed "Big Daddy" Roth. I was surprised by these guys. It was nice to have a twenty-first-century kick in the ass by a whole new attitude that came up from the underground.

My earliest memories are from the '50s. My dad was a bit of an eccentric wacko and he was a second generation used furniture man. This meant that I grew up in a house where when you left your bedroom in the morning to go to grammar school you couldn't assume that the furniture was going to be the same when you came home. My dad would pick up and change things. In my home there was an appreciation of a curatorial sense of different styles of furniture and periods of furniture. Or an appreciation of antiques as opposed to just used things. That was my dad's business but it was also an education for me.

On some occasions my dad would make weird trades with people who were moving. This is before flea markets and yard sales. If you were moving, you would call the used furniture guy and he would buy your stuff. On some occasions my dad would come home with strange birds and more than once he came home with old jalopies and antique cars. In the '50s that would have been an old

'55 Chevy: Ricco's Custom Auto, Brooklyn

Izzy driving '55 Chevy: Ricco's Custom Auto, Brooklyn

Ralph Torres and El Diablo

Ray Ray's bike at Coney Island motorcycle event

Parked bikes at Coney Island motorcycle event

President of Redrum (murder spelled backwards) motorcycle group, Coney Island

Coney Island Tattoo and Motorcycle Festival poster

Jeff Rogan's Limey Lucas business card

Jeff Rogan, Limey Lucas Motorcycles, Triumph custom build:
"I'm into Triumph. English bikes have a reputation for being temperamental but I like taking those machines and making them reliable. I just like the way a Triumph motor is put together. The rockers are all smooth, they have their own character. The intake manifold has its own character; the timing cover has its own character. It is what it is."

Coney Island Tattoo and Moto-cycle Festival poster

Ralphy Boy's ride

Motorcycle event attendee

car from the '30s that was unrestored. Some people thought that was really cool and some people were embarrassed by an old car like that. There were times he would drive and drop us off at school but not in a new car; in a 30-year-old car and the windshield wipers didn't necessarily work.

In the town where I grew up, there would be an annual summer festival that would include an antique car show. So, even in the 1950s there always was an appreciation for antique cars. I had an uncle in Freehope, New Jersey, who was a butcher by day and he collected used fire engines. He had a business card that read, "Same Day Fire Company." We'd drive around town in antique fire trucks which was cool when you were a kid. But his was all stock "as is" stuff.

This all changed in the 1950s with Ed "Big Daddy" Roth and his Revell models. When I was a kid Soupy Sales was a counterculture kid hero, but so was Roth. Not only Rat Fink but the whole assortment of models. Roth was from the West Coast and that was a specialized thing and a fantasy thing for an East Coast kid like me. But at that time very few people on the East Coast were doing that kind of thing with cars. My family had old cars, restored or unrestored but people weren't really doing hot rods here. It happened, but it was really private. That was coming from a West Coast sensibility.

There has been a huge shift in America regarding what is called popular culture. My efforts at Sideshows by the Seashore have followed this process of cultural change. You have to remember that is wasn't so long ago popular culture was completely unrecognized as a legitimate form of expression. In America this process has had a lot to do with the growth of youth demographics and identity since the 1950s. The baby boomer generation represents an explosion of youth demographics in America.

The struggle and intent to achieve what has happened with Sideshow by the Seashore was done with a sense of place in mind. New York City is arguably the cultural capital of the world and Coney Island is the natural place to create a center of Americano Bizzaro. A place that explores underground culture. We have worked hard over the last 30 years to legitimize American popular culture here. High culture is fine, but we've really succeeded in our 30-year argument saying that all this American popular culture is important and influential and fuck you if you dare to keep saying in the twenty-

Motorcycle event attendee

Motorcycle event attendee

Ray Ray

Louie, member of Wolf Pack AC, Brooklyn: "The car is a '67 Plymouth Barracuda. The car is set up as a pro-touring car. It has a 360 cid engine from a '70s police interceptor. The motor has been bored and stroked. I took an oath not to reveal the inner workings, however. It is pushing about 500hp. Also, it is backed up by an automatic overdrive transmission. The suspension up front is a custom tubular k-frame and control arm set-up with coil over shocks; not common to these cars. When I am out for a run on the highway the car just comes alive—I could cruise at 130mph or better without a shutter. (The car was clocked at over 150 last summer).

The Wolf Pack AC is a family. It is a one-of-a-kind. We pride ourselves on brotherhood. We hold a three-piece patch which is more common to the outlaw biker world, and we keep our discipline as such. We would pick quality over quantity any day. The man makes the patch; the patch does not make the man. I know that any one of my brothers would be there for me for any reason as I would for them at any time."

first century that it's not legitimate. That argument is over and we won.

When I was in college at Yale I was exploring popular theater forms like burlesque, minstrel shows, side shows, and strippers. My teachers thought I was out of my mind. Now, there are a number of universities that offer degrees in burlesque. That's the way that whole thing always goes. Believe me, this is now happening with subjects like hot rods and custom motorcycles, car clubs, and motorcycle gangs.

To me, Ed Roth was a real person from the West Coast, and as a kid I would go to the store and buy a Revell model. I'd buy a magazine and there would be Rat Fink. So that's what popular culture is. It's disseminated everywhere. So, in terms of Roth's effect, I never met him but yeah, he wasn't just West Coast—he was American. Roth's ascendency was connected to several cultural dynamics in America: The growth of the number of young people and the growth of popular media. For a while that has been what popular culture has been all about. Previous to mid-nineteenth century and my patron saint P.T. Barnum, culture was either folk culture that the folk could do or it was imperial culture that had the stamp of approval of your king or queen, or your Czar.

P.T. Barnum comes along and in a country with an emerging working and middle class and he says culture is what people are willing to pay for it. He had his wacky museum and he starts what became modern advertising. And now these earlier popular culture forms have grown exponentially. The President of The United States or the Queen of England have little power and control over this process. In the world of popular culture, people get what they pay for. The market decides rather than the elite.

Today, a place like New York City is a part of the overall post-modernist dynamic. Hot rods, custom motorcycles, car clubs, and bike clubs have increased exponentially in New York and they are a part of this process. The younger generation and clubs like the Rumblers are interesting because these young people have grown up in a world that supplies unprecedented amounts of information. These people have Direct TV or cable TV with 150 channels. Young people today have seen it all. They have seen motorcycle builders like Jesse James and Indian Larry and then groups like the Rumblers have come together and imposed standards. They have a strict attitude about what they like and what they don't like. If it's newer than 1965, get

Louie under the hood

Louie's 'Cuda

your fucking vehicle out of here! To some people this might be intimidating; to others it makes them a better club with better artists who are more interesting.

There is a big element of nostalgia about all this, but it goes deeper and I find this fascinating. For me a club like the Rumblers expresses a form of wisdom. They are weighing the history and making choices about values with cars and bikes. People today can access any variety of nostalgic information about anything, but the Rumblers have chosen to access the specifics about machines. Watching the membership of a club like the Rumblers, you get to see how people value the information. How they make choices and how they understand how this process works. How they exercise their wisdom and translate it into their machines. These guys are getting older and I feel that their decision-making process is influenced as a by-product of getting older and having a sense of perspective.

When I first met Indian Larry he wasn't a famous person on a TV show yet. He was just a very cool guy who started coming to the tattoo and motorcycle shows. He had, not so long ago, come out of prison and he was doing great work. We talked a lot and found out we had a common interest and respect

Indian Larry build at Coney Island motorcycle event

Indian Larry build at Coney Island motorcycle event

Ed "Big Daddy" Roth tank

Lenny Donghia, Rumbler member

Mike Palazzo, Rumblers member, in his garage

for Ed "Big Daddy" Roth. Then Larry starts building bikes on television and the cameras are here from the Learning Channel and he is becoming well known and he creates all these great bikes and then he's gone.

Now you have a new generation that didn't grow up on Ed "Big Daddy" Roth but instead they grew up on Larry. And now it's post-Larry time. But that's the popular culture recycling and renewing itself. Roth filtered through Larry filtered through the Rumblers. And that's an interesting dynamic and that's how this goes in the twenty-first century.

Indian Larry build at Coney Island motorcycle event

Lenny Donghia's '51 Chevy Bel Air, work by Lenny

Surf Ave., Friday night

Surf Ave., Friday night

Rumblers wipe rags

Lenny Donghia, Rumblers member, with his motorcycle at his firehouse in Brooklyn

Surf Ave. Nathan's, Friday night

Brian standing at one of his garages

Brian Darwas

IT'S NOT HOW FAST YOU GO, IT'S HOW YOU GO FAST

Bronx

When I was young I always had the shittiest bicycle in the neighborhood. I would take the parts that the other kids didn't want and I'd build my own nicer bike. So, when I got older and had a license I had a shitty car and I went through the same process. I'd take other people's thrown away parts and add them to my car to make it better. When I was a teenager I kind of liked muscle cars. Then I started liking older '50s cars. By the time I was in my twenties I started to like hot rods. I guess that I just sort of applied the methods I had developed when I was younger about swapping parts. Taking a wheel from this bike or that bike turned into taking a part from this or that car.

Brian Darwas under the EL in the Bronx near Zerega Ave. "It's a 1932 five-window coupe. It's got a Pontiac 326 motor, a 1940 Ford rear axle with a Winters Quick Change center section, a stock 1932 front axle, a spilt 1932 wish bone in front, and 1940 Ford hydraulic brakes all around."

Brian driving in his Ford

Brian pulling out of his Bronx garage

I never went to school for any of this. It has all been trial and error. It came down to wanting something that I couldn't afford. Building it myself instead of buying it. I guess that I'm mechanically inclined. I've always found it easy to build stuff or fix stuff. I was always the stupid type of kid that took stuff apart to see how it worked. I've always been more interested in knowing why it works; knowing that it works isn't enough. I need to know. In my life I have broken many things and taken them apart. I have always been that way. I see a steering box on the car and I have to open it up and figure out how it works. The worm gear and all that.

I was born in '77 and raised in the Bronx. I went to Lehman High School right in the neighborhood. Before that I went to Catholic grade school. I was an altar boy so I could get out of class to do funerals and weddings and stuff. All the bad kids always tried to be altar boys. In Catholic grade school life is strict. So when I went to public school I immediately grew my hair long.

My family lived next to the Hutch [Hutchinson parkway]. When I was a kid my brother and his friends would go to the Howard Johnsons restaurant near the Whitestone movie theater and they would have a weekly cruise night. All the guys would talk shit to each other and challenge each other. They'd make their bets and then go onto the Hutch a little past the Orchard Beach exit. Three cars would stop on the highway to stop all the traffic and then two cars would set up and race. As a kid I would go with him and watch the races.

The first car I owned was a '72 Chevelle. I was seventeen. It was a total shit box. I did all the body work on it and pulled the motor out. I bought another motor. Through trial and error I learned how to fix that car. I worked on my car in the street. My family lived in an apartment building at that time, so I worked in the street. I got all the body work done on the car and had the car all in primer and I was going to paint the car. I was driving near Gun Hill Road and fishtailing around a corner and the gas pedal got stuck open. I went around the corner and I was going really fast towards a school yard with all the kids playing basketball so I threw the wheel the other way and I skidded into a telephone pole. I pushed the door jamb halfway into the car. I just totaled the entire car. I had no seatbelts so if I had had the window rolled up I would have smashed my face through the glass. The way I hit the pole I flew three-quarters out the window. I was hanging by the backs of my knees. The kid who had been sitting in the passenger side flew across the seat and smashed into me and knocked me out of the car.

I drove the car home and when I was at a light a guy pulled up next to me on the other side of the car and said, "Wow that's a nice project you got there." From his angle he couldn't see where I had hit the pole. I was fucking pissed off. I was just about to fucking paint the car until 30 minutes before. I drove past people I knew who were on the other side of the car from where I crashed it. They were waving at me like; nice car. I took the car apart and sold the parts. I sold the engine and every last piece of metal on the car. I probably still have a couple parts someplace. I'm the type of person that can't throw old car parts away. I know that there's somebody somewhere that needs that part. I hold onto stuff. If somebody needs it I usually give it to them for free.

The second car I built was a '66 Pontiac Le Mans. This is going to make it sound like I am a bad driver—I did all the body work and everything on that car and got it all nice and I was driving on Tremont Avenue and an off-duty police officer coming the other way made a left hand turn and for some reason floored it right into me. There was a pregnant woman in his car. I shut my car off and heard this woman screaming.

Front door of Willie Gee's Bronx garage

Rumblers members Lil' Chris (L) and Lenny (R) at Willie's garage

Brian and build in Willie's garage

Brian and Willie at work

There was a fire and her legs were all burnt. The paramedics came. I was bleeding out of my head. Some off-duty cop came running over yelling and the paramedics dropped me and went to help the cop and his wife. An hour later they came back and checked me out. That fucking drunk asshole drove into me and because he's a cop they ignored me. They refused to give me a police report. They reworded the report to protect the drunk cop. They said I drove into him and all that bullshit. I was a kid and they knew they could get away with it. I ended up only getting 600 bucks for the car from the insurance company. I got screwed.

Brian's '32 parked in the alley at Willie Gee's garage area

I took that Pontiac engine and put it into the first hot rod I ever built, a '29 Ford roadster. I was in my twenties. This is like in the early '90s. I was a little ahead of the curve in terms of interest about this sort of thing.

My parents moved out of that apartment and we moved into a house in the Bronx. We didn't have enough garage space to work on a car so I built that roadster in the basement of the house. When I disassembled it to paint it I brought the pieces into the back yard, painted them and put the car back together. It was a roadster pick-up. I carried the chassis, the body, and the bed outside one piece at a time. My parents were cool with it. It took me a little over six months. It was the first one I ever did. It was kind of a learning experience.

This was just me and my brother figuring this car stuff out. We really didn't interact with other people about this. We'd build the chassis, we'd do the body work, the engine work, the paint. I'd build the entire car from the ground up. I wouldn't farm out the chassis to one guy, the body work to another guy. We'd do all the steps. We'd do the engine work. I couldn't do the machine work, but I did everything else. The last car we built we did the interior work on it, too. I got out the sewing machine and started stitching the material together. I was trying to do everything. I am a control freak about all this. The slightest little detail being off will drive me insane. When I look at upholstery work, if some guy stitches the line crooked it will catch my eye and drive me fucking crazy.

People from different parts of the country have no idea what people in New York go through to have a car in the city. The most basic problem is where are you going to keep it? There is no place to park in New York. Most people can't even own a car. This is very different from a place like California. I have a garage that I can build in, I have a

Brian taking a break from welding the frame

garage around the corner where I park my hot rod, and I have another garage where I keep my parts. So, when we build a car, we mock up the chassis, take the body off, and move it to another space. We are constantly moving shit to make room. These kinds of situations about space add to the time it takes to build a car. It's not like I can close up my garage and leave. I got to clean up and put the stuff away. I have to drag everything in and then I can leave. It makes it harder but I guess that is the way things are done in New York. This is how I make my living.

I have always had an aversion to working a straight type job. I have never been able to hold a regular job for any period of time. If I am working on something for myself I can do it for 10 hours a day. When I am building a car I work on it 12 hours a day for four months and I don't even bat an eyelash. If I worked in somebody's shop for eight hours a day, just knowing that I can't leave when I want, I couldn't do it.

I have had a number of jobs. I worked as a barber but I walked out in the middle of a haircut. I was doing a haircut and I asked myself, "What the fuck am I doing?" I just left. Fuck this. Half a haircut, see you later. I worked at Yankee Stadium selling Cokes and hot dogs. There were days I'd say, "Fuck this," half way through the day. I'd drop off the hot dogs and the Cokes and the money and just leave. I couldn't be there; I had to leave.

Then I got into music—we'd go on tour. The last band I played in was the Disasters. I played with Roger Miret from Agnostic Front. I played in that band for five or six years. A lot of hot rod guys in New York City have all come from the same Punk Rock scene. We all got together and started the Rumbles Car Club. With playing in a band and going on tour I didn't have time to have a real job. I can't read music but if I listen to it I can figure it out. Kind of like when I was a kid and I'd take stuff apart and figure it out. Kind of a savant thing. I'm a hot rod savant.

So the music and the car thing kind of came together. I was able to go on tour with the Disasters and then I'd come home and build the frame of the car. Then I'd go on tour again and come home and mock up the body. Then I'd go on tour again and come home and finish up the car and sell it. I would build one or two cars a year that way and I was able to scrape a living together. It was good that I didn't have a boss that would fire me because I'd have to go on tour.

This is how I make a living; I build a couple cars a year. When I build cars for other people, they are complete, finished cars. They put the key in the ignition and turn it. I do not build fancy show type cars. I build traditional hot rods. I am strict about what parts I use. All the parts are from the early '50s or before. I try to build all the cars to look like if you took a photo of it now, you couldn't tell if that photo had been taken in 2010 or 1950. You know? It's all old parts. It has taken me time, but I have built up a network. People know that I build cars and that I am serious about it. They know that I usually build cars for people. If somebody has a part they want to sell they know I am going to step up and buy it. People know that I am not fucking around. People that have rare parts save them for me because they know I will pay a fair price and use them in a unique build.

I have been doing this with my brother for some time. I do not look at this as trendy shit. There have been some people over the years that I have looked to for inspiration and guidance. There was always my brother and some of his friends, but looking back now, they were teenagers at the time. They didn't know much but they definitely planted the seed in my head. I have a degree of confidence and my brother and his friends always enforced that in me.

Willie Gee

Lenny

Bronx neighborhood troubadour

Willie's garage

Bronx neighborhood troubadour pistolo

The hardest part of building a car for a lot of people is taking something they built and doing 90 miles an hour on the highway. They are not confident in the fact that what they built is going to stand up. For me, after building and driving cars in New York City, I am pretty confident with all these shitty streets that my cars will do well. I played music in a touring band so I have driven in every state in America and every city in the United States. I can confidently say that New York City streets are the worst of anywhere I have ever been. Most urban areas in the Northeast have bad roads, but New York has the gnarliest streets in the area. You have to build it better. You can't just say it's good enough. If you don't weld something right, or put enough gussets on it, the whole thing will break apart. There are so many potholes it is unbelievable.

I taught myself how to weld and I look at the streets of New York as my welding test. If I can weld a chassis together and drive it through New York without it falling apart, I guess I taught myself the right way to do it. I go to shows in other places and I see stuff that is put together in such a way that it wouldn't have a prayer in New York. I have to build it the right way. When I am building a car for someone, they are putting their life on the line driving it around. If I build it half-assed someone could die or get maimed in a car crash. So, in New York you have to overdo it a little.

This is tough because I am big on aesthetics. Everything has to be overbuilt but not look that way. I try to reinforce things in places that are important but in a way that you won't notice it. I'll see guys do a heavy welding job to reinforce things but it is done in such a way that looks terrible. For me, that won't cut it. I got to make things strong and also make things look good. My builds are probably done a little more than a guy in Florida might do it. Sometimes I'll hit a pothole and it feels like I drove over a tall granite curb at 70 miles an hour. Driving in New York is a very serious thing. You got to worry about all the bad drivers, all the bad road conditions. It's like an obstacle course. You have to avoid all the other assholes; you have to avoid all the potholes. Everyone else is on top of you and right up your ass. You don't have that moment to think about avoiding the pothole: Either you do it, or you get creamed.

Height is also a big issue. Obviously you can't build a low car here. This isn't LA where guys build cars four inches off the ground. If you do that here you will lose your transmission pan, your oil pan, you'll break something real quick. This is normal for me. When I go somewhere where the roads are nice I am shocked.

There are standards that are pleasing to my eye: The way the car sits. For me, the stance of a car is probably 75 percent of the look of the car. The way the car sits is so important. I have seen a lot of cars where the body work is nice and the paint is nice and all the right parts are on the car but it just didn't sit right. So it ends up being a totally ugly car. There is something off about it and your average person knows they don't like that car but they can't tell you why. I have also seen cars that are a little rusty or the body is a little shitty but the stance is perfect, and the car looked badass. It just sits right.

Lately on the East Coast there has been an interest in building cars with a high-boy stance. No channeling. This is because of the road conditions. During the '50s and '60s on the East Coast there were channeled cars that weren't chopped because guys were in the car bouncing all over the place hitting their heads on the roof because the roads were so bad. I build my cars a little bit higher than if I lived in Los Angeles. I do see guys on the East Coast building cars that are low. They are so low that the cars cannot be driven on the East Coast. You have to use a trailer if you want to move the car. To me

Willie grinding a frame weld

Coffee break time

Break time

this is fucking stupid. It's not a car; it's a life-sized model.

I have to drive my car. The only time my car is on a stretcher is when it breaks down. Because it's a car, half the fun is driving it. I'm not just going to look at it. To me, owning it to look at it is a waste of time. I drive my car through my neighborhood and people take notice. They have to; my car is loud. People turn around to see what the hell all the noise is and then they see a 1930s hot rod driving down the street. I always notice this sense of connect/disconnect in their faces. They have this look. I have explained that this is the closest I am ever going to get to knowing what it's like to be a good looking woman. You know what I mean? Every good looking woman goes through this. Ten guys are trying to talk to her or whistling at her trying to get her attention. So, at least in New York a lot of women develop a bad attitude towards men because they won't leave them alone.

Alley at night

I understand the drama of nostalgic things. This is one reason people honk at me and my car. I wasn't alive when my car was built the first time. My Ford is from a time when people were more hands-on about things. Today, eight out of ten guys can't change a flat tire. My car and cars like it are from a time when a high school kid wanted a race car so he bought a junked car from the '30s and he worked on it himself and he made a hot rod. The main passion in his life was his car. I am attracted to that aspect of it. It's my car and I built it. I'm driving it and if anything goes wrong I can fix it. It is more personal to me. Nowadays someone writes a check to buy a car. It just isn't really personal to them. They might not have the time or the skills to build a car. So, they ask someone like me to build it for them.

This kind if interest in cars has become popular recently. There are good and bad aspects to popularity. For example, there is a huge aftermarket for all the parts. Before, you would have to search really hard to find things. Now people are reproducing the old parts because they see that people want them. It has become profitable. So, in that aspect popularity is good; but then, when it becomes too popular, it gets burned out. So now all the rare stuff is bought up and a lot of people that can't build a car are taking a lot of good bodies and butchering them and ruining them for the next generation. A lot of ugly cars have come out of this kind of thing. Unskilled people will build unsafe cars and then people get hurt and that looks bad for everything. I am not an elitist, but the popularity is good and bad. I have respect for people who try to apply themselves and build a car correctly.

I follow a few builders: Vern Tardel in Santa Rosa, California. He builds extremely traditional, early Fords. He and a guy Mike Bishop wrote a book, *How to Build a Traditional Ford Hot Rod,* and that's kind of the hot rodder's Bible about how to build these cars. There was a guy in the '50s named Doane Spencer. He had a really popular car called the Doane Spencer Roadster that was really far ahead of its time. He was one of the first guys who didn't just bolt the car together. He made his cars functional and stylish. If you look at my car I have the front of the frame pinched in. He was one of the first guys to do that. I like the guys the Rolling Bones that I featured in my *Road to Bonneville* movie. As far as I'm concerned, those guys build some of the best looking hot rods of this generation. Their cars are perfect: aesthetically and functionally. They are really good car builders and they are nice guys on top of it. That means something to me. I've seen a lot of cars I like but the guy that built it is a fucking asshole, so suddenly I don't like the car that much anymore. Know what I mean?

A lot of these things were worked out in the '50s and early '60s. Now the street rod industry has pretty much turned into a formula. Now, traditional hot rodding that was going against the grain has become formalized. I would call my car a traditional hot rod. I search out original parts, and for safety I completely rebuild things if needed. But I try to use period-correct parts all the time. The word traditional hot rod is a little confusing because traditionally a hot rod was making your car fast. So, if you were being traditional now, you'd go to the junk yard and get a Honda Civic and make it as fast as you can. That's the tradition of hot rodding. Taking something that is available to you now and improving upon it. I try to build everything in the late '40s early '50s style.

If you think about it, in 1945, a '32 Ford was a 13-year-old car. It was a piece of junk in the junkyard that nobody wanted. So that is equivalent to buying that 1995 Honda Civic and making it fast. There are different attitudes. I am of the mindset where it's not how fast you go, it's how you go fast. For me I am interested in old cars because it is aesthetically pleasing to my eyes. It's something about that time period and the cars from that time period that strikes a chord in me. It's hard to explain—I like late '20s up to about '34. Maybe it's the simplicity of it. My car is the bare minimum. You take one part off and you can't drive it. Straight axel, simple. That's the way I like it.

It's funny but people in my neighborhood know I build cars. Sometimes they'll drive up in their 2010 Acura and say, "There's something wrong with my car, can you fix it?" I look at them like, "What? Take that shit to a mechanic." They look at me confused.

I like taking something that is destined for the junk yard and giving it new life. When I first got my car it was just a pile of parts. Now that I have turned it into a hot rod it might be around for another 100 years. I like that idea. I enjoy preserving the car. You look at the old parts and think, this served its owners, this logged however many miles. Now it's obsolete and people want to turn their back on it. I like taking this car and putting it back into use again. I like doing that. This is like somebody that turned their back on their friend because they were no longer useful. I like taking these old cars that are kind of lost and forgotten and turning them into a car again. In a sense I am preserving time.

I'll get an old axel and there will be a moment where I sit there and look at it and think, "*This is 75 years old and it's still around.*" I think of the car it was in. It could have been involved in a bank robbery or a baby could have been born in it. There are so many things that could have happened in that car. I like that. I know guys that have found old cars in the woods and they find a frame in other woods, a door in other woods and they put them together and now they are driving in these cars. These cars that were rusting in the woods will be driving around for another 50 years.

The car club I am in, the Rumblers, we all have this attitude. We can find it and we can build our own cars. We can do all this by ourselves. This is how life was in the '40s and '50s. I think my generation is unique in terms of where it sits historically. I'm 33, I got to grow up being hands-on but I am not too old to be out of the loop in terms of technology. I feel that I grew up in a good time. I grew up in a lower-middle class household. My dad's car never saw a mechanic until after he had tried to fix it 50 times. Know what I mean? That's just the way it was. We didn't buy a new blender to replace the old one until my dad had taken the old one apart and tried to fix it. That's always the way it has been in my family. This is one of the reasons I became hands-on about things. My father, even to this day, he will not throw anything out until he's at least tried to fix it. Then he'll give it to my brother, then I'll give it a shot. If it's still broken then we'll toss it out and get something new. Now, nobody has to fix anything. They just buy a new one and put it on your credit card. Pay it off 50 bucks a month.

Up here in the Bronx, I still see guys working on their cars in the street. The laws about things like this aren't enforced too strictly up here. I see guys doing oil changes and doing front end work and the police don't say anything. It's just rough. If you live in a building and you want to work on your car you have to do it in the street and chances are it's a busy street too. Hundreds of cars driving by as you work, people walking by who want to talk to you while you work. People who steal your tools when you're not looking. Working under these kinds of conditions is definitely a different atmosphere. This is fucking New York City. At any given second there is somebody who wants to be in your business and wants to know what the hell you are doing. That's how this city is.

Brian's '32

Peter Hunstein

I WANT TO GET
MY HANDS DIRTY

Manhattan, Jersey City

Peter Hunstein

During the 1970s, I monkeyed around with my father's lawn mowers. I finally wound up getting a go-kart running and on the road. There was a junk yard in the next town over from where I lived and I would go in there and scrounge around for stuff. I found a snowmobile engine that was big and a two stroke and it ran. I put it into my go-kart that had golf cart tires on it. I had welded the frame together out of heavy gauge water pipe. I fudged my way through it. It's called rabbit shit welding. But it worked.

When I was young I was into cars. I was a gear head. In high school if you weren't into sports you were into cars. I got into playing music and then later the technical aspect of music production just as the digital thing took over. I got good at it. I ended up meeting people and working for big acts like Sting and Kiss as a programmer doing the album work. I did okay during those years but the schedule was grueling. I moved on.

Now, I have a big space over the river in Jersey with some friends who all work on and ride race bikes. I have been here for a couple years. I like the symmetry of air-cooled engines. My favorite Harley engine is the Shovelhead. Purely from an aesthetic stand point. It was not the best motor. In fact, it became pretty crappy and it was the motor that almost put Harley Davidson out of business, but it looks aggressive, it's unrefined, totally unapologetic. And it also looks like somebody chopped two cylinders off an old radial aircraft engine. I am a big fan of radial aircraft engines.

What little history I know about all these things is that there were so many guys squirreled away in so many sheds in so many countries doing so many things that there is controversy about who invented what and where. People still argue about who invented the internal combustion engine. Me, I like the old technology. The simple pushrod, two valve, air-cooled finning. Leaking oil all over everywhere. I have total appreciation for that. This sense of appreciation grew because I was lucky to spend time with a few of the guys in New York who were very influential with their ideas, designs and builds.

I knew Larry [Indian Larry] and watched him work in his "Shop under the stairs." He had a little motor building shop. He used a chest of drawers for his tool box. I knew Larry and Steg after Steg left Don and started Psycho Cycles on Avenue C. I was a hang-around and I'd come in and see them working. We all had a mutual interest in burning gasoline on two wheels.

It was a bit of an accident—these people and their skills and ambitions kind of coalesced in the East Village area. I moved to this area completely unrelated to motorcycles. During the '80s the East Village was the center of a vital music and art scene. It migrated to the area because that's where we could afford to get apartments. At the time the East Village was a ghetto. Burned-out buildings on every block. When I moved to my block on 8th Street there wasn't a single inhabited building on my side of the street. From Avenue B to Avenue C, every building that was still standing was abandoned. Junkies, squatters, a social club maybe. I was there as a musician and I played with various bands and I also happened to start riding a motorcycle. I couldn't have a car because I didn't have space for it so I bought a Moto Guzzi Le Mans.

I would hang out at the bar Side Walk on Friday nights. On any given night there were a bunch of British bikes out front or Motor Guzzis or whatever. I met Hugh [Mackie] and became a part of this movement in New York. My choice of apartment was dictated by whether I could get space for my bike. In the late '80s I lived in a storefront on 4th Street so I could bring my bike right into my living room. I converted the basement into my workshop.

Larry used to hang around Side Walk every now and then around '91–'92, so I knew who he was. I didn't start interacting with him until '93–'94 over at Psycho Cycles. I was wrenching on my bike but I was also a painter. In high school I had worked in an auto body shop. I was sweeping and washing cars and dealing with customers but I was always looking over the shoulders of a couple older guys there and I was always fascinated with painting.

My first car as a kid was a '68 Mustang that was completely rusted out. So, the older guys at this shop taught me how to weld in body panels. I never got into lead work. These guys always had old Mercedes and BMWs that they were restoring. These guys would do lead work and the cars would get the lacquers and enamels and the new cars would get the urethanes. I worked with a guy who taught me how to wet sand this BMW that had like 20 coats of lacquer clear as the first round. That paint had depth. I ended up painting a few bikes and guys saw them. I set up a little spray booth in the back of my shop on 8th Street and was painting and I actually got to the point when people started coming to me. I did some metal flake and special effects. Tape-outs and some stencil work.

Bikes are deceiving in terms of the square inches that need paint. It depends. A lot of the Harleys that were being built when I was doing paint work involved painting seven pieces of body work. There's

Workspace, Jersey City garage

Peter Hunstein standing in Jersey City garage

East Village garage

the tank, fenders, the side covers, an air cleaner cover and maybe a belly pan. That's something. That's not a lot compared to cars but by the same token, the first thing you see when you look at a motorcycle is the paint job. And that's part of the reason why I got into it. When a person encounters a custom bike, the first thing they notice is the paint. You can have the most amazing motor or transmission but most people wouldn't know the difference or recognize anything. There is an overall aesthetic about motorcycles, but if you want to get noticed, it's the paint work. Motorcycles are a complete statement. The Guggenheim didn't have their motorcycle show for no reason.

So, with a motorcycle you are limited to the amount of area you can use to paint and create a sense of the machine and its aesthetic. It's a lot of work. It's a lot of hours to get it right. Bikes have a certain line to them. Different brands have different lines and traditions of design. Triumph, Norton,

Peter Hurstein painting a tank

Peter Hunstein mixing paint at his bench

Peter Hunstein

Ducati, Moto Guzzi, Harley. The aesthetic of the entire thing is taken into account. Early on I wasn't known as a painter. I used to paint in the basement of my building when I lived on 4th Street but that got me into a hell of a lot of trouble with the people on the second floor. I had no ventilation. I didn't know any better. I'd paint at two o'clock in the morning and fill the whole building with paint fumes. People would be banging on my door screaming, "What the fuck are you doing?" I'd climb out of my basement holding a can of acetone and say, "What's the problem?"

I had a place on 8th Street and a guy moved out and Larry moved in. I didn't know him well enough to know that I shouldn't have let him do that. Actually in retrospect, if I had spoken with a few people first they all would have said, "What are you nuts?" I didn't know any better. I had a little shop in the back for wrenching and I put a spray booth in. I started painting some things for guys and Larry was there and saw me doing it. He had me paint some stuff and it took off from there. That whole shop was tiny. The spray booth was nine feet by ten feet. I'd have to paint a couple pieces at a time. With painting there is definitely a technique in terms of a quality job. The paint lines have to be smooth, the paint has to adhere properly. The metalics and flakes are tricky and there's a lot of technique involved. A few tricks.

I am a systems type guy and painting and motors are systems. If you understand mechanics then you can understand the system and then you can trouble shoot because you know what should be happening to figure out what parts of the system are not there to make it happen. I understood this stuff so Larry and I would talk motors and boring and his choices in terms of compression ratio and the bore and stroke. We'd talk about his deck height for his cylinder heads in order to get the compression ratio he was looking for. His valve springs, his push rod lengths, his cams etc, etc. I knew what he was talking about and he appreciated that.

Larry was definitely a larger than life figure. Everyone knew who he was. He worked at a few places and as a low-level mechanic at American Dream Machine. It wasn't until he started going to meetings and sobered up and then his reputation started to come together. I was hanging around Psycho Cycles when they were on Rivington Street because of Paul [Cox] and Larry. He was working in my building and there was always cool stuff going on there in the basement.

I have been in this new space for three years. It's bigger and liberating, but again, I don't have enough room. I got bikes everywhere that block my benches. I have a pretty open mind about motorcycles. I ride a 2008 KTM. I am into modern, electronic control systems. Anything from a jet turbine to a solid propellant rocket motor—I'm interested in it. I want to know about it. I got a CDI Diesel [common-rail diesel injection system] sitting right over there. I have ideas to use this for a project. These engines didn't exist ten years ago. I have an appetite for this. I am fascinated by all of it. This is one reason Larry and I got along so well. To him technology was fascinating and it didn't matter what it was. His bikes were very old school but he loved the whole idea of watching automation and a CNC machine. Larry was totally fascinated by all of that.

I tend to be a loner and I enjoy working by myself on my projects. In New York there are any number of guys working in their garages and nobody knows about them and they don't know about anybody. Some of the guys who work in this space are all about the weekend scene and going to all of the races

Workbench area

Garage work area

Hunstein build with New York City skyline in background

to see their buddies. Being part of a scene. Me, I could care less about most of that shit. I like to see what other people are working on but for me it's not a social event.

Yes, I see my friends and there is some social aspect to all of this but that's not why I do it. I am involved in this because I want to get my hands dirty—do something and make something. As far as I'm concerned, every guy I know needs to make something. They need to be productive. This is something that took my wife a long time to understand. That if I am not making something, I don't feel so good. It's so important for me to get out to my shop every day and work on something. I like to do something physical. I worked for companies as a machinist or a welder and that means something to me. At the end of the day I looked at a rack of parts I made and said, "I made that."

This is interesting to me because I feel that a lot of this doing and making of things has been lost in a place like New York. Life here has changed. One of the reasons my wife and I ended up in the East Village was at that time you could do what you wanted and people left you alone. People didn't give a shit. They had bigger problems. In the old days we'd be working on our bikes at two o'clock in the morning. Nobody would mess with us.

Now, I look at the people that have moved into my area and they all have straight jobs. They work five days a week and this defines their life. Whatever they do outside of their job, whether it's their hobby, their girlfriend, their clothing, going out to eat. It's all weekend shit. For these people, most of what I would call an all-encompassing passion about machines or hands-on things is gone. I don't see it any more. The thing that defines this new sensibility is not the artist, the mechanic, or the machinist. It is defined by consumerism. At the core of the machine guys in New York is a passion to make something—to produce something. Not some interest in living life vicariously, watching sports on TV? Watching some mass media market NASCAR bullshit on TV? What?

When I was growing up my friends had interests in tangible things. Doing something, making something. Not sitting on the couch and being a bystander. You know? For some of my friends it was photography, art, and music. For me it was all of the above. You walk around my shop and see 40 different disciplines here.

I was brought up here. New York City is definitely a part of my identity. I spent most of my life here. It's important but it also means that I have to put up with a crowded environment and a bunch of people who don't necessarily understand what I am doing. I go onto the Internet to various bulletin boards and talk with machinists in other parts of the country who have as much space as they need. Me, I'm in New York; I want more machines but I don't have any place to put them. I know guys who build 15,000-square-foot garages behind their houses because they can. Their property is measured in acres and not square feet. I do have a predisposition towards turn-of-the-century red brick factory buildings and all that they represent. Thick wood floors, heavy beams, exposed red brick, cobblestones, and iron railways. I love that shit.

I don't think about it too much but I do look back at when I was a kid in New York. I lived in areas that were not necessarily gentrified. I was lucky and survived through a lot of different situations. Everyone was constantly getting beaten up and robbed. All your shit was always being stolen. I know many people who did not survive. New York is like that. New York is a learning curve—if you live long enough to get to the other end of the curve. Walking home, you knew you had to watch your shit. Doorways, stairwells, what was going on between the cars and on the subway platforms. You needed a sense about where you had to go and what you had to do if all hell broke loose. And believe me, all hell did break loose. I grew up with that. These were the ground rules. If you weren't paying attention, somebody was going to hit you and somebody was going to take your shit.

Garage workspace

I know that this New York sense of things is inside me. I know it influences my creative impulses about how I do things and how I make things. But it runs very deep; and I'll be damned if I can actually break it down and explain how it effects me. It's just there because I'm a New Yorker.

Garage workspace

Osa Koyama

NEW YORK CITY BOSOZO-KU

Brooklyn

Osa Koyama with his Yamaha SR500 in his garage/workshop, DUMBO, Brooklyn. His team name, Kaminari, is after the nickname of Kawasaki H1.

I was born in Nagoya, Japan, in the Midori-ku section. In New York I ride with a small group of Japanese guys and we all have older style Japanese motorcycles. We have a team leader, Shinichi Ikeda. We have a team mechanic Mr. Takasaki. He has a motorcycle garage and if we have any problems we can work with him. This is New York and we are all working hard to make money to pay the rent but we have our minds on our motorcycles. We customize our bikes in certain ways. We have been doing this for six or seven years.

Osa with his Yamaha SR500

Manhattan Bridge, DUMBO

The major cities in Japan like Tokyo, Osaka, and Nagoya have groups of motorcycle gangs. These gangs are called *Bosozo-ku*. They race around these cities and are known for making a lot of noise. Their engines are known for that high-pitched racing sound. These guys like the sound of their bikes and it is like a badge of honor for Bosozo-ku. Normal people in Japan are very quiet. They don't make a lot of noise. Noise is seen as a dirty thing. So, Bosozo-ku like to make noise. This is a counterculture statement. These guys race around the city streets in a place like Tokyo and make a loud statement about their life.

Now, in New York we ride around downtown streets in the East Village or in Brooklyn or Coney Island and we make this same Bosozo-ku noise like in Japan. *WHAAAaaa ma ma ma ma ma*. This is Bosozo-ku. One time we were on St. Mark's Place and the police noticed our group and this making of noise. They walked over to us and started talking with us. Then they noticed we were all speaking Japanese. We were polite but nobody spoke English. The police looked at each other and just walked away.

In Japan the Bosozo-ku guys are the ones that did not do so well in school. They did not study a lot and then they did not do so well on their exams. These young people just hang around and maybe they get some job doing something. They finally get the money to buy a motorcycle. After they get the motorcycle a lot of these guys join the Bosozo-ku. It depends on the person, but they find a job doing construction work. They can make a lot of money doing this. They probably get paid cash for their labor. So, the money they make they put it into their motorcycles.

So, then they have a life of going fast, hanging out, finding girls. They hang out in bad areas of the big cities. Like in Tokyo, these motorcycle guys hang out all night in Kabuki-cho. Gambling, sex bars, crazy

Osa's Yamaha SR500

clubs. So, from 14 or 15 years old to maybe 20 they are Bosozo-ku. After that some of those people stop riding in the streets like that. Then a percentage of these young guys go into the Yakuza. They do jobs for the family. They know how to sell drugs so they can make money. They get a job on their motorcycle taking certain packages to certain places.

Here in New York we don't behave like this. We ride our motorcycles and we make noise but we don't take packages around to places. We work as designers or sushi chefs in Japanese restaurant. We are legal Bosozo-ku. We are already old now and not young guys anymore. My team leader is already 38. So we are getting old. So no more of that crazy, crazy life. Now we just customize our motorcycles and we are just riding. Maybe we still make a little noise.

Basically, the guys in my group are collecting 1970s, 1980s Japanese motorcycles. No American, no European; just Japanese. Older Kawasaki two-stroke motors. These motorcycles are almost considered vintage at this point. The bike I ride now is original Yamaha SR500 but I have changed everything. It took me two years to finish customizing this motorcycle. I bought it in 2001 just before 911. We have twelve people in our group and we all do our own work on our motorcycles.

Japanese motorcycles have made a reputation for themselves. Honda made a four-cylinder piston system and this changed everything. If people want to make a fast bike the four pistons are very powerful, but also smooth. This arrangement changes the torque. The members in my group, we ride Japanese motorcycles because we like Japanese motorcycle. I like Harleys, too, but they are expensive.

I like riding in the city because it attracts people. They hear my motorcycle; it's loud and then they see it. It looks racy and kind of custom. It's not normal. My pipes are a little high. People like it. I work on my motorcycle and nobody else touches my motorcycle. I do it myself. If there is something wrong, it is my responsibility. I try to be safe. I check over my bike. This is important to me. I constantly look at the different parts of my motorcycle and think about improving them. Like my brakes—recently I looked at my calipers; they are from '76 and this is pretty old. The rotors and master cylinder were old. I couldn't stop if it was raining. I did not want to ride this way in a place like New York. There are enough problems riding in New York. I do not need new problems of not stopping.

Osa with his Yamaha SR500

Team bikes at Work's Engineering summer event

Team mechanic, Mr. Takasaki

Osa's Yamaha SR500

Team member at Work's Engineering summer event

Osa's team under Brooklyn Bridge

Team mechanic, Mr. Takasaki

It is important for me to ride in New York City. This is an important city. People respect this place. I tell people that I ride the streets of New York and they respect this. For me this is a good feeling. I like riding in Japanese cities, too. Riding in Tokyo is pretty crazy, but riding in New York is a different kind of crazy. For me there is something more futuristic about riding in New York. It is a really old city but still it's like a progressive place. Late at night, when you ride through the high buildings of mid-town this is a little crazy. This is like riding through an Akira [Katsuhiro Otomo] animation. Post apocalyptic, neo-Tokyo. That is the type of feeling I get when I ride at night through mid-town. New York is a very beautiful city to ride a motorcycle. At night, on Madison Avenue around 46th street, it is very quiet. The buildings are very tall and it is dark and I can hear my motorcycle echo off the buildings down the streets. My motorcycle has a special sound.

Team bikes at Work's Engineering summer event

Team bike

This is not just noise. This is different for me. My motorcycle sound is controlled. A lot of motorcycle people just make loud noise. I don't think this is that cool. I like when the sound is controlled.

My motor is made for off-road so it's pretty loud. I have a SuperTrapp exhaust for better performance. I can control how much air goes out. This type of thing is important for a racing machine. Every day the temperature and humidity changes so I can change the way the system works. My carburetor responds differently every day. For me, this keeps it more interesting. Of course, some days the air is heavy, some days not. This changes the way the air comes into the engine, mixes with the gas, and burns.

I don't change the mixture every day, but I am sensitive to this and how it affects my motor's performance. The needle and jet settings. I don't think Japanese motorcycles are more sensitive, just different. Any motorcycle is sensitive to these things. But I do notice that riding in New York is different than riding in a place like Tokyo or Nagoya. The motor behaves differently because the atmospheric conditions are different. The ride is different. I am not talking just speed; I am talking a sense of ride. This is different. In New York I like being sensitive to my motor and I like being sensitive to my ride.

Osa and his bike in Sapporo East, 10th Street and 1st Ave.

Osa and his bike outside Sapporo East, 10th Street and 1st Ave.

Grant Ray of *Hell For Leather Magazine* at Aprilia Motorcycles event in Brooklyn

This is a particularly interesting period of time for motorcycles. In terms of a market, the average age of a person who buys a motorcycle has been ratcheting up. It's already around 45 years old, but it's rising. A lot of manufacturers have a hard time getting in touch with a younger demographic. This is a decision they have made. They wonder why they can't get younger people on bikes but then they won't make bikes for younger people.

People in their twenties have a different mind-set. They want to go fast. But the industry tries to project an aura of safety. The reason Honda made such a splash in the 1960s is they hired an advertising company named Grey. They came up with, "You meet the nicest people on a Honda." You still hear it to this day; that's how good the slogan was.

A lot of motorcycle culture and marketing is influenced by California and the culture there. A lot of the motorcycle culture in California won't even deal with New York and the East Coast. They feel the biggest market is in California, so why talk about any other place.

So, thinking about this kind of situation, what's really incredible is the design and building that is going on outside of the corporate brand box. It's not just outside of the box in New York. It's happening in LA, it's happening in San Francisco, it's happening in Seattle, it's happening in Portland, it's going on in Chicago, it's kind of nationwide. There is a group of people in their twenties and thirties who are all skaters, surfers, designers, artists, punk rockers, and indie kids. It runs the gamut. These are urban young adults who are into cool things. They don't want to go fucking drink Pepsi. They think, "*What is that? I don't want to wear a shirt with your brand logo all over it. I don't do that stuff because I know what that advertising and marketing is all about.*"

They get it, they're educated. So, instead of all that crap, they are going out and doing something completely on their own. As they say, they want to take a motorcycle and strip it and black it all out. No nothin' on the bike. And they are going to ride around like that.

You'll see the guys who are deep into 1960s motor culture but they are doing it their own way. This is what each generation does. They say, "That looks like fun, that looks cool, but I don't necessarily need all the accompanying imagery. I just want a cool motorcycle and go out and drink some beers." But these guys are tactile, they are craftsmen, they want to work on the machine at the same time. These guys keep track of people and what they are making and they appreciate the work other craftspeople are doing.

A lot of what's going on with this movement and the young people who are a part of it has to do with the nature of our times and a sense of dissatisfaction with the machines of this time. They want to touch on something that is a bit more real than what they've got. They are driving cars with automatic transmissions, they've got traction control, everything is a perfectly wrapped bubble for them. They look back at their dads or their uncles or grand dads and they say, "These guys were building things." They think about the computer chips in their new cars and they question that.

There is a whole segment of this new movement where the people are saying, I want to get my hands dirty. I want to live and I don't necessarily want to be safe dammit! I want to ride a motorcycle and I will make an existential choice to not wear full body armor. I am making that choice. I'm going to be like a smoker and say, "Fuck you."

This is not some nutty nihilistic death wish, this is more. This is saying, "I am not afraid to have fun. And I'm going to do it on different terms." There are all these packaged ideas about what fun is, what culture is. It's become so refined. These people get all that, and they just want to do something else.

In the 1980s everyone was coked out of their minds, in the 1990s everyone was pissed off, saying, "I hate you." Now, young people are saying, I don't care about all that, I want to drink beers and have some fun. Go hang out at a skate park. The kids are flinging themselves in the air. Or the BMX kids are in the street doing stunts on their bicycles. It's the same thing with the Kustom Kulture. This is expression.

A lot of the mainstream messages today are about standing up, being strong, being brave. What the fuck does that mean? Things now are getting pretty skewed. It's always been pretty skewed. Things have never really been a black and white although it has been presented that way. So in American culture things have been presented in a this or that format. Things are validated as correct/incorrect. Now we don't really have a this or that situation. Now there is a total barrage of information. And we have generations trying to find out where the boundaries

Aprilia Motorcycles event installation, Brooklyn

Aprilia Motorcycles event installation, Brooklyn

Aprilia Motorcycles event, Brooklyn

Attendees observing Aprilia installation

are. People are going in different directions trying to find that.

There are different reasons why some of these guys get into old cars. A part of it is about exploring old machines, but a lot of it is also about who even wants a new car? I can't afford a new car. They cost $40,000. And if I do get that new car, I kind of like doing stuff with my hands and fixing shit, and I can't fix any of this new shit. I would need $40,000 of equipment to fix this stuff. Basically, I want to know this is a carburetor; I want to know how to adjust it. I want to know how to change the filters. Maybe it's a move towards simplicity as well. Yes, there is a sense of nostalgia, too, but it's more than just that. Its more; if this thing breaks I want to fix it.

Our world today has become hyper-technologized. We don't have the same relationship with things any more. Now we have to have specialized people who come in and take care of everything for us. So then some people ask, "What's going on here? What qualifies as having some sense of engagement with what's going on around me?" I don't feel that any more. What qualifies me as doing something that says, "OK, you are now a capable man in society?" What the fuck tells me that? I drop off my laundry every other week but is that enough? No, but now I can't work on my car because the industry has made all the stuff so complicated that if I do start to get into my engine, the internal engine sensors will freak out and the whole thing will shut down.

So, to work on my modern machine I would have to go into certain computer programs and update my system so that I can actually work on my own machine without pissing it off so that it shuts down. So I can't do that anymore. And I can't work on my house anymore because its state coded that only properly licensed people can fix shit. So, there that goes, too. So you start to have all these layers of separation. Of course a percentage of people start thinking, "*Well, what qualifies me for doing anything anymore?*" Some people say, "I got to do something."

I can't just sit in front of a computer at a desk all day and hit the keys and then punch out and go home. What did I just do all day or all week that was valid? I have no clue. So I may as well find something to do in my spare time that makes me feel relevant. Some people may get philosophical about it or some might just say: "Hey, my dad had one of those cars, maybe I'll get one too." You got to remember that this is a generation that grew up watching *Fight Club*. That movie resonated deeply with a percentage of this new generation. Some young people are asking, "Why am I buying all this stupid shit? What's going on here? All this shit doesn't mean anything to me as a person."

The people who are working on these bikes and cars in this way have a deep sense of appreciation about the materials and the machine and the historical processes about how these things work. A historical sense of doing something and understanding boundaries and appreciating these boundaries. Then changing things in certain ways that acknowledges this process.

Aprilia Motorcycles event installation

Aprilia Motorcycles event installation

A lot of time you do see a class orientation to some part of this appreciation. You do not see a lot of white collar kids getting into this process. They appreciate people who can do it right but they will never be the person who does it right. They will buy these guy's bikes, they will love them, they will do small things like polish them correctly and clean them correctly and then they will ride the fuck out of them. But, they will never work on these machines the way the young guys do who are actually building them.

New York City is interesting in terms of the small communities of people who work on their machines. They all represent small worlds and pockets of ways to do things. There is no real sense of a large community. It rarely happens that people from these groups all come together. Maybe the Indian Larry events or the Brooklyn Invitational events or the Rumblers events. You almost never see that. It is rare to get that many disparate types of people together in a space. This almost never happens. The city is just so damn big and everybody's busy. There are circles of people that run into each other at certain times and they mention each other and keep track of what's going on, but they never really hang out together at one time.

My website attracts all kinds of people. A lot are into new motorcycles but I am tiring of the motorcycle industry and how they are not speaking to anyone. I will probably go more towards hand built motorcycles. We get a very healthy cross section of people who interact with the site. At the site we talk about what's going on with motorcycles and motorcycle design, the industry, the culture. It has been really interesting.

There is definitely a specialized scene in New York in terms of motorcycles. It is not like the LA chopper scene. If you look at what's going on here, these bikes are well built and they are built hard for hard handling. They are not delicate the same way some of the machines are in LA. Here, these fucking bikes have to last. In New York it's got to be rugged, strong, and powerful. The streets in New York are shit. The roads on the East Coast are shit. People talk about The Dragon's Tail [Deals Gap, Tennessee/North Carolina]. You want good roads? Go west.

Grant Ray at Aprilia Motorcycles event, Brooklyn

Eric Ahlquist

A GREASY LIFE

Brooklyn

Eric Ahlquist

There are a lot of different subcultures within the car culture. There are these generalized terms like Restoration Rods or Rat Rods, there are early hot rods, and then people get more specific. Some guys are just into making a copy of a Salt Flats racer. It can get very specific. For myself, the thing that always drew me to old cars was that I could afford them. Initially, it wasn't cool old cars; I bought a '46 Ford truck for a good price. It was poorly built and was falling apart. So I put time and money into it and built it into something that's pretty decent as far as craftsmanship. But the truck is a thorn in the side for a lot of guys. It has a Chevy small block motor in it which a lot of guys hate. A lot of guys would say you don't put a Chevy in a Ford. They are brand loyal. At the time, that's what I knew how to do. It's built as a sleeper [an unassuming looking car that is actually high performance—all go and no show].

"My Truck is a 1946 Ford pick-up. I have owned the truck for 13 years. It has a 373-cubic-inch small block Chevy V8 motor with a turbo 350 transmission. I set up the truck to be a sleeper. It basically looks stock but drives fast, turns, and stops well."

Eric's '46 Ford tail gate

For me it's the custom thing. It's not about the brand. For me it's arbitrary that it's a Ford. It happened to be the car that I got, but it could have just as easily been a '46 Chevy. Because what I made is not that much about the brand either. It looks like the original car from a technical standpoint but it's totally custom. It's got a motor that is not really a Chevy. It's based on a Chevy but so many of the parts are aftermarket. The motor was built by an automotive machinist. It's not stock. It's a mix and match of different brands and makes.

It's a funny thing. A guy like me, I don't really fit in with the guys who are Ford or Chevy purists. But I don't really fit in with the guys who are full-on traditional hot rodders either. Personally, it doesn't bother me to put a newer motor into a car. There are guys who only build a car with parts that are 1955 or older. They would only work with vintage speed equipment. I don't take it to that degree personally. This world quickly periods of time. A lot of it can become a rich man's game; buying a muscle car with a powerful hemi engine gets expensive.

For me, the interest in this kind of thing is about being able to build what you want to build. If it's too new, you can get into all the regulations about emissions standards. But I like the way the older stuff is put together. It's a lot more solid. There's a quality to the materials you don't see with newer products in general—cars or otherwise. And they are simple enough machines where you can work on them. I just really like that streamline era. I really like the stuff that came out of the '40s. That whole "going fast standing still" thing has always caught my eye. The way designers were doing stuff with the lines, early concepts of aerodynamics. Everything is kind of rounded. I don't know where that really comes from with me. My parents didn't have cars like that. My parents had old Volvos. Maybe that's where my sensibility comes

The pre-show line up at the 2010 Rumblers BQE summer event

I know that a lot of guys in the Rumblers club have gotten into learning about this whole thing as a way to get into better cars. A lot of the cars that guys started with were what they could afford at the time. My thing has always been that it's better to have one nice car than five crappy ones. Which is part of the dilemma with my second car. From a practical standpoint there is no reason to have more than one car living in Brooklyn. I pay a lot of money to house that car. My truck, which is relatively nice, lives on the street and it has every winter for years. So that's a bummer. I did all the body work and it was perfect and nice and now it's starting to deteriorate into a used antique truck. When I lived on the West Coast that wasn't that big a deal because the weather wasn't rough, but here in New York it's a different story. The truth is, I'll probably end up driving that thing to a junk yard because it will rust apart.

I have been interested in photography since I was young. For lack of a better description, I guess I am an art photographer and I pursue photography as an art. I have worked in a lot of creative areas. I went to school for industrial design for a while and then I dropped out and started working as a model maker. I was doing color matching and lacquer painting and finish work. Then I got a job working for a company that made shifter racing go-karts. I was working on motors and so I started learning a lot more about machines and machining. I worked on building custom carburetors and porting techniques on two stroke motors. Recutting the shape of the head and changing the volume of the head for different types of high compression.

Around the time that I quit working there was when I moved to New York. I went through a lot of different creative jobs after I got to New York, but then I started working for Paul Cox. This has been a good thing and

Pre-show line up at the 2010 Rumblers BQE summer event

Rumblers 2010 BQE summer event

I enjoy it. Working with Paul energized me again. There is a lot of new stuff that I am learning and the focus is different than a lot of the jobs I have worked before. There is overlap with it all and a lot of it has to do with having a critical eye and understanding proportion and having the hand skill to be able to go from drawing to concept. Cut and grind and finish a part and make it work. This is a unique situation, and working with Paul is an opportunity that was too important to pass up.

When I first moved to New York I tried to get a job working at their shop on 14th Street when it was called Gasoline Alley. Indian Larry was working there; Gerard [Mortillaro] was partners with him. It is an interesting experience to watch this come full circle and be working with Paul. I have to think that this is one of the common threads with this new bike scene in New York. A few different groups of guys with some kind of artistic background: Painters, photographers, coming out of the art school background. Ray Abeyta and this Brooklyn group, we all sort of have this common thread of being artists and also being interested in custom machines. Many of the people are interested in Low Brow culture influenced by Ed Roth, Von Dutch, and Robert Williams.

For me, the tattoo culture has influenced me a lot. I started getting heavily tattooed when I was 21. I got a lot of my tattoos from Tim Lehi on the West Coast when I went to Ed Hardy's shop. I knew some of Ed Hardy's history and was really inspired by his art work. I am originally a southern Californian and my parents are the same generation as Ed. My father was a huge surfer but that never really did it for me. When I was a teenager, which is when I would have gotten into surfing, my father passed away. I didn't have any way to access surfing. I didn't live at the beach. I lived over the hill 30 miles away.

Rumblers 2010 BQE summer event

Rumblers 2010 BQE summer event

I got a car and tried to go surfing but I was a little stupid and stubborn about it and went to surfing areas where beginners weren't supposed to go. I got beat up a bit and kind of gave it up. But, I've been a skateboarder since I was five. It would have been difficult to be a kid growing up in California during the seventies and eighties and not have been exposed to skateboarding. For me it was skateboarding and bicycles. My parents were outdoorsy people. I was exposed to Yosemite and camping.

The thing that got me hooked to the motorcycle thing was my dad. He had a couple Vespas and also a pretty big Honda and he took me riding on the back of it when I was seven years old. He would ride us up through the twisty roads on Routes 84 and 35 and that was it. It was a done deal. I was introduced to all that stuff at a really young age. I still skateboard, maybe to my detriment.

It seems to me that for young people in America, and probably everywhere, so much of the interest in bikes and cars has to do with what region you grew up in. Of course in California, automatically there is a lot of car culture. You look at a lot of the high-end restoration hot rods in *Rodder's Journal* and the owners are almost all from southern California. These are the guys

that grew up with the monster t-shirts that Roth was making and they finally got the money to buy a car and fully restore it. I love that stuff. If I could get Roy Brizio to build me a car I might. I might feel better about building it myself. But the difference between cars I have and cars I'd like to have is money.

I am not one of the guys who's dad was deep into this and grew up with the whole culture of customizing machines. Cole Foster is a good example of this kind of knowledge. His dad, Pat, was a skilled drag racer and Cole is a descendant of this kind of knowledge. I am not one of those types of guys. I was an only child raised by my mom and I always had to reach out to other people to learn about stuff. How else was I going to get the information?

The thing for guys my age about being connected to skateboarding or BMX bikes is the question of being introduced to a world of subcultures. These are subcultural scenes and there is an outlaw nature to skateboarding. A destructiveness to skateboarding to a certain degree. There are a lot of clichés that go along with that whole thing but some of my skateboard heroes, the first thing they did when they got some money was to build custom cars and custom

Rumblers 2010 BQE summer event

Paul Cox and Eric Ahlquist working in Paul's garage

bikes. And then they would go raise hell with their custom cars and custom bikes.

It made sense to me somehow that I would adopt some of the same interests as those guys. These days the sponsored skate and BMX bike scenes have changed into a jock culture and I feel a total disconnect to it. It is very big money these days. When I was young the guys who were sponsored were not paid a lot of money. Now of course all that has changed. Tony Alva and Tony Hawk, these guys made a lot of money.

There has been a lot of concern voiced about my generation and our sense of direction. As a kid I played video games; there was a time in my early twenties when I was really into that kind of stuff but I grew out of it. Some people don't. But the thing that is encouraging about my generation is that yes, some kids are really into computer tech and games, but there are a lot of young people who are not into it. There are members of my car club the Rumblers who are 19 and 20 years old, but they obviously see that there is something else out there to get into. They do not just break it down to sitting around and watching MTV or whatever.

There was a great *New York Times* article and argument that advocated working with your hands [Mathew B. Crawford; "Shop Class as Soul Craft: An Inquiry into the Value of Work," 2009]. It talks about the process of so many young people coming out of college in the mid- to late-nineties being promised they would have great white collar jobs; but they don't know how to make anything or get their hands dirty. The article mentions how there is now a little more attention and respect being given to people who are craftsmen and know how to make stuff— automotive repair and motorcycle repair. There is a sense of mystification now about a guy that can actually work on machines. The guys that sit in a cubicle all day working on a computer just don't get it and are confused by guys that make their living using their hands. I find it's weird when I meet people and they don't have a clue. Maybe my resume comes up and all the weird jobs I've had and they sit there and just look at me with this, "How the fuck do you make a living?" look on their face.

Ten years ago I was asked what would make me happy? At that time my answer was to make a living working with my hands. I wanted to be a fine woodworker. And I think it's still kind of true. I need to be creating something. There is a part of me that needs that, whether it be a hobby or a way to make money. I need to be doing that with at least some of my time. I certainly love to be doing photography and other artistic things, but for me there has to be a balance. It can't be all about computers. Now, a lot of the time computers seem to be distractions that prevent people from accomplishing anything.

Computers have to be a part of the process; they are a tool. In terms of rebuilding a car? You couldn't do it without a computer. You couldn't find the parts without the Internet. The old methods for getting stuff don't exist anymore. You can't go to a swap meet in Brooklyn and find an old wheel to a car. It's all connections through the Internet and connections to outside of New York. You have to be connected to a place like California where there is this historical car culture. That's where the parts are. The car scene has always been very limited in New York because of an unfriendly climate and unfriendly street conditions.

You can see how difficult it is to build and then maintain a car in a place like New York. The cars are a lot more beaten down. Here, you might only find the fire wall and cowl of a car [the top portion of the front part of an automobile body, supporting the windshield and dashboard]. You won't find the back end or front of it so they make everything using sheet metal. They make it from scratch using photos and reference books. This is where the computer stuff comes into play more. Just to be able to have more information. Today, if you want to find, build, or restore a car, you need a computer. That's just the way it is.

Working on my truck or my car helps me to negotiate the spaces between our current technological world and the world of getting your hands dirty making stuff. Both spaces are relevant but I just need to know I can move between them.

Eric's '27 Ford T: "My hotrod is a 1927 Ford Model T coupe. It has a 331 hemi motor with a Weiand intake and three 97 carbs. It has a 3-speed Saginaw manual transmission. It's a 'bitsa'; you know, a bit of this and that. It's a pretty rough car. I am considering a redesign. I drove it a couple times during the summer and have not had it out since."

Eric and Paul Cox

Eric working in Paul Cox's shop

Eric grinding

Eric's '27 Ford

Sal Pepe

IT'S FUCKING DANGEROUS, BUT IT'S FUN, TOO, YA KNOW?

Brooklyn

Sal Pepe — Hard Life Cycles

I'm 30 years old. I used to run BMX bikes as a kid and for a couple years I got sponsored. I got paid and shit and I went riding around. Yeah, I was really into BMX bikes and I was into hot rods, so I kind of merged them together.

Sal's Shovelhead

I used to race cars on the street. Over here in Brooklyn that's tough to do unless you have a house with a garage. Me and my buddies, we all lived in buildings. That's a different story; we had no garage. Our cars sat in the street and once you start street racing, people would either steal your shit, or burn it, or break into it. Guys would hunt around for the competition cars and pour ball bearings into your oil. You'd have to try to lock up your hood. All the guys I knew had bikes so I just got into bikes. It's a lot simpler.

I had a couple cars. I had a '85 Cutlass, like a normal passenger style car with a 455 Old's big block with a turbo 400. It was a fast car for the street. I used to street race it. Guys been doing street racing for ever in Brooklyn. Like Fountain Avenue, and the East New York area. That was probably mid-'90s, right when I got my license. Then racing faded out because of law enforcement. A car flipped over and people died and another guy lost his arm. A girl who was standing with them died also. On Fountain Avenue, Flatland Avenue the city dug like ruts—reverse speed bumps. Late '90s I got out of it. After like five years of fucking having my cars broken into. Ya know? But guys used to race for big money. I've seen guys almost get killed over big money. People would tell stories about the amounts: forty, fifty thousand. People didn't believe them but they did race for this kind of money.

Everyone would show up with their crew and they would agree on an intermediary—a guy in the middle who would hold the money. Then they would race. But, when they are racing for that much money the guys would knit pick over everything. They'd say the guy jumped the start and this and that. Shit got more out of hand than the actual racing. Sometimes you had two guys who were straight up and they knew what they had and they would just race. Somebody would win and get paid. But most of the time, guys who were racing for big money, they would complain more than they race. That's the other thing that killed it. People didn't want to deal with it any more. Then the cops just started taking people's cars. That was it.

I had that Cutlass. It was a high, ten-second street car. That's a fast car for the street. That was also my regular drive around car but it's the city. It's difficult. So I got sick of it. Alternate side parking laws in the city, parking tickets; I just got sick of it. I said I'm just going to build a bike in my fucking bedroom and I'll just buy a pick-up truck and that's it. So that's what I did. I got into bikes. Guys in my family had been into this for a while. I wasn't going to school and I went to work with a friend of the family. He was good friends with a guy who was HA and we went to visit and work with him in upstate New York. So, this guy asked if I liked bikes and at the time I was into anything, so I liked sport bikes and Jap bikes. This guy says, "You wanna see a real fucking bike?" That was one of the first times I'd seen a real chopper. He had a real nice Panhead in his bedroom. So, I was like, "Fuck—that thing is awesome."

Sal's first bike build in his apartment bedroom

Sal's money car, 1997-98: '85 Cutlass, 455 Old's big block, Grand National rear, Grand National transmission

Sal's '85 Cutlass

Sal's tank

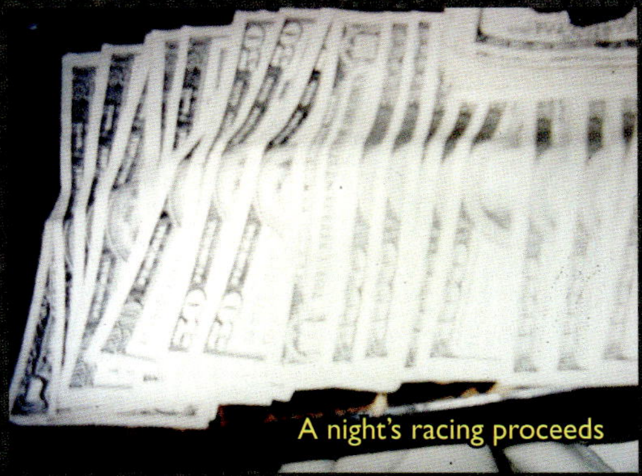

A night's racing proceeds

Sal's burned '68 Firebird, 400ci, money car

Sal at his bench

Inside the shop

Inside the shop

My uncle had lived in Long Beach all his life. Everybody out there had bikes, but they were more into the vintage thing. So I'd go visit him and shit and they had Pans and Knuckles and stuff, but they were just kind of stock old stuff. I would think that they looked stupid and slow and goofy looking and my uncle would say, "You'll see—one day you'll want one of these old bikes." Sure as shit, I ended up wanting one of those bikes. He actually used to race 45-inch Flatheads, the WWII-issued WLs. He used to race those on the sand-drag racing out in the desert. About three years ago he gave me an old forty-five as a Christmas gift.

My first bike, I built it in my mother's apartment—14th floor. She wasn't too happy about that. We fucking stood it up in the elevator on the back wheel and a few friends held it up. I rolled it out into the lobby. You know? The building super hated me.

I'm still learning shit. Like I said, I used to race cars and then bikes are just an easier thing. You can build a motor on your fucking kitchen counter. Ya know? I have a Bridgeport and this makes it easier to do tricky engine work. I didn't go to school to learn this. I grew up around guys that raced bikes and they had tools. A Bridgeport lathe that you use to spin the metal around and take off fins and shit. Fender mounts, brake mounts. A lot of guys in the city ride with no front brake. Guys do it just for the clean look of not having a front brake. You learn how to ride with no front brake. You can't be blasting around in New York traffic with that set-up. That's suicide.

As far as me and being around the old bikes and working on the old stuff—once you get into it you won't even look at anything new. The simple mechanical old stuff grabs you. Then it becomes a part of your life and starts to drift into everything else. You don't want to deal with the whole computer world, all that Internet shit. Working with the old stuff changes you. You end up feeling that everything new sucks.

Timing and carburetion with motors is a big thing. I've had guys bring in big powerful bikes but they run like dogs because the carburetion is off and the timing is off. I have built 74-inch Harley motors that beat 120-inch motors because the big motors aren't set up right. They are not taking advantage of all the power. It's a waste. There's a whole aesthetic about spark plugs. Some guys run a tight gap, some guys run a wide gap. All these things come into play with tuning an engine. Some guys will set it up with a dyno. They use a laptop and an oxygen sensor. See if it's burning rich or burning lean. There's an aesthetic to this. You'll get guys who'll know how they want it to run and feel. They know the mixture should be richer or leaner but they don't know how to do it.

I got customers who ride long distance in the summer. They know they are going down south and they'll be in the mountains. They don't want the bike to lean-out. They'll be at five and six thousand foot elevations but their carburetor is set up for New York City and their bikes will lean-out [bad air to fuel ratio—not enough gas]. The higher the elevation the more "Ping." Sometimes the cylinder will get so hot from being too lean that the whole thing will blow out. The valves won't seat correctly and you're not getting any compression. Air's the biggest thing.

These guys who race these top fuel dragsters that are 8,000 horsepower, they are the fastest things in the world. The guy that gets paid the big money, the crew chief or head mechanic, he makes that thing go down the strip. All he does is carburetion and spark. That's all he plays with. He knows when it needs the spark and how much gas it needs. There are other things—the clutch guy comes in and he adjusts. He makes it slip a little or grab a little. He's putting 8,000 horsepower to the ground. That's all it is. Gas and spark.

Build by Sal, dished tank by Sal

Dougy, shop owner, with his Caddy

Dougy's Caddy hood with Mercedes black paint

Sportster tank, custom flame paint

That's why turbo and supercharged stuff is so efficient— especially turbo stuff. It's forced induction. You can dump all this gas into the cylinder and make tons of power. Ya know? It's the same with nitrous. It's just cylinder pressure. How much pressure can you get and how much gas can you put in there while you're doing it. Tons of times the pressure gets to be so much that you blow the motor. There'll be a rod sticking out the side of the fucking engine. You don't see too much of this turbo with Harley, but it is happening. I know a guy who is doing it with an Ironhead. You can put a lot of torque on an Ironhead. Its small bore and the head bolts are in a tight configuration. It helps to prevent blowing a head gasket.

When you build a Harley motor, especially a stroker motor, you do like a half case set-up. You do the motor, your fly-wheels, your pistons, and everything. Your cylinder and head on one side of the case. Harleys don't have blocks; they use cases and its half and half. So you set up everything with the cylinder and head and then you can check for clearances and shit like that. When you do a stroker motor in a Shovelhead, the oil goes up to the rocker box and then drains down. A Harley don't make that much pressure: The Evolution motors make no pressure. Shovelheads, Panheads, Knuckleheads, all the old stuff—if you got an oil gauge on them and you're sitting at a light and it's a hot day, if you look at the gauge it will be reading zero. That's just how they are. They don't need a lot of pressure. It's not like a car; they don't have as much stuff going on. So, when you do a stroker motor, you have to move stuff around in there because you are moving the cylinder. You are running a taller cylinder. These motors are actually pretty tight. People think they are leaky but no; that's usually because guys aren't taking care of them right.

Hank in his garage

Twisted frame work by Hank

Hank's build

Sal sitting on his bike behind the shop

Setting up these engines is actually pretty straight forward. You got a fly wheel, you got a timing mark. So, you find the timing mark and eyeball it. When you are running a twin-plug stroker motor, everything is off from stock. So, rule of thumb for the twin plug is you run it real retarded. You retard the timing. For me, instead of 30...32, which is where you usually set the degrees—mine is like 25. So it is really retarded back. So instead of using a timing light and all that, you just eyeball it and set it up. You develop a sense about these things.

Some people are speed junkies. I was like that for a long time. My Shovelhead, the motor I have in that bike, is like overkill. It's all this horsepower in a bike with no front brake. It's pretty much a race motor short of compression, ya know? The compression is just low enough so you can run it in the street. If I put big compression pistons in the motor, it would be as powerful as a 98-inch, 106-inch. I do this to keep it interesting but you also get addicted to it. The bike could be a rocket but after a while it's just like anything else. You get used to it. You get bored with it. It's fucking dangerous but it's fun, too. Ya know?

Steve Iacona

I HAVE ALWAYS FELT COMFORTABLE MAKING THINGS

Brooklyn

Steve Iacona at Indian Larry event, Brooklyn

I spend time thinking about what things I want to try to accomplish when I build a bike. This is a machine but there are a lot of different elements that come together. These machines have shapes and they have histories. There are definitely sensual aspects to a motorcycle. When a guy refers to his bike he usually talks about it as if it's a woman. That look—the high tank, the seat, the rear. There is definitely something beautiful about this. It's all a part of life. The whole shape of something that pulls you in because it's attractive. A motorcycle is a beautiful object. I squint my eyes and look at the shape—yeah, a motorcycle shape is pleasing to the eyes. If you are into machinery, it could be anything. All kinds of builders will always get along together and have a good conversation. We all appreciate these machines.

Iacona build

Iacona build

I just opened a new shop and I have been moving things in. I knew a machinist where I work. I used to bend his ear to bounce ideas off of him. He was selling one of his Bridgeport's. The day I signed the lease on my shop he called me and said, "OK, come and get the Bridgeport, I have to get it out of there right away." So all in one day everything arrived. I used to work out of my house for a lot of years. I grew up in that house. I worked in that garage since I was a little kid till today. I had a lot of stuff in that garage. So, it will take a little time to personalize my new place. Of course I feel a sense of accomplishment that I am putting this new shop together. It's a whole different thing.

I've been building some sort of something since I was 14 years old. I have always felt comfortable in my space making things. I have been doing it for like 30 years. The bikes that I have worked on all contributed something to where I am now. Everything I have built has left a little something behind. It's like walking up a flight of stairs little by little. I think that I am coming into my own now. All the stuff I have done, I have liked it but at the same time I saw it as a process. I hadn't quite gotten to where I wanted to go. Now, I feel that I am coming into stuff that I really like. My earlier builds were earlier versions of me. Decisions I made before. I still like my earlier builds and I am proud of them, but I wouldn't do it like that now.

A lot of builders deal with this issue of looking at their earlier work. I am proud of my earlier work but I don't think it's really what I want to show at this point. The process is what it's all about. To be honest, I don't think too much about where it all comes from. I always just did it.

I'll never forget it. A few years ago when I was doing the race bike thing I was in North Carolina at a brand new track. We were riding all day and during the last session I

Iacona shop machines

Steve Iacona with build in progress

Iacona build in progress

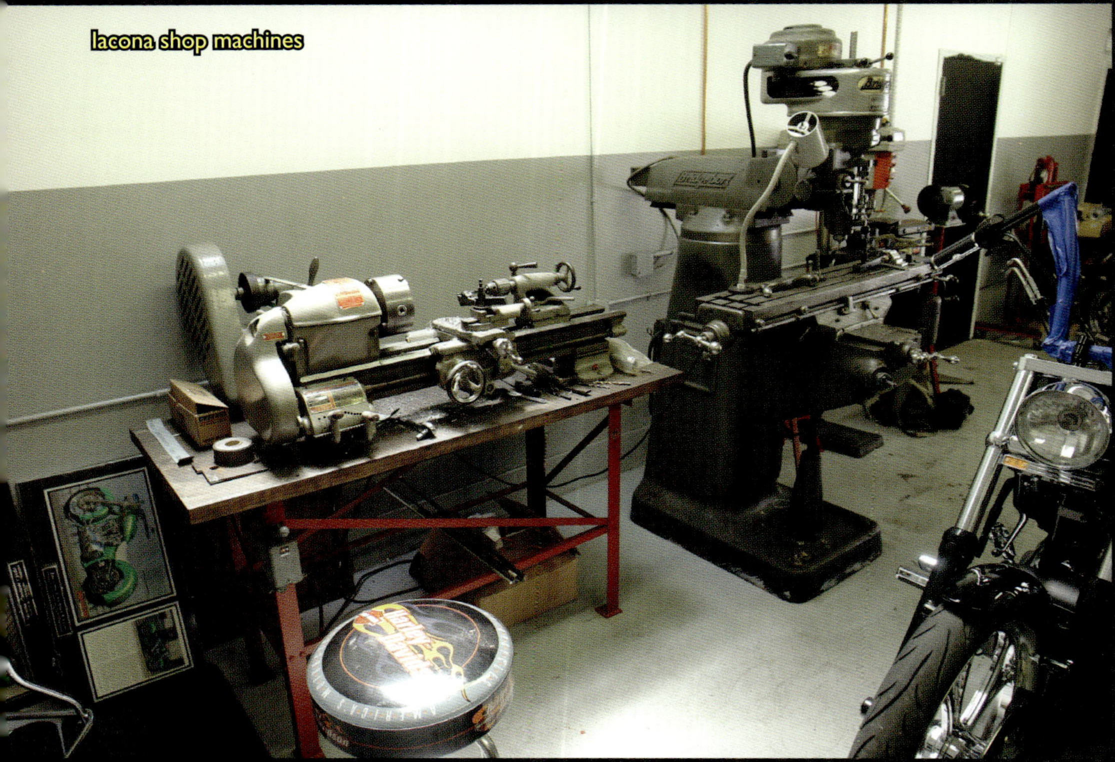

Iacona shop machines

was in a turn with my knee on the ground and I thought to myself, "*I don't want to do this anymore.*" I just stopped. I finished the day and I never went back. I went home and I never rode on a track again. Something in my head said, "*OK, I've had enough.*" I sold my Ducati and I ended up getting into Harleys. I knew I had to go a different way. I guess I felt that I had gone as fast as I could go on a track and the fun factor started to go away. It started to be a job. I went into that turn and that was it. To this day, I remember that spot on that track and the position I was in going into that turn. That image has never left me.

I am that kind of guy. I don't get too brainy about it. I follow what I feel—if it feels good, it's good.

Iacona work

Steve Iacona's father

Steve Iacona's business card

Ricco & Izzy

I WANT TO PASS
THIS ON TO MY SON

Coney Island

Ricco doing body work at Coney Island garage

Ricco and Izzy
'55 Chevy rebuild
(Two-Lane Blacktop
homage car),
Coney Island

Garage interior

Garage interior, Vette rebuild in progress

Garage yard

Ricco and Izzy Chevy rebuild

Ricco and Izzy Chevy rebuild

Izzy

Friend of Ricco and Izzy

Ricco and Izzy Chevy rebuild

Ricco and Izzy re-builds on street

1000hp Camaro in garage

Cadillac, 1950s, forms side view

Ricco and Izzy Cadillac rebuild

1000hp Camaro

Ricco

Dennis "D Man" Vazquez

PIT STOP

Red Hook, Brooklyn-Union City

Dennis "D Man" Vazquez in storage area of his Pit Stop shop

I was brought up in Red Hook, Brooklyn, and I lived in the Red Hook projects. The Ching-A-Lings motorcycle gang had a chapter in Red Hook. Today everything has changed in New York, but in the late '60s and early '70s you wouldn't go to a place like Red Hook unless you lived there or you had some kind of business there. The Red Hook projects had a reputation. The police didn't go there because there was a good chance they would get shot at.

Dennis's jacket

I was a kid but there was an older gentleman in the neighborhood named Black Tony. He was the president of the Ching-A-Lings chapter out in Brooklyn. I don't know which chapter started first, whether it was the Red Hook chapter or the Bronx chapter. I was young but I remember being told that the group started in Red Hook and it started with Black Tony. This has got to be 40 years ago.

Tony had a shop where he worked on cars and bikes. He was into Harley Davidsons and cars. He was real big into drag racing. As kids we used to go into the shop and he'd show us his new motors and new cars and new kinds of slicks. I remember Tony burning out in his drag cars down Richards Street. He would do a burn-out just to see where the tire had started to grip. He would measure things but instead of taking a tape measure he would burn out and then walk the rubber trail in the street. This is how he would measure his torque. He didn't have a Dyno, so he worked out his method to measure the torque of the engine. He would measure the width of the slick tire and then he'd walk the length of the burn-out to find out how much power he had.

As a kid I understood why he was doing it. I watched it and I understood why he was doing it. It was pretty cool. That was his way for measuring power. He would take the seats out of the car, all the excessive weight out of the car and then he would sand bag the rear. There used to be a place called Long Dock in Red hook on the waterfront. The place was falling apart and every year that place would get worse. This was an abandoned place, so this is the place where everybody raced. It was a narrow place to race; if you were set up in the far lane towards the water you were at a disadvantage.

It was a two-lane street and the racing there became more and more popular. People started to travel there to race their cars. There were spectators walking the race course looking for a place to stand, but it was very narrow. People would be standing right next to the street where the cars raced. If a car lost its line you had no choice but to jump off the edge of the street into the water. Jump or be run over and killed. Guys would crash all the time and people were always jumping for their lives into the water. It was crazy.

One day Tony had a big race and we were all watching but he lost his line and he hit a pole. He hit that thing so hard his steering wheel caved in up to the dash board. Tony was really strong; he was built like an ox. When he hit the pole he held onto the wheel and crushed it in his hands. He was OK, but the car was totaled. I remember as a kid we all ran to look at the car and we could see where Tony had been holding the steering wheel. We were like, "Holy shit. How did he survive that crash?" There was Fountain Avenue, Long Dock, and Flatlands. Guys risked their lives there every night drag racing. There is a huge history in Brooklyn about Latin and African American drag racing. Tony was Latin but he was dark skin so they called him Black Tony.

Tony was a great inspiration in my life in terms of fabrication and the respect factor. That guy was respected. As a kid you wanted to be respected. Sometimes in a place like Red Hook you had to hold yourself in an aggressive manner. In Red Hook there was a different kind of walk and a different type of look. A different approach to how you looked at some one. It was very distinctive. People knew that if you had that Red Hook swagger in you they'd give you a pass. You were OK. Nobody was going to fuck with you.

The area had originally been Irish and Italian. Then the Puerto Ricans came in and then the African Americans. Everyone packed a weapon. That's what it was. My dad was a neighborhood type of guy. Protect your family, protect your neighborhood. I learned a lot of good lessons from my dad about how to carry myself and how to have a sense of respect.

I was young, but early on in the neighborhood, the Irish owned the neighborhood stores. They would give trouble to the Puerto Ricans. Break their

Pit Stop track bike

Dennis and father with Red Hook altar boy crew, c. 1980

Dannis "D Man" Pit Stop build, 2009-10

balls and take their money because they couldn't speak English. One of my early memories is one evening a friend of my dad's banged on our apartment door and said the Irish guy at the store had taken his money. My dad very calmly got his pistol and everyone went down to the store. My dad walked in and introduced himself to the Irish guy. Then he took his pistol and put it right in the Irish guy's mouth. He asked the Irish guy what was the problem? It's one of those childhood memories I have, the Irish guy mumbling with a gun in his mouth that everything was OK.

I was into athletics and discipline and I was into gangs. Back then you'd get together and go to a neighborhood and bang it out against a different gang. We were fortunate that we always walked away. We were in good shape, always doing push-ups and pull-ups. We'd go to the park and do our exercises. We'd take cement and pour it into buckets and put in a piece of pipe. We'd let it set up, flip it around and pour cement into a bucket with the pipe to make bar bells. Those was our training weights. At first I really liked cars. As time went on I started to appreciate bikes. I used to run a '69 Camaro. That was my favorite car. I still own one now. My original desire was to get into cars—racing cars. I was hanging in that area with tough guys that were into cars. And yes, they also owned a bike.

For me the whole motorcycle scene had started with bicycles. I always wanted to build my bike to look like a motorcycle. I would go to the Sanitation Department on Atlantic Avenue and get scraps of metal. As an eleven year old kid I didn't have any money for buying anything. So I'd find my scrap but then I'd have to weld something and I didn't know how to do that. Black Tony was always welding something so I'd ask Tony for some help. He was very cool with young people; there might be a bunch of bikes or cars outside his shop, but he'd take a break and weld my stuff. I would get him to weld up these crazy extended forks for my bicycle and I'd put things together and then go show Tony. He was always interested in my creativity. My bicycles looked like my version of a show bike. He got such a kick out of that.

I was a hustler: I'd fix kid's bicycles, tighten their spokes, whatever. I made a couple dollars. I was always out there to earn a dollar with my skills. I went to Catholic school, but we were from Red Hook and pretty bad ass, so I did some things I am not very proud of, but I got an athletic scholarship to college.

Dennis "D Man" Pit Stop build, 2009-10

Dennis "D Man" Pit Stop build, 2009-10

Dennis "D Man" Pit Stop build, 2009-10

Paint work by Giancarlo "Snek" Silva

Painter Giancarlo "Snek" Silva

When I got out of college I got into motorcycles— racing motorcycles. Racing cars is too expensive. You need a lot of money to do that. So I put out the word in the neighborhood that I needed a bike and I got a bike. I started to race it at the track. That's a trip. I never did any hard drugs in my life. Smoked a couple cigarettes, sniffed a little glue with the guys, but it gave me a fucking headache so I said fuck that. Racing a motorcycle at a track became my drug.

I love V-twins. I had a Wide Glide and a '78 Sportster. I had watched Tony work on his cars and bikes. I watched him burn his tires to measure the torque. He was a good teacher. I watched and I learned. I have always been good at taking things apart and putting them back together. At my shop now I teach guys to take things apart and not be afraid to put them back together. I think one of the most difficult things about trying to build something is the fear factor. Once you feel comfortable with the process, you get over the fear factor. As you take things apart you become a mechanic, a designer and a fabricator. All these things together make you a skilled builder. I am fortunate that I enjoy designing and making things.

I have been around many of the traditional forms. Watching a man like Tony helped me to appreciate the old forms of cars and motorcycles. Now, I take things to a different place. I have a new set of customers that look for a different design and a different solution. I build for rap stars, performers, athletes. These people come here looking for a different style and solution. I try to make all my projects impressive to people. I have never pushed a bike out of my garage that I am not impressed with. I am now exploring the whole sports bike element. It's an urban, inner-city thing.

The world of sports bikes and V-twins do not necessarily mix. At times it's like fire and ice. These are different machines and also very different lifestyles. If you had a V-twin you were considered a harder kind of guy. If you had a rice rocket you were like the upper echelon of the racing motorcycle or urban world. It was not viewed as a hard core element. We never got the thumbs-up from the V-twin guys. Some of this is a pro-America thing; part of it could be a racial thing. These are two worlds that exist independently in New York.

But let me tell you, today there are some hard core mother fuckers in the sport bike world. There are some young guys in the sport bike world that stand around and talk about it, but let me tell you, there are some real G's out there. Gangsters. Believe me. If they say they're going to hug you, they'll hug you; if they say they're going to stab you, they'll stab you. Today there is a new world of hard core outlaw sport bike groups. There is definitely a 1%er element to this world. It's not my world, but I respect it and I respect the process. In New York there is definitely a metro sport bike lifestyle of tough guys.

I've had this business for eleven years but I have been working on motorcycles for about 20 years but not to this extent. I have always fixed my bike and gone to the race track. Eleven years ago I decided to really wrench. But I do this as a labor of love. I am 48 and I still consider myself a student and I am still waiting to work on my next build. I am a two-wheels guy. First it was the V-twins, then the Kawasaki LTD in-line four. The transition is crazy. The V-twin turned into the custom world but the rice rocket world hasn't really done that yet. There is a lot of engineering involved. They are adding a lot of technology like onboard computer technology and video camera technology. This transition about adding electronic technology to fill out the bike is interesting. I have to stay on top of all this stuff to keep on my game.

Shop floor, Pit Stop

Katana knife detail

Firearm details

Fairing windscreen fabrication by Dennis "D Man" Vazquez

There is an Old School and New School perspective about bikes but with one difference: Rice rocket people can look at a 1960s rigid frame V-twin and respect where it came from and what it means. Old School V-twin guys cannot do this about rice rockets for the most part. There are V-twin clubs in New York City that will have parties where they hang a rice rocket from a tree and charge money to smash it with a sledge hammer. I understand the perspective, but I try to respect everyone. I don't see sport bike guys getting into smashing a V-twin with a sledgehammer.

Bikes get stolen in the city. This is always a concern for bike owners. A few years ago one of the guys in my crew had his Kawasaki stolen. He had just finished doing a lot of work on it so he was pretty pissed off. We got word that some guys from Newark had come into our neighborhood to take the bike. I have friends in Newark so I made a call. They had heard about the bike and who stole it. Things were going to get crazy and people were going to get hurt.

I called back my Newark friend and we talked about trying to work things out. We got some guys, an SUV, and a pick-up truck and we went to meet the assholes that stole the bike. I told my guys to hang back a couple blocks and not to roll down the tinted windows for any reason and to stay inside the SUV. I was in the pick-up with the bike owner. The location for the meeting was in a fucked-up Newark neighborhood. We pulled up and right away I noticed some guys wearing long coats. I knew what that meant and I told my friend not to get crazy. We noticed two guys looking at us from over the edge of the roof of a building.

A guy approached my pick-up and said they wanted $5,000.00 for the bike. My friend almost went crazy. I had told my guys in the SUV that if anything went bad to come up quick and try to run as many guys over as possible and get the fuck out of there. I had dialed in the location on my GPS so that there was a record of where we were.

I told the guy to produce the bike so he made a call and then some guys showed up with a van. They opened the van doors and we could see the bike. I thought my friend was going to lose it. He could see his bike and these guys wanted him to pay $5,000.00 for it. I made another call to my Newark friend and said these fucking guys were pushing their luck with this. He said he would make a call. Nothing happened for ten minutes but finally my phone rang. It was my Newark friend who said we could take the bike. So we got out, took the bike, rolled it up into our pick-up and we got the fuck out of there.

Erik Green, Works Engineering

I've been on North 14th in Brooklyn for only a couple years. Before I was on Wythe and before that I was next to the Matchless Bar that I have. Back in '99 I was in DUMBO. I was there for probably five years. I have always seen my places as some kind of a resource for the people involved in motorcycles in the city.

Erik Green

Works Engineering

I started working on bikes after I got out of college in Georgia. I had a Ducati 350. This is more than 20 years ago. At the time my only resource was a shop in Athens, Georgia. A really grumpy guy named John ran a shop out there. Now that's the way I'm getting to be these days. He had a very cool shop that was dealing with old Italian bikes. I was totally in heaven when I saw his shop. And for me, that's kind of what this place is now. But this kind of thing wasn't around back during that time in Brooklyn.

I have a degree in mechanical engineering and years ago I had a real job in Atlanta. Then I went to work for Team Obsolete. They have probably the world's biggest private collection of GP bikes. They are the real deal. I worked there for ten years as a mechanic.

Most of the time I see myself as some kind of a facilitator for people that want to work on motorcycles. There are a few other shops like this in Brooklyn but Works is unique in many ways. There has always been an interesting group of people coming through here. So I deal with all the idiosyncrasies of people and their machines. This is a big space and there's a lot going on here. This place boils down to some kind of a labor of love.

We all work together and we try to lend each other a helping hand. We have a welding shop, a woodshop, and a bunch of things that work together somehow. There are a few artists like Bobby [Garey] and Ray [Abeyta] that have their studios here.

I get bounced around between a managerial role and then getting some time to work on a project. These days it seems more managerial. It is good for me to try to keep three of four mechanics but this is tough. It's hard to find three or four qualified mechanics that can handle complicated projects like these old bikes.

I have a young man, Irving, who has been working here five or six years and I

Works Engineering

Matchless Bar, next to old Works Engineering location

Ray Abeyta's Triumph parked outside old Works location

Basement bike storage, Works Engineering

Dice magazine release event, Matchless Bar

Old Works Engineering location/Matchless Bar Dice magazine release event

Dice magazine release event, Matchless Bar

Dice magazine release event, Matchless Bar

Erik and Works team racing

got to train him from the beginning. He is energetic about learning stuff. That's the best situation, but it's hard to find someone like Irving walking in off the street.

We are lucky here because there are some very interesting people coming through. There's a whole group of people that comes with this place. My ideal shop would be to have my space rented and other people renting their bike spaces down in the basement. Then I could just help people work on their bikes and I could also have some project bikes that I wanted to work on. I'd rather be able to just help someone work on their bike than be put into the role of managing a space. I probably rent out 30 bike spaces and the rest of the motorcycles you see here are our obsession about what we collect. So there are 30 people renting space and there are well over 100 bikes in here. So do the math on that. All the people here are very enthusiastic about having motorcycles. The bikes add up quickly.

Personally, I am interested in project bikes—restoration. I really like to work on race bikes. I don't necessarily discriminate about makes and models. I prefer old and I am getting into these side car racers. If I could work on old bikes and also build a cool little café racer every so often and help people prep their bikes then I would be a happy person.

Irving working at Works Engineering

Sidecar racer

Ray Abeyta at Matchless event

My uncle came back from Vietnam and bought himself a BSA. I was so intrigued by that bike. It was the most beautiful thing I had ever seen. As a kid living in Panama, in the Canal Zone, all the American kids had British bikes. The parking lot where I lived was full of glittery, shiny machines. That's probably why I like British bikes so much. It's something I grew up with. This connection to vehicles is a part of my background. Cars and Hispanic guys have always been connected. It started in the 1940s.

Ray Abeyta's Ford pick-up

Traditionally, people of Hispanic descent were always on the lower economic rung. The cars that they could afford to buy weren't in good condition. So what they would do is buy an old car and fix it up. But these folks are Latin so they fixed it up in style. Make it your own. Make it cool. Stylizing your car. You might have been poor but you still wanted to look good. How you gonna pick up chicks if you don't have a cool ride?

I see this process of culture, memory, power, and realization with machines too. Some say that New Mexico is the Lowrider capital of the world. Some claim that Lowriders were invented there. Los Angeles might think otherwise. This is what I grew up around. My father and his buddies; me and my buddies were always into cars. Our cars were always done up. One of my father's oldest friends, his son was an upholsterer. This was during the first days of that glitter fabric. He had a '49 Mercury. The interior was all done up with dark green glitter upholstery with silver piping. He also had an old Ford pick-up he had done up Old School, neat and clean. He had a buddy who rolled around in a totally shaved '57 Chevy and he did the upholstery on that. So I was brought up in a world like that.

This whole thing about machines is pretty much a twentieth-century phenomenon. Young guys have always been attracted to things that are fast, powerful, and bold. Before machines it was horses. It has always been defined in a cultural sense. Everyone did it in their own way. All the white guys were doing it their way. We used to call their cars "Road Sniffers." They'd jack up the back and drop the front. All my friends were into the Lowrider thing. So, everyone had their style, but everyone had to make it unique to themselves.

Once kids started getting a hold of old cars they started to ask what they could do to them to make them look different to scare adults and piss off the citizens. Like the bikers from the post-WWII era and their use of the swastika. It came from all the GIs coming back from the war with their Nazi souvenirs and paraphernalia. You take a bunch of young boys and teach them how to be stone cold killers, they will have the potential to act wild. Race around on motorcycles and fast cars. The whole thing with the iron cross and the swastika in the sixties was just a way to piss people off. To say you are an outsider and different from the norm. The fifties were a horribly conformist time and in the sixties things just went through the roof.

I think hot rods, motorcycles, like choppers that have been messed with, it's a way to try to be different. Of course in the end things become codified. It becomes a mystique. I am infatuated with many different kinds of tradition. I am a painter and I enjoy expressing myself this way. But it's an ancient way to communicate. People were doing it on caves. But I think for the people who are getting involved in this motorcycle and car scene it has a link to a past. And that past has taken on this patina of gloriousness. It's something that people used to do. And now you have young people re-exploring this aesthetic and getting into the whole seventies chopper thing. I think this is perfectly fine. Trends come and go.

I have always had machines around me. I have been into Triumphs but someday I'll get my Harley. I'm not in any hurry right now. I just want to do some painting. Building stuff takes a lot of time. I don't know, the appeal is just that when you get on them and you ride them there's nothing like it. Especially if it's something you have built yourself. Like my Triumph; I built it during a time when my Pops was going out with cancer. Me and my daddy never had much of a relationship. He was one of those fifties guys who didn't know how to talk. We had no conversational relationship. When he was dying, all this stuff between us that I had

Ray Abeyta's Truimph parked at old Works location

put to bed in the past came bubbling back up to the surface. And I started thinking about it and I couldn't paint. I'd go into the studio and stand there and stare at the canvas. It was like I forgot how to do it.

But mechanical stuff has this very different kind of focus going on. It's like a Zen thing. You compartmentalize it. You take something apart and then put it back together in a different way. But you can only do it in so many ways. Otherwise it's not going to run and it's going to kill you. So I decided to work on this motorcycle. To fixate on it and not what was going on with my Pop so much. He finally died right around when I finished the bike. So it's kind of a tribute to him and the things he did teach me. Things I did see when I was growing up because of my daddy. That kind of lineage is important. It's important to understand tradition and your past and history so that you don't make the same mistakes again.

You can make beautiful things in this present moment that refer to something that existed before you. With that bike, I wanted it to look like it had been kicking around for a few years. I patinaed the paint, did the old logos on the oil tank, like it had been sitting in a garage since the 1960s. It's not just moving through space. You want to move through space with a certain amount of style.

I have a buddy who owns a Ducati Monster. He was always after me to ride it. He'd say, "You gotta ride this thing. It's so fucking Italian." So I take his bike out and I'm riding it around and it's a nice motorcycle. It's fast and it stops on a dime, it's got a nice sound to it but for me I just don't know. I come from a Lowrider culture. It's the difference between getting into a slammed-down Impala or a store-bought Subaru. Which one you gonna feel cooler in? It's all about the cool. But, sometimes other people's bikes and cars are like other people's tattoos. You see them and scratch your head like, "Why the fuck did you do that?"

Side view, Ray Abeyta's Triumph

When you build a motorcycle you are taking something and turning it into something else. Painting and putting paint on a canvas is different. You are starting from scratch and turning it into something. I think they are very different processes. With a machine you can tweak it a bit but there are tolerances and there is a range of where you can go with it.

My painting started out as an investigation about who I was and where I came from. I was born into a certain artistic style familiar to New Mexico: Santo Esta. A lot of this stuff was done during the seventeen and eighteen hundreds. It is an American folk art form. What happened in New Mexico was basically it was a very isolated place. It was disconnected. A lot of farmers and ranchers. People that came from Spain were basically on their own. So this culture from 1600s Spain kept going and stayed intact. There were fraternities that were associated with various saints and Jesus and they had their own chapels and community based religion. With everything being Catholic, there was a need for images and statues. Paintings and alter pieces were done by people who were not academically trained but had a flair for using a paintbrush or using a carving tool. They developed a very interesting style. It stressed the suffering aspect of Christianity and it was very bloody. I grew up around this stuff. My mom would drag me to church every Sunday. I'd sit in

Ray Abeyta at Matchless Bar

church and look at these images and it made quite an impression on me.

At first it scared the piss out of me. All this creepy dead Jesus stuff with blood all over it. But later, as a young artist, I started thinking about it. It was powerful and visceral. I wondered, "*Where does this stuff come from? Why does it look like this?*" I started to do all this historical research. I went back to pre-Columbian times in terms of what had happened in the Americas to produce this kind of aesthetic. In the end it turned out not to be related so much to my small little patch of New Mexico but it went all the way from Canada to the tip of Chile. It existed before the Europeans got here and changed after they got here. The Mestizo-Baroque. Religious and secular imagery that traveled from the Old World to the New World. I became intrigued by the way images are translated and retranslated and become other things. How the images were stylistically keyed into the places where they were being made. Peru translated the images one way, Mexico one way, Argentina one way.

I wondered about the European and New World cultures coming into contact with each other quickly in a short period of time. I likened it to a car crash. Two forces coming together violently. So, in trying to figure out where my past met up with my future, this became more of how we as people move through space. How we are trying to find our points in time and space. How we give meaning to these spaces and how memory plays into it.

I am working on a painting now that focuses on the character Queequeg from Melville's *Moby Dick*. For me, he is a bridge between all these things. He is introduced in that book as a mystery. The mystery that the "Other" always has—primitive, savage, unknown. Different and scary. In the end he winds up becoming a noble innocent but no more so than anyone else in the book. He is just another human being. When I think of that book *Moby Dick* it is so relevant to what's going on in the world today.

I don't know how existential it all gets with motorcycles. For me, you get on the thing and they're fast, their powerful, and there's a certain element of being out of control. The thing could kill you. Riding on the machine pushes all those adrenalin buttons. I mean, if you go down on one of these things, you go down hard—even if you're going slow. I wonder sometimes if that's not the main appeal. It's an accelerated life basically.

You look at people and the way they move through the world. This has changed over time from the days of ancient discoverer's ships, and then people moving around with horses or chariots. The physical sense of speed was always there. How fast are you moving? This has been a question that has followed mankind for a long time. Of course this sensation has changed over

Williamsburg, Brooklyn scene

Ray Abeyta in his painting studio with Moby Dick-inspired paintings

Ray Abeyta's Ford pick-up parked in north Williamsburg

time, but that need for speed has followed us as a species. Going fast is amazing, going fast is fun, going fast is sexy. Machines make a lot of noise. Riding around New York is a blast. It's dangerous, but it's a fun way to get around. As long as the cops aren't watching you, you can split lanes and you can go fast enough to keep it interesting. If you know how to work on your machine then it's even better and there is something very satisfying about it.

That first Brooklyn Invitational bike show in 2009 was a very important thing for me to see. There were all these motorcycle kids. They rolled in from Chicago and from all over. They were so excited to be doing this. I really liked seeing what was going on with that show. The whole custom movement in cars and motorcycles is very interesting to me. It says so much about people and creativity. A lot of this creativity has been minimized over the years. Like with cars, during the late '60s, the whole invention of the muscle car had a lot to do with the fading of the hot rod. The industry co-opted it. It's the same with motorcycles. The industry reduced the whole thing to consumerism. Pick out what engine, how big, what paint you want to buy. The industry changed the process of guys building cool bikes and cars. They were still out there, but the process changed.

I recognize that it's gotten people thinking about the process of making machines that are not industry controlled. So that's cool to me and that's important. That Brooklyn event is put together by young guys and it's important they are doing this.

For me the whole thing is more than a hobby. It's more like a therapy. Sometimes you're working on stuff and shit is hitting the fan right and left and then you get on that motorcycle and it's just you and the machine. You are moving through space and for those few moments you just own the world. It's yours and you can do anything you want. All your troubles, all your cares are just blasting off into the wind.

Ray Abeyta

Bobby Garey

IT RUNS FAST AS HELL

Brooklyn

Bobby Garey and his Sportster in his studio

Motorcycles are an aesthetic thing. I can be objective about it but there's something about these old bikes—the castings, the chrome that they used, the engineering. They are beautiful. Old tools are the same way. A machine like this is the epitome of all that. I have had this bike since 1988. I started riding when I was in my early twenties. The first bike I had was a 1972 Sportster.

Bobby's workbench

Bobby and his '49 Plymouth

Bobby's first Sportster

I built this bike. The frame is original and the motor is a 1966. I built it from a bunch of parts. In my mind I built this bike to look like what a Sportster is supposed to look like. It's tough, it's fast, and it's beautiful. It's a beautiful mean machine.

Old tools and old metal. The shape of it. For me this look comes from the era I grew up in. I was always fascinated with cars and motorcycles. My dad had a 1961 MGA. I used to work on that with him. We did all the work on that together. The first car I had was a 1949 Plymouth. I bought it for $75. The compression was gone so it couldn't go up hills. I pulled the motor out, got a manual, and learned about that engine by wrenching on it. There's something about a continuum in my life with old motors and old cars and motorcycles that just feels right. I came from a family that was gifted mechanically.

My dad was a chemical engineer. A smart, talented dude, ace mechanic, and an amazing artist. He was a WWII fighter pilot. He raced British motorcycles when he was back from the War. My grandfather had a cabinet shop. I worked in it as a kid. I have always made a living doing things that I learned as a kid. So there is something that ties me to working on things like this motorcycle. A life-long love of it. Painters from the WPA period. The aesthetic goes back and this motorcycle's design is a part of that era. The shapes of it, the way it rides. I have lowered it about four inches by switching the rear shocks and rear tire size. That decision has to do with outlaw style bikes.

I was brought up in the south and all we ever rode was Harley Davidsons. The chopper and bobber style bike. That whole aesthetic was a part of my growing up. Strip it down to the bare essentials. Louder, ruder, meaner. There were some groups down south and in the old rust belt states that

Good ol' boy

Bobby's first Sportster

helped to form the outlaw styles. We would see these guys and their bikes. These guys had seen bikes from the West Coast. The style traveled with the bikes. Today, a lot of this has been reduced to a "look" but one of the things I like about this motorcycle is that it predates all the bullshit.

This motorcycle represents how I feel about the whole thing. It is nuanced and subconscious, but when I made it I was really just thinking about building a bike that runs. Something that I could use to get out there on the New York streets that runs mechanically and safely and is in tip-top shape. Particularly if I was going to ride the hell out of it and that's how I like to ride.

Riding in New York is an intense thing. I like the intensity of it. Jamming the bike, splitting lanes; it's exciting. The adrenaline pumps. It gets hairy. So many close calls. It's constant. I always have this thought of breaking down in the middle of the Holland Tunnel. Riding through that tunnel is actually pretty nice. It has this long curve and late at night or early Sunday mornings when there's no traffic it's quite nice. Or I'll take the FDR to the Harlem River Drive and then down the West Side. Make a big loop all the way around Manhattan. That's a real good ride. I appreciate things like that and this Sportster helps me to appreciate things like that.

Recently I went on a night ride with Ray [Abeyta]. We hit the BQE [Brooklyn Queens Expressway] and Ray was gone. I was probably going 60 miles an hour. I could still see the potholes and I was dodging them, my eyes were tearing and all I could see was Ray's tail light off in the distance way ahead of me.

The stance of this Sportster is important to me. I have rear shocks but they are tied down and have no travel. There is a reason why this works. When it is lower down in the back like this, the front end changes the angle and gets a perception of a little bit of rake. When I hit the throttle with this bike it squats down like it is getting ready to leap. I don't know if you can articulate that but that's what it looks like.

The look of early outlaw bikes looked like this and this was a statement. These guys were exploring how to make things look fast. They might not have been able to put it into words, but this is why they were doing it. These guy's bikes looked like they were going fast even when they were standing still. They looked like they are going to blast off. Like when you look at an old photograph of a race car driving around a track. All the cars are always pitched forward. So these San Francisco outlaw stance bikes were exploring this same perception of velocity. They might not have been able to talk about it but that's what they were doing. This had to do with blood knowledge and muscle memory. These guys were riders and they were building fast bikes. They knew what it felt like when they hit it. So they were building a bike to look like that. They had an internal knowledge about this and blood knowledge of what the machine should look like.

So then, were these guys in San Francisco thinking about what and how they were making their motorcycles? Maybe, but maybe not. They just made them like they wanted. I just made my bike like I wanted. But the stance and the look of these bikes had come from someplace. Nobody could even talk about it, but their machines just affected people in deep ways.

In terms of motorcycles, people will talk about East Coast-West Coast styles and I think a lot of the East Coast style is in New York. Narrow bikes that you can cut through traffic with. But that style goes back to the California outlaws and their bikes. Frisco style tanks. The Sportster tank was the prototype for that style. There is no motorcycle tank that comes close to it. Two and a quarter gallons of gas. I can run for about an hour and then I need more gas. You can change the tank a bit. Raise the cap and add a petcock so you get about a half gallon more gas. Guys in San Francisco invented that style tank. That's an aesthetic I like.

I finished building this bike about five years ago. It took me more than four months to build it. My friend Billy Phelps, the photographer, was working on something for Harley. He called up Ray and me and asked us to meet him over on Front Street. He did a photo shoot set up of us and our old bikes and he sent it to Harley. So, Harley went for his idea and then he set up a big shoot for the advertisement. There was a tractor trailer full of new Harleys that he used in the shoot. The representative was there from Harley overseeing the shoot. My bike was parked there and the representative looked at it and said, "Ah, there's that bike. Whose bike is this?" The rep said that he had showed a photo of my bike to the president of Harley and the president said, "This is what a Sportster should look like. This is it."

I am a southerner; I love to ride down south. That's where I grew up riding. Country roads with smooth surfaces. It's relaxing. I am very aware of my connection to a region. And from that I have an understanding of other regions in America—southwestern, Appalachian culture. As a kid I hitchhiked all around the country. I am acutely aware how in America there are these great epic stories: *Huckleberry Finn*, *Moby Dick*, John Steinbeck, and the Civil War. I am aware of this and I try to explore this narrative approach with my painting.

My painting style and how I like to paint has a lot to do with craft and a sense of tradition. My Sportster also has a lot to do with a sense of craft and tradition. I've been drawing and painting for a long time. I've been making pictures with people in

Bobby's studio

Bobby in his studio

Front door Works Engineering

them since I was nine years old. Now I see a lot of this kind of thing disappearing. I have done all these paintings of people and places in New York and it dawned on me sometime during the process that I was painting things that were going through a process of disappearing.

This space here at Works Engineering is an important place. There are some creative people here. A lot of the mood that surrounds motorcycles is going through a gentrifying process now. But the people here at Works are just living their lives. This place is a stronghold for the people working here. There is work being done here that is really creative. It is not a part of this ham fisted, ham-bone motorcycle sensibility that is out there.

A few years back I went down to South Carolina to take my motorcycle license test. I talked to the gal in the window and she asked what kind of bike I had. I told her a 1959 Harley Davidson. Everybody in the office got all excited. The motorcycle trooper lady who gives the test said she wanted to see my bike. She took a look and asked me to turn on my head light. I told her I had to kick the bike over to do that. "You don't got a switch for the light?" she asked.

"No Ma'am, all I got is a magneto," I replied.

"Where's your turn signals? I don't see none," she asked.

"I don't have any." I replied.

"Well I don't know about that," she said. She asked next, "Where's your speedometer?"

I replied I didn't have one.

"Well I don't know about that," she replied. She asked me to toot my horn. I told her I didn't have a horn. She asked me how the heck I was expecting to pass this test? She said she was going to call her office and see how to handle this.

She came back in 10 minutes with a big smile on her face and said, "My supervisor up in Columbia just told me that if you want to take the test on a 1959 Harley Davidson then you deserve to take the test even if you don't have no horn, no speedometer, or no turn signals.

"Thank you, Ma'am," I said. She passed me on my test and stamped my license. As she was giving me my license she looked at me real serious and said, "That's one fast looking machine; I bet it runs fast as hell."

"Yes Ma'am," I said.

Bobby's Sportster

Bobby Garey

Drawing by Bobby Garey

Bobby with Sportster at Works front door

WHITE KNIGHTS GARAGE

BROOKLYN

AJ Herold

SOUTHBOUND & DOWN

Brooklyn

AJ with his truck and '47 Flathead on the West Side

I was making my first road trip to Daytona for Biketoberfest 2003 on a 1947 WL that I picked up in the summer of 2001 with some help for my friend Sully. In NYC we exchanged the cash at a bank next to the Trade Center. Unfortunately for me, I picked up this bike from a grifter in Portland, Maine, 3,000 miles of NYC driving, the whole bike fell apart, blew half the pistons off. They made them tough in '47, but as I drove it to the shop I could not get it over 30 mph. Thanks to Joe and Andrew on Route 1 in Rahway, this old bird got a fresh drive train for the trip south.

I had my father's ashes in the saddlebags and I had a lot of time to think; it was a little better than a 1,000-mile ride. I wasn't breaking any land speed records on this run.

"A phony, a fake, a fraud," 23 hours of riding to figure this out. "No tattoo's, no club."

I left at 6 A.M., bike pre-packed. The night before was long and rainy, the bike and its contents baptized; the Staten Island Ferry slammed into a pier that morning killing many commuters. The wind that day kicked my ass all the way to Richmond, Virginia. I stopped for the night in Lumberton, North Carolina, and reflected. I wrenched on my primary chain after checking in at 7 P.M., "that was fucking scary", and noticed my father was sneaking out all the way down 95. I smoked some grass and ordered my first meal, a few beers, and thought about how I got to this point, and this time around if anything, had I really changed. I just spent 13 hours on the road; my usual trips are 6–8 hours, stop and go, on the streets of Manhattan, bouncing off cabs, and bar hopping 35 miles from home. 573 miles down 95 with my father on my trail, our time together is now; day two, with a deteriorating primary chain situation, it is not looking very promising.

My first Harley was an '81 shovelhead, my second Harley was a '47 Flathead, and I don't know what my third will be, but I will build it for my son; I have some time to get it together and it's looking like a 93-inch Pan-Shovel, maybe a '50s straight leg. The boy picked out the tank online from Gasoline Alley—my 7-year-old wants to find Brother Rat Fink, and already a fan of Big Daddy-0. His Grandfather was a truck driver and his uncle is a truck driver. I know of the road and have been on it my whole life on one set of wheels or another; sorry to say, any form of transportation I could get my hands on. My brother and I started to mess around with bikes in '84; he, unlike me, is more of a biker, but I got the Harley thing started in our immediate family around '87. It would be my first loan; I could not afford it straight up cash. My brother was the first one to get to Daytona for bike week in '89, at that time he told me the only biker build-off was at the Rat's Hole, and it was for the best rat bike, and other mods in town. I would not make it there until much later in life, right around the second chopper explosion.

Born in Rahway, New Jersey, 1965; raised in Iselin. In the '70s, when we were kids, all we would see around the neighborhood and at the annual Catholic church fair were hardcore choppers and 1%'ers drinking Pabst on the keg under the biker tent. It was unreal, what seemed like hundreds around the oak tree getting boozed up and stoned out on weird smelling cigarettes, then blowing out at midnight with hole shots and wheelies after the last polka and the wrestling bear were put away for the night. In the name of the Roman Catholic Charity, we donated beer money for the saint of the highway I suppose. The lifestyle, working class, where the wave broke back, East Coast style, and hardcore outlaw biker, that was the undercurrent in our neighborhood (which my parents were not too happy about).

Things in town started to change, the old timers moved out of Middlesex county in the '80s, I was in college playing football for the state university so I missed most of the local fun prior to the exodus, but not all of it. I picked up my first Shovel from Tim at Ski Towing in New Brunswick, he had his father's bike in the shed under a cover and an old FL Panhead with a sidecar. He sold me the shovel, an '81 Lowrider for $4,500, and said it may need a counter shaft 2nd, it started going on his way back from Sturgis in '86. I believed him. I am pretty sure he was well versed in the ways and the codes, like old friends Johnny and John back from Avenel. Tim's ink and his demeanor reminded me of the Hilltop Crew by Shop Rite back in Iselin, the biker Gods I used to see from the car window and at the fair as a kid. Soon after that my brother picked up a Shovel bagger, stripped it down, and we were on our way. Where? I am not sure, but we were going to get there. The Lowrider burned to the ground on Grand Avenue about 6 months later, August of '87. The insurance, since it was financed, set me free—the money forced me to take it apart down to splitting the cases. Hubs and Wayne from B&D in Rahway helped with the lower end and the heads, as well as the transmission. They sized the jugs with new pistons and gave me a Sifton 440 and I was on my way to put that bike back together in my basement. I would help the biker crowd out in other ways, ways in which I was into at the time, "a decadent and depraved" lifestyle of sorts. As the build got under way, my mother told us she had cancer and died of it on Thanksgiving Day of that year. The Shovelhead helped me through the pain, the loss, and the suffering. I had it back together for the spring and needed to figure out how to get it out of the Bilco doors in the basement, it was a good thing I went with drag bars and four-inch risers. It took five of us, and my old man was right there. I think deep down he would have loved to ride, trucking was his thing. He turned me on to all the trucker movies of the '70s, *White Line Fever*, *Smokey and the Bandit*, *Duel*, and *Convoy* were the most memorable. We would truck often together through the years, he could keep his eye on me in the summer, and night jobs running into NYC through college for extra money. He would try to stop the hustle that I picked up at the university.

I graduated university on that bike, stomped people and got stomped on back in those days. I learned a few things about the cops, dealers, and dealing—when a son of a detective breaks your head open with a

AJ Herold

AJ and Wes Lang at White Knights Garage, Brooklyn

baseball bat, don't expect him to get more than a third-class misdemeanor. If it was a biker on a Harley, all greased out, it would have been attempted murder. It's not that I don't like the police, but they take care of their own just like everyone else. Lost a few along the way, Johnny G died in the streets of NYC and Mark drove his Pan into a tree one early morning. They were from the Clinton area of New Jersey, and the accidents happened six months apart. After all that went down so did I. Burned the Shovel again right in front of the Kings Inn Route 1 in Rahway, New Jersey, 10:00 P.M., just back from Brooklyn—shut the whole south side down as flames shot out of the tank 30 feet in the air, fuel hissing and spewing out. The sky lit up like the refineries on Exit 13. I tore that Shovel down and started to rebuild. In the end it was sold to Leo and Gary on Rt. 1 in Rahway as a basket case for $2,000—one of the biggest regrets of my life. After that it all ended for a while, I lost my first fiancé, moved to NYC with my future wife, and for 10 years became a "biker"? without a bike. Yeah, everyone knows that is the lowest form of shit talker.

6 A.M., day two. Packed and ready for the road, "I got to let all my shit dry," and de-ash in the Motel. It was a fucking mess—soggy, mildew smelling, cremation soiled. I put my father, whom I had zip locked, in the old chrome stamp metal WLA tool box—his dog tags fixed to the vessel that would find its way to the depths of the Atlantic and down to the Gulf Stream by way of the Sunglow Pier, Daytona. He died at Halifax Medical Center the year before; he is back in the saddle riding shotgun ready for the rest of the ride. I remember my father more vividly since my brother and I just took him off life support. He outlasted my mother 17 years to the ripe old age of 64; he never drank never smoked, that German walked the line, and was one tough motherfucker in his day. One of the best wheelmen you would ever meet, and could turn a wrench on most anything. He knew, and he knew I knew what to do when the time came.

The fog was rising in Dixie just as I crossed the border; the swamps of South Carolina are pure as the sun rises through the mist between the moss and the sycamore. I was freezing my balls off in mid October 1.5 hours in. For the second day, hypothermia was setting in, and my primary was rattling around like 10 penny nails banging in a coffee can. I pulled over and cracked open the primary cover. I readjusted the stretched-out primary chain of the 45. That bitch was dried up and stretched like an old whore. I only had 425 miles to go and I could see the pins in some places, the clutch basket sprockets were worn like a saw blade and the chain whipped through the front of the primary cover. "Oil, oil lubrication," I shouted as the cars and trucks passed buy. Shit, it looked like I was the only crazy bastard on a bike that morning.

I guess it was around 11 when this 18-wheeler hauling hogs blew buy me, I smiled and snorted at those hogs as they where probably going off to be breakfast for some retirees down in FLA. I was thawing out, smoking grass, forgetting all the bullshit back in NYC, exit 131 New Jersey. Just as sure as I was wrenching that fucking primary chain with full transmission adjustments 5 or 6 times, I was a greasy sweaty fucking mess by 4 P.M. when I hit the FLA state line.

I slowly rolled into Daytona not sure where I was; north of downtown in some poor ghetto, I could see the streetlights were coming on and I got closer to some of the main streets. I could see the sights and sounds of the pent up event—Bikertoberfest in it first Friday night. I rattled onto International Speedway Drive looking for the Ramada I stayed last year, right across from the Daytona International Speedway. I rode into town burnt out, greasy, looking for my second meal

AJ and John Copeland at White Knights Garage

in 36 hours. All I could see from stop light to stop light, and east to west were the "trailer" crowd, fresh out of the shower, polished up in their billet. I must have looked like a "Coney Island Freak" to most of these well-manicured folks—my face swollen and wind burned, eyes of Mr. Gasser, greasy, a ratty old bike, a ratty 3/4 leather jacket, a degenerated, stoned-out, beer-swollen 38-year-old, white dude, crew cut, blue eyes, thick in Jersey accent, large, greasy-handed cretin. The receptionist at the Inn remembered me from the year before and got me a room on the ground floor east side. I parked, off loaded the saddle bags and stripped myself down for a long hot shower. The pool of oil and dirt in the bottom of the tub looked familiar, all the towels covered with motor oil and highway grime; the maid service needed a good tip.

I had cleaned up my act, burned some grass, and turned on the news: The miners were saved in Pennsylvania. Holy shit, that was the year before, I was having a flash back to my Halifax Medical Center experience the year before. It was a miracle, those miners getting saved. I thought to myself, "*God takes some and spares others like those doomed commuters on the Staten Island Ferry, or as HST would have put it 'Fear and Loathing on the Staten Island Ferry—a savage journey to work.*'" Everyone is spared once and a while, well, except for those pigs I saw hauling down 95.

Assessing the damage after a pork ribs dinner and several taps off the keg, I tore down the Achilles heal one more time, and found out our 1,053 mile journey must have been made with the wind south of Dixie. A saddlebag with the best wheel man God had to offer, we made it, we were halfway through the pins, but we made it. All the Saints had to cash in their beer money for this ride, but by the grace of God we made it.

I was finally vindicated of my own conscious, my internal lack of intestinal fortitude, sitting back seeing the chrome triangle box with the army dog tags, and knowing that I can get someone somewhere they wanted to go and get the job done in the honor of a highway man. It might have been for both of us, and maybe with the way it all unfolded, the gift may have been truly for me. I was only three miles away from the Sunglow Pier.

The hotel was full, checked in next to me was a trucker and a biker from Canada, Big Billet R., he checked out my ride and said, "What's your deal?" His old lady was headed down via 727 in the A.M., so we rolled in the bar for a few. He had a well-appointed, polished, lowered, diamond cut, 103 ci, half-orange half-black, full customize, full of glory, 2,000 bagger, a big new trailer to match, and a huge pickup to haul his shit from the land north of the greater 48. Big Billet offered to drive me around to the local vendors, a brother who looked familiar told me to try Red at Alley Cat who offered us a beer as we drove up to his one-car garage storefront. I noticed he was a Pan and Shovel man, located close to a 1%'er club house, and knew I was close, he said, "Good luck finding a 100 plus pin 45 primary chain down here, try Black Gold, he might. I doubt it, but might have what you're looking for. What the fuck did you do again? Good luck." You see, Billet was a fresh rested truck driving man on a mission, so he wouldn't give up the search, I would have just went with Reds advice. I was just a fucking beat up mess by this time, buzzed on lack of sleep, lack of food, strong grass from NYC, 1,053 miles, 25 hours of a rigid '47. I was out of my mind by this time and hardened as steel pins, and noticed I just started passing a kidney stone. As we headed to the truck, Red said, "Black Gold is not open until the morning."

I said, "Lets go to the Beach Beauty Club." I just rolled with it in a sense of defeat; my job here is not completed yet. I never got to the Beach Beauty Club, or Boot Hill, that night, but I talked to every billet pimping vendor on Main Street catching the local scene. One guy gave me Old Dude's number in GA, but I had no time for UPS or FedEx.

I woke up at 5 A.M. blowing ribs and beer out of my pie hole; the stone passed, I was doubled down in pain, the blood vessels broke right out of my eye sockets. I went back to sleep, I woke up at 7 put the old man on the back of the bike with the bags, and I set off for the Sunglow Pier. Buy the time I got off the bike, walked through Crabby Joe's, and out to the end of the pier with my tool box, tags, and precious cargo, I was an emotional mess, thanking everyone I ever met in my life to help me get this far, then that last long talk with the tool box—all the usual shit. I was really broken down and emotional, reliving the talks you have with a soon-to-be corpse and a heartbeat monitor and respirator giving you hope that he will just sit up and say, "Hey, how's it going. Good you could make it down to Florida to see me." But that never happened. Before I hauled that toolbox and tags and Dad as far as I could, I put a knife through the zip lock and locked him down in the box. As I sent my father in to the great Atlantic like a discus, he moved out toward the sea, splash down, bubbled down ash sprayed out to the sea with the off shore breeze and with the sun on the rise it was all I could hope for that desperate Saturday morning on the Sunglow Pier.

As I made that long walk toward shore, I called my wife and my son and told them I loved them and would be home soon.

Fancy-ass boots, White Knights

My mother loved Elvis and my father Cash. I went to the Lighthouse Diner right off A-1-A. As I looked at the pictures of all the lighthouses around the US, I felt as if I had been here before. I flashed back to my father, mother, and brother sitting here in the '70s on our way back from Hialeah after our annual trip to see my grandfather and the half of my half family in Florida.

The load has been lifted, promises kept; I felt free, a great burden lifted. That night as I slept, I would feel the ocean and the undertow pulling me into a good night's sleep, but right now I was headed over to the Boot Hill for some beer and some

Johnny Cash—"Sunday Morning Coming Down"—and a few Buds for breakfast after breakfast. Three or four beers before 10 A.M., it was a few puffs and a kick start and I was off over the Main Street Bridge, a right on the other side, and to Black Gold, my savior; $55, a new primary chain, and I was ready to ride home. I went back to my room and crashed for four hours, woke up, and tried to get that new primary on. It was not fitting for some reason, not enough pins? Fuck it. I called U-Haul, $250 for a box truck back to Jersey, done.

Big Billet had his old lady with him now, his truck, his trailer, his hot bike, and said, "Do you want to grab some lunch, Hooters?" He told me she wasn't really his girl, just a friend with privileges. I said, "Cool, try marriage." A lot of people his age seem afraid of commitment, I guess it is not outlaw enough. The toughest men I know are married and walking the line for their family. But to look, talk, and laugh at a titty bar is just good old fashion fun, I told him. I don't know why we never made it to the Beach Beauty Club like the year before with my brother, but at Hooters the chicken wasn't bad. I drove shotgun to Main Street with Big Billet and his old lady, looked for booze instead of a longer primary chain. The two of them didn't drink, so bar hopping was out of the question. I smoked some reefer and limped around holding my kidney with a feeling of remorse that I would not be able to ride the bike home as I intended. I was sad to go home in the U-haul, figuring my plan failed—the mission was half lived.

In the end, I went down my way on that old bird and home my father's way via diesel. I am still not sure if I am a biker. In the end I know my father was with me because if I tried to head north on that '45 it may have killed me and I would definitely not be a biker then? For some reason I felt like my father knew my son and wife need me still and probably said getting there with him on that bike was just fine. I trucked back Sunday morning 16 hours straight through, heard a little Cash on the radio. It was coming down like a couple Sundays at the Boot Hill Saloon with my brother the year before, when we got the call from the Halifax just as we cracked our first can of beer. All in all it was 2,100 miles in four days. Biketoberfest 2003 was a success for me. The Marlboro Man and coffee got me home. I picked up some fire works for the kid at Lucky's. Other than that it was the diesel doctor all the way up 95, a comfortable ride compared to the battle south. Had I really changed in the past 20 years, no not really, am I a real biker, well "no tattoo's, no club." No, no, I can't say that I am a real biker either, just a fan of the proud highway. An independent, like my father; all I could think about on that diesel blazed trail, petal-to-the-metal tear back north was Laconia early summer '04 and meeting up with my brother, and a 101 other places I wanted to go on the road.

AJ's Shovelhead in front of White Knights Garage, Brooklyn

Wes Lang in his studio with his bike built by Keino

Wes Lang

THERE IS A HISTORY TO THE MACHINES WE BUILD AND RIDE AROUND ON

Brooklyn

We rip around the city sometimes. We can get stupid—that's the thing; we go out together and it turns into a race. Absolutely. John [Copeland] taught me how to ride. He can ride the fuck out of a bike. So I learned how to ride with him. So yeah, we ride too fast. The streets are a disaster but that's why it's fun and that's why you do it. The basic principal of why you ride a motorcycle is because of the feeling you get. It is absolutely pure exhilaration. When you add New York into it, the whole thing becomes insane. You almost have to be stupid to do it. But every time, when you are done with your ride, your head is so clear and you feel like a million dollars.

Wes Lang and John Copeland

White Knights

One of the best rides I ever had was with John and Jeffrey and a guy Rich who made that *Free to Wander* movie. We rode up FDR to Dinosaur BBQ and had a big meal. Then we rode down the West Side and fuck, that West Side Highway ride with John was really nice. We killed that thing. We were just fucking hauling ass on a Saturday afternoon.

Our bikes move pretty well, but you are dealing with a primitive technology. A primitive breaking system, a primitive everything. You are not doing 110 mph, but you might as fucking well be. But the people driving cars in the city are fucking idiots. I have seen a friend wreck because this dude flipped a U-turn in the middle of the street right in front of him. The guy hit the curb and my friend had nowhere to go. He ran right into the side of him: T-bone. That was awful seeing something like that happen. But at the same time, you can't think about that kind of thing too much. If you are scared, you are more likely to fuck yourself up. A healthy fear is one thing; being afraid is something different. You can act stupid and really hurt yourself.

You have to pay attention. You are responsible for your bike. Everything is working at once. That is a pretty rare thing for the body to go through. It is like fucking. When you ride a bike around the city, you get a smile on your face this big. It's the greatest thing in the world. Recently I was about to go to Denmark. I went on a ride with John and Jeffrey down to Red Hook to clear my head out. I went back to my apartment and my girlfriend looked at me and said, "Wow, you look like you won the lottery." It's the same fucking feeling.

At times the police become more interested in motorcycles—what kind of helmet you are wearing, your eye protection. They will pull you over and inspect things. A little while ago I was pulled over—he asked for my paperwork. I didn't have my license with me and my insurance papers were for another bike. He looked at me, he looked at my bike, and says, "Have a good day." It goes like that sometimes. Other times you hear from guys where they get a $200 ticket because their eye glasses aren't DOT approved. Who the fuck knows.

Bikes and riding can become complicated in a personal sense. There are nostalgic things going on. A sense of a time line. I bought my bike because it was made the same year I was born. That's as good a reason as any. The bike popped up and I had to buy it. The bike has been good to me. There have been times when I've been afraid, but I worked through that sense of fear and I kept doing it. Riding a bike helps you deal with a lot of shit you don't even realize. I have always been a very confident person and riding has helped me to take that part of myself higher. Having this group of guys to do it with is very important. You can't ask for a better thing. We have similar interests, but everyone can express themselves very differently with their bikes. The gender aspect of it definitely plays a part. It's a macho thing to do. That's not why you do it, but it's definitely a part of it. When we are riding, it's a private thing that we are doing in public.

What could be called the "Private World" of motorcycles and cars has absolutely changed in recent time. During the 1950s this private world was very different than it is today. Back then some guys explored this different world using cars and bikes. This was counterculture—to take an old car or an old bike and change it into something that talked with a new voice. Young people did this in their own way.

Today there is a new sense about what is going on with a lot of young people. Everyone is plugged into some form of personal hand-held technology. Some of this is useful; some of it is a total waste of fucking time. For me, my interest in motorcycles and my artwork is wrapped up all together.

John Copeland working in White Knights Garage

Andy Camay

Wes in his studio

There is absolutely a counterculture aspect to it. I live this shit all the time. I am trying to operate in the most cluster fucking city in the world. For me it is very important to be an individual and to sustain a good lifestyle and make money doing exactly what I want to fucking do. I take no bullshit from anybody and my motorcycle is just another part of this whole mentality.

I am extremely lucky yet I also know that at one point I made a conscious decision at a young age to do this. This is the only thing I ever wanted to do with myself. As a kid when I was in school, I really sucked at that. I am not a schooled person in any way. I never went to art school. When I got out of high school I worked in a tattoo shop. I worked at a dance club, Limelight on 20th Street, during the club kid days. I was a part of that thing.

I grew up in a really, really conservative town in New Jersey. It was a small, ultra-white, WASP town. No Jews, no Blacks, nothing. WASPs and Catholics. That's it. In that town I grew up getting the shit kicked out of me because I was fucking weird. I was always in kind of my own space. Every once in a while I will run into one of the guys who used to fuck with me. Now these guys work in the city. Now they look like piles of shit. It's the classic fucking story. They see me and they want to be nice to me…? It's fucking weird.

A lot of the guys involved in the motorcycle thing are the guys who were involved in skateboarding. That was our anti-social behavior back in those days before we could do this. That was our way to get a thrill back then. A weird thing that kind of bothers me is this new strategy at Harley. They are getting into a new branding thing. They are targeting the 20-something skateboard kids and their sense of alienation. Harley is creating an accessory for them. I understand why they are doing it. That's just the way the corporate world works. It's blatant marketing.

I have a major love for this country. Probably to a fault. A lot of art work that I made is about this country. If you saw what I was working on a couple years ago you would see that I was exploring history. I was retelling the history through tattoo imagery and country music and American symbols—Willie Nelson, Waylon Jennings, George Jones, and that kind of thing. The kind of guys who wouldn't take no for an answer and would do whatever the fuck they wanted to do. I was interested about this kind of attitude as a sense of unique American truth.

Wes' bike in his studio

Wes' bike in his studio

I got into trouble. I did a lot of paintings of old Sambo imagery. Big fucking paintings. I got kicked out of a pretty big show for showing images that people did not like to see. A 14-foot tall golliwog doll. I got kicked out for showing that fucking painting. I just kind of went through that to do what I am doing now. Most of my paintings now are about my friends who have passed away. More of a personal history than American history. I am focusing more on painting than just drawing now.

All of my friends are here together. We are making art. The whole thing is evolving. Motorcycles, pick-up trucks, history, different senses of right and wrong, different cultural senses. Alternative machines that are a part of a set of different values. Different codes. The guys that beat me up in high school had their own set of codes. The guys I hang around with now have their own codes. We don't talk about it but we know. We know that there are other people out there who might share in similar things and that's cool, but it isn't all that necessary for us to meet them. We have ours and they have theirs. We like to keep it small and simple and tight so it doesn't turn into something fucked up. This is intentional. We all just came together at the right time.

We all are creative people who are becoming successful doing this. We are making our mark: Vince, John, Jeffrey, Neil, Keino, Paul. It just came together and fucking happened. We all pretty much work in the same area and we are always kind of around each other. These are my guys and we can depend on each other. That is a very important thing. A lot of people never feel that kind of thing.

New York is a very intense place but it doesn't have to be an uncomfortable place. Life has always been like this. I keep focused. I keep my head straight and focused on what I want to do. I study people I respect and their artwork. I study people whose motorcycles I respect; I study writers who I respect. I focus in on what I respect and I try to believe in myself. We operate in a major city and we have a super small thing going on. We keep it precious and we like it that way.

Yes, there is a history to the machines we ride and work on. Some of it is aesthetic, some of it is physical. Yes, we are reacting to nostalgic things. I own a bike that was made the year I was born. I have an appreciation for my art and my machines and my lifestyle. As a kid I was brought up and supposed to be a certain thing and I was never that thing. The guys I hang around with feel the same way. There just always seemed like there was more we could do, so now we're doing it and we're doing it together. We like machines and the culture and history that surround them. We like it that you can't just go out and buy machines like ours. I am constantly looking through old motorcycle magazines trying to find things. You can spend hours on the Internet looking for things. The prices have become astronomical and this drives you back into your shop to try to make it rather than buy it. For all of the guys there is a huge respect for the history and for this process.

A couple years ago we went out to Sturgis with Keino. If you go to a bike event with Keino you meet a lot of very important guys. One day we took a run out to a horse ranch where there was a BBQ. I ended up sitting down next to a black guy named Sugar Bear. He was there just hanging out in a rocking chair. A very influential 1970s chopper builder. That was very important for me. I started talking with him and his wife. But at the same time there were all these idiot guys behind us riding their bikes through giant piles of horse shit and acting like assholes. The contrast just seemed surreal to me. This contrast is a part of the whole biker thing.

Wes in his studio

Wes painting in his studio

Wes Lang installation, Partners and Spade Gallery, 2011 NYC

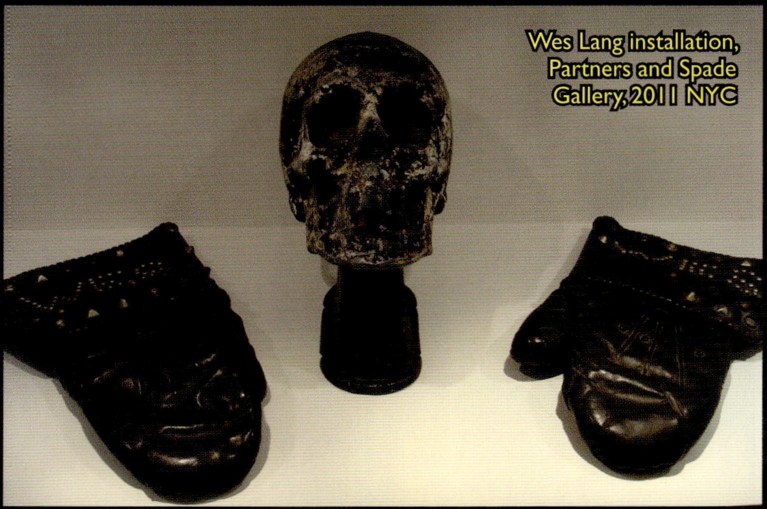
Wes Lang installation, Partners and Spade Gallery, 2011 NYC

Maybe I have only been riding four or five years since I got my first bike. Once I got into it I became very serious about it. The history of motorcycle culture, the history of the machines. This has all become very important to me. At Sturgis when I was talking with Sugar Bear, I was reminded of the traditions and the history of these machines. One thing about machines is that they don't go away too easily. The woods everywhere in America are full of rusting machines.

I am working with Keino now creating a one-of-a-kind motorcycle. This is the ultimate experience for me. I am drawing on all of these memories I have about motorcycles since the first time I saw a motorcycle. I think this is what all these guys do. This is what John and Jeffrey and the other guys do. I have a strong affinity with the late sixties and the seventies about the music, the popular culture, cars, bikes, whatever. This motorcycle is hyper aware of all of the things that were going on at that time. Some of them are cliché like the prism gas tank and the king and queen seat. The raked out front. The 1969 Harley motor and transmission. I intentionally searched out the '69. It has thousands of references to bike culture. So the motor is a reference to bike history and the rest has been handmade by Keino in 2010. This is the process for me. We found that '69 on Craigslist and Keino split the cases on it and the engine was pretty much unscathed. Having that engine was the place I wanted to start and then Keino built something that blew people's minds. These days I am having these dreams of riding a bike with a jockey shift. I remember as a kid I had dreams about driving cars with a stick shift. This continues to be a deep experience. I had this bike made by someone who I respect very much. This is a major part of this bike, too. Taking that trip with Keino to Sturgis was a changing moment for me. After that I saw things in a new way. I rode my Super Glide out there and people were buzzing by on these custom bikes and Keino said I needed a custom motorcycle.

Motorcycles are representative of people who don't want to have anything to do with normal society. And that is important to me. Operating in New York City is different. You have to be really dedicated if you want to have a custom motorcycle in New York. You have to pay for space. Our shop is a collective of guys who made the decision to get the space and put all our tools together so we can work on our projects. It is a very specific subculture. And it's important to us.

Drawing by Wes

Jeffrey working on High Lil' Pony

Jeffrey Schad

WITH MOTORCYCLES THERE IS AN INTERESTING RELATIONSHIP BETWEEN THE PRESENT AND PAST

Brooklyn

Jeffrey's workbench

I am originally from upstate New York and I just turned 33. My dad was mechanically oriented but he was not into cars or motorcycles. He was a tool kind of guy with a nice workshop in the basement. I basically grew up in a country setting and we just made things as we needed them.

I never really worked in metal when I was younger. I learned a lot of this stuff about engines and motorcycles much later on. I didn't learn how to weld until I was around 20. As a kid I was into motorcycles but I grew up in a family where they were shunned because of their safety concerns. One of my dad's best friends had a bad accident and I was never allowed to get one. After I graduated college at Parsons I bought one. I was living in New York at that point and I bought a Sportster off some guy. I brought it up into my loft and took it apart. I was like, "OK, I am going to figure this thing out."

This was probably around 1999–2000, when Indian Larry's shop Gasoline Alley was over on N.14th Street in Williamsburg. He had been at New York Dream Machine on Watts Street in Soho. He had a reputation in New York motorcycle subculture, but this was before all the TV shows. So, stuff that I couldn't do, I brought over to his shop and I met Keino and Paul.

I rode my Sportster down to one of the Horse Smoke-outs in North Carolina. I put all my tools into my backpack with the factory manual. It was pretty uncomfortable and I must have looked strange. Some old biker guys saw me at a rest stop with all my tools on my back and asked what I was doing? They told me to bungee cord them to the back fender. Good idea. I met a bunch of really interesting guys at the event and I ran into Keino and Paul and Larry. I rode back to New York after the event and realized that my Sportster wasn't going to cut it. I needed to make my own bike and I started collecting parts for what became my Root Beer bike. I was probably 22 but I was spending time with those guys and I was learning from them.

I have been at this space on Johnson Ave. in the Bushwick section of Brooklyn for about three years. Before this I was over on Lorimer at the old Rumblers garage with Dan and Eric "Wing Nut" Ahlquist. This is an important creative environment and this is an important group of people here: John Copeland and Neil Fenton and a couple other guys. We are all inclined to build things and there is a wealth of knowledge at this shop. I'll be working on a motor and then the other guys can look at it and we can talk about it.

The guys that I work with are aware of all the TV culture that now surrounds working on machines like hot rods and motorcycles. For some people there is a degree of trendiness. Matthew Crawford's book, *Shop Class is Soul Craft*, has codified this kind of thing for the mainstream. Most of the guys I know have been into motorcycles before this massive bubble of interest blew up.

From a value standpoint, all this trendy interest has inflated the market extremely. It is now harder to get hold of certain things than it was before. Now there is a whole subculture of motorcycles. They are definitely cool machines.

There is a crossover world of skateboarding to motorcycles. I skated pretty much my whole early life. As kids who were skateboarders back in the early '80s, we had a sense of the counterculture that was a part of why we skateboarded. The punk and hardcore music that surrounded it was a big part of the subculture. Everyone started to get tattooed. We started to tattoo each other and that became a part of the whole thing, too. We explored music, tattoos, and motorcycles out of a sense of friendship and all of this became a part of our personal sense of expression. Myself and the other guys in this space do not make motorcycles to sell them. We don't do work for other people. This is not that kind of thing because we all do other things to make money. We don't build motorcycles as our trade. We do it for other creative reasons.

There is something very mechanical about building a motorcycle. I do not consider them to be art objects. For me it's a mechanical thing and the process of building one is very methodical and also very meditative. For example, you work on a lathe and you are cutting ten-thou at a time. You have to make a hundred passes to make one change and it takes four hours. It is very calming. Working like this creates a balance in my creative life. For me I am interested in making my motorcycles work as well as possible and also look as beautiful as possible.

The guys I know are now talking about making a new drag bike but making it show quality. Something that will look impressive but also set a speed record at the strip. Between Keino and Paul and John and everybody, we have been talking about doing a project like that. For me, some of the motorcycle stuff has become a little too precious. Especially the vintage stuff. It has become very precious and very hard to get a hold of. So I wonder about playing with that sense of preciousness. Taking a $10,000 Knucklehead motor and making it go very fast. If it blows up, it blows up. Do you think that somebody in the '50s would care about blowing up that motor? Maybe not. That's what they were working with. I like the idea of taking a bit of that preciousness out of it.

Years ago, when guys worked on something like a motorcycle they did it inside a small, closed community. There was no wealth of information. Maybe a guy knew a guy who knew a guy. This has changed today, but I think one of the reasons we get

Jeffrey working

Jeffrey working

Jeffrey Schad (L) and John Copeland (R) at their Brooklyn garage with their bikes

into this is for that same feeling of private community and private knowledge. The best and most valuable information is still passed word of mouth. I think that this still exists and I know that this process is what interests us about working on machines. There is a wealth of oral history that a builder like Krazy Kevin had and he passed it on to us. I know that process is exciting to all the guys that work in this garage.

We're here now and we're younger and we're building these bikes in our style and we get to learn about how this has been done before us. For us this goes beyond some momentary trendy situation. We are interested in learning about this process and appreciating it.

New York does not necessarily have a historical reputation for its machines. People do not necessarily make that association but that's not correct. There is a history and a style and a sensibility about machines in New York City. Its deep and its private and it goes back.

For example, when I first bought my '66 I was looking for an Electra Glide. I found this flat side Shovel with a DC carb. It had a seat with a scroll back rest. So I went over to Harley to get some parts for it and that's where I met Krazy Kevin. I told him about the bike and he instantly lit up. He was like cool, a young guy riding an old bike. He saw the bike at some point and noticed the metal scroll on the seat. He knew it had been made by a guy who was a member of one of the old Puerto Rican clubs in Brooklyn.

When you talk with a guy like Kevin you immediately know that New York has a deep but private history of machines. There were different types of stylization by different people and clubs that lived in different sections of the city. There were guys in the Bronx that drilled out their Kelsey Hayes rims Swiss cheese style. They had a very particular style. In New York there are these chunks of history. In the Bronx or Brooklyn in the '60s there were these clubs and then in the '80s there was Larry and Steg and that crew at Psycho Cycles.

That's one of the reasons John and I started the Brooklyn Invitational show in 2009. We wanted to get back to something and create our own scene. At that point we got all the guys together: Wes Lang, Paul, and Keino and we talked with all of our friends and we tried to plan it out. We thought maybe 500 people would come but 3,000 people showed up. Then this year [2010], 4,500 hundred people showed up. People came in from Japan, France, Belgium, the Netherlands, Brazil. It was a powerful event.

For the most part I enjoy working with a Harley Davidson. I have worked with other kinds of bikes like Triumph but I focus my work on Harley. For me, and I know for many other people, there is an interest in Harley as an American machine that has an important past. The design, engineering, history, and culture have a folklore connected with them. I definitely think about issues of the preservation of an aspect of American history when I work on my bikes.

I have been accumulating knowledge about these bikes for maybe the past 12 years and I guess in a way I am conscious of my decisions when I build something. I have chosen certain kinds of styles and designs to use when I am working on a bike. I am definitely giving an historical nod to a specific era. There are people who have built things that I respect. There is a mythology to

Bike with scroll seat rail (L)

The Rootbeer bike parked under surfboards in garage

The Rootbeer Bike: engine is a 96c.i. S&S with a Bob Woods cam, high compression pistons, and head work done by Hillside Cycle.

High Lil'Pony: matching numbers front loop and engine 1969 Triumph 650cc. Rear loop hand-fabricated and chromed 3 inches shorter than stock. Front end is a highly modified showa 39mm. Country bar and seat tube hand fabricated. Exhaust, controls and sissy bar hand fabricated. Oil tank handmade by Keino. Seat made by Paul Cox and paint by Vincent Szarek

these machines and it is interesting for me to see the bikes that guys are making in a place like the Netherlands for example. They are making very specific 1960s Americana period style bikes. These are not accidental looking machines. It is very deliberate and researched and formalized. Then of course in Japan everyone is into the super vintage, really rare stuff. They will look for really obscure rare parts. Personally, I do not fetishize parts that much, but that's just a different point of view.

Only recently have I felt like my builds are a part of some kind of continuum. I have become more aware of the process as I have gotten to know people like Keino and Paul who have an historical background in New York City motorcycle culture and history. I am also aware of being a part of a generational thing where people my age are working on these machines for certain reasons. I think that we are keeping the continuum going in our own ways.

But I don't over think that whole thing. Yes, I am making my bikes in certain ways for certain reasons, but ultimately the greatest satisfaction is being able to ride them. Ultimately, that is the only reason I know any of us in this shop make them.

There is something particular about being an American and there is something particular about being in New York City. There is definitely something particular about riding one of our bikes in New York City. Guys look at us riding our bikes and they say, "That is definitely a New York City style bike." And a lot of it comes from Larry and Steg and the guys at Psycho. If you read some of those old *Iron Horse* articles about why they built certain things the way they did—you gotta have good brakes and you gotta go fast. You gotta build them strong so they won't fall apart on the BQE. All these things.

These were functional decisions that resulted in the formation of a style and an aesthetic. I think it started out as complete functionality and it morphed into a way that these particular machines look. In that aspect we are carrying on this niche aesthetic of New York City bikes. You can say, "I know that southern California bikes look like this and that New York City bikes look how they look." There are people who know how to connect the dots and know why certain bikes look the way they do. I am aware that the bikes that I make are a part of a lineage of design. So yes, the guys at this garage understand this and we are learning and interacting and we are aware of the question of lineage.

Sometimes this is a conscious way of doing things and sometimes it an osmosis thing. For me, I live and work and ride in New York City and I am surrounded with certain things that influence me whether I realize it or not. I take these things in but I am not necessarily thinking and doing things based on this knowledge. The decisions just naturally flow in certain ways for me because I am doing it in New York City.

The whole information thing has changed about bikes. Back in the '60s, bikes were material forms of traveling

Jeffrey relaxing in garage

Panhead built by Jeffrey

information. Guys traveled back and forth across the country and the styles traveled with them. Now of course there is the Internet and information about bikes travels differently and people pick up on that. There are two ways to look at it—instead of riding across the country and sharing the information that way, now you can e-mail and everyone has blogs. This is interesting because through the Internet you are introduced to more people who will come to visit you or you will go to visit them. As things are shared on the Internet, connections between people grow.

This year so many people came to the Invitational show from all over. We had six bikes from LA and Max rode from Oakland and that's the thing that is really exciting about being connected together through the Internet. It is acting as a catalyst to physically connect people. One of the greatest benefits of the Internet is in its power to create a resource base. It has become a great archive of history and also the present.

With motorcycles there is this interesting relationship between the present and the past. How you are going to make something now and the process of that making as it has been informed by the past. A lot of this has been figured out so you follow in certain footsteps. For example, Harley Davidson figured out a long time ago that a 30-degree rake worked well. To alter the geometry of that is a stylistic decision. If you are going to really ride your bike and you want it to perform well you are going to stick to what they figured out. Guys have certainly changed the rake and trail over the years with different stylistic ideas. Back in the '70s, bikes with longer front ends stood up in the front. That was the look for that period of time.

You go back to Denver's Choppers and Lil' Freddie Hernandez, they were running thirty over tubes with no suspension and that was the style of that day. I suppose we are kind of doing the same kind of stylistic thing here in Brooklyn. John and I talk a lot about this issue of style. For us there is a subtleness of clean lines and that is one of the harder things to do. It is so easy to go overboard. When you keep a sense of restraint in motorcycles, it comes off as not being really wild, but people who know what it takes to create something like that find the restraint more impressive.

Schad and Copeland bikes parked out front

When I was trying to do the pipes for Vince's Triumph I knew I wanted high shot gun pipes and I knew it would be a bitch to weld those pipes perfectly straight with an eighth inch gap between the two—to make them parallel, straight, and level. It's difficult to do and it is more difficult to do than some wild pipe design. But that is the look I wanted and that is a New York City look which goes back to Larry and his early bikes. That aesthetic goes back to the decisions he made about simplicity and functionality—super minimal, built to go but also very aesthetic and very intentional. This is a part of some tradition that I feel is important. Pipes like that take ten times longer to make but that's the way I wanted to make them.

I definitely get sentimental about my machines. When I build a bike it might take me more than a year. It gets exhausting. I get into the garage and 12 hours later I notice that its 12 hours later. The question of the bike as an art form definitely comes up. Motorcycles and cars are now being shown in galleries and one thing I think about is how are we supposed to contextualize this? I don't necessarily think about it like that but if you want to put my motorcycles into a gallery, well then go ahead; it's a piece of art. If you want to ride it on the highway, well then it's a vehicle.

This goes back to our Brooklyn Invitational bike show. We are all artists and we created an environment that showcased these things in a different way. We are informed by our day jobs and then of course we are bringing this artistic sensibility to this part of our lives where we are making motorcycles. Some people might be sensitive to this and say, "Hey, you guys are just gentrifiers." And that discussion could go on forever. For me, I see us making our bikes by hand and I would rather let the bikes speak for themselves. I like the history to these bikes and I guess you can say nostalgia if you want. But I like working on them and keeping them going and I like doing this in New York City. The guys working in this garage are totally aware of New York and its access to history. It can get overwhelming so you have to be selective. We are aware of having a small community of friends who feel the same way and work together and support each other.

Neil Fenton in his workshop, winter 2010, 36°F

Neil Fenton

I LIKE THE SOLITARY THING OF BEING ON TWO WHEELS

Brooklyn

I've been seriously building things for the last five years. I have been learning about the things I need to know to make bikes. Learning to weld is an example—you can't make things like a gas tank if you don't know how to weld. Sheet metal is an important material to know how to manipulate. You can't make things out of it if you don't have the skills. If you are serious about making motorcycles, all these abilities are a part of the learning.

As a kid I surfed and skated and did some BMX and tried not to have a job. We'd compete with each other on bikes and boards. We'd steal wood from construction sites and make ramps and jumps. Basically, I always had the cheapest cars available and I had to work on them myself because I never had any money. I always liked old cars. Having a nice looking car or a fancy one was not a priority. I liked to design things but basically I needed a machine just to get places. I did not cherish my car and make it all pretty. I needed it to get to the beach.

We were all racing around using a minimum of things. A BMX bike, a surf board, a skateboard. We weren't using a lot to get around. It got more complicated when we wanted cars and bikes. I got a Vespa and made it so I could go about 65 miles an hour. I told my mom it only went 40. She was nervous. I was attracted more to two wheels than four. I could maneuver better through traffic and get around better. I also like the solitary thing of being on two wheels. You can ride with other people, but you don't need a whole team to get something done.

You can skate by yourself or you can meet up with some people. You have the option to be on your own. This is one thing I like about being on a bike. I don't have a radio. When I ride I talk to myself. It becomes a solitary thing. You are removed, you are thinking about things.

I remember my first skateboard had ball bearings and clay wheels. I remember taking a wheel apart and all the ball bearing went all over the place. As a kid I took a lot of things apart and I didn't always get them back together. My dad had a garage full of junk. I was always taking everything apart. I would find bicycles in a trash can and fix them up and sell them to kids in the neighborhood. I just like taking things apart.

My dad was an accountant and then he got into making boat docks. He liked fixing things, but the family car was always breaking

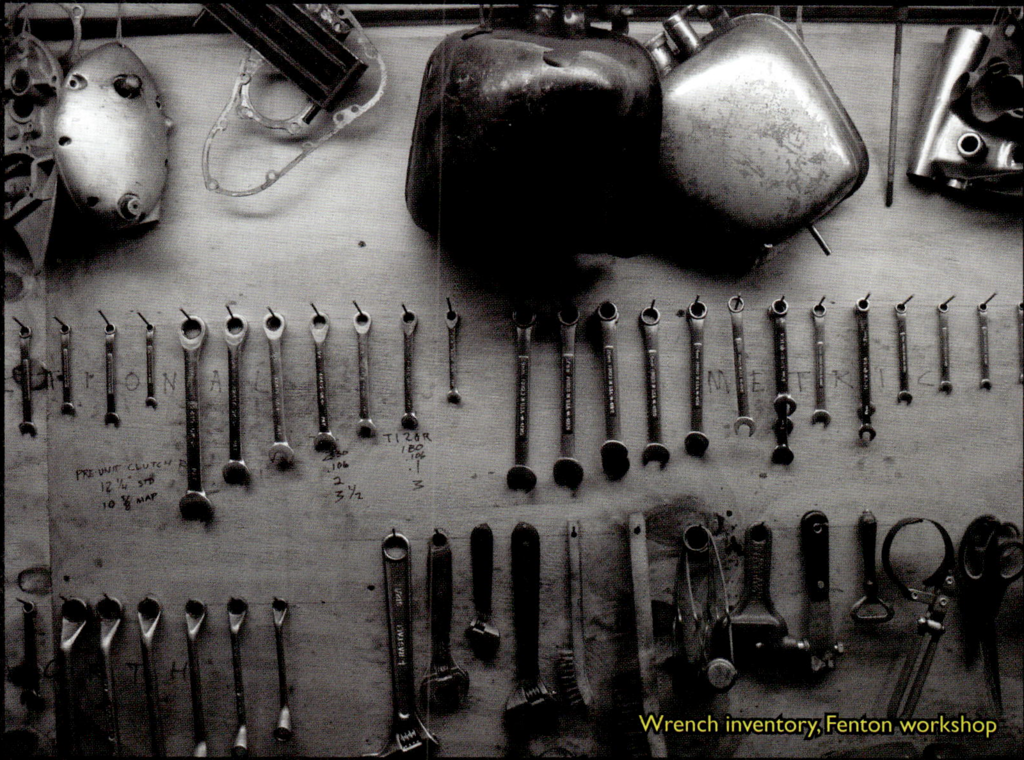

Wrench inventory, Fenton workshop

Fenton Brit bike project

Parts inventory, Fenton workshop

Neil Fenton

down. As a kid I was always thinking, "*Why didn't he bring it to the mechanic?*" But his attitude was, the mechanic doesn't know what he's doing, why not fix it myself. When I was 17, my VW bus would break down. My dad would say, "Here's some wrenches, here's a book—fix it." I slowly learned about these things.

I would run into people and look at what they were working on. I learned that some people have a better eye and a better way of doing things. I have been working at this garage for about eight years. It has changed a few times. People coming in and moving out. I like working on American machines. I have a few British bikes that I have worked on over the years. I like them both. Somebody said that the big Harley is your wife and the Triumph is your mistress. They are both fun for different reasons.

If it's crowded, the Harley is a pain in the balls to move around the city, but the Triumphs are a lot of fun moving through traffic. In the city it's one thing to have an expensive custom Harley but do you want to park it in front of your apartment at night? Most of the guys I ride with or do work for ride their Triumph around the city. They park them on the street and they get dented and knocked down. But if you worry too much about something, well maybe you can't afford to own it. I don't worry about my old Harley too much.

Motorcycles have become a bit trendy lately. I think some of this has to do with the TV shows that focus on some aspect of this. This has opened up the sensibility. People are impressed with things that are hand done. A percentage of people like something that is built by hand. A percentage of people rebel against mass produced life. There is something to be said about hand made things. Yeah, there are machines that can crank out things one after the next. These things work well and are reliable, but there is something impressive about something that is one-of-a-kind and handmade. Like with a surfboard. There are board shapers who learned from older board shapers and these boards are the best. These sensibilities move around and go back and forth. With making machines, there are the guys who like the whole CNC machining process and then there are the guys who say, "No, I don't want to use a CNC machine."

In my work I am thinking about these kinds of things and how it affects my process. I am striving to get the things I work on to be good but I still take into consideration that my abilities are not great yet. I am learning and will probably always be learning. I still think a lot about both sides of the making process. When I am making things I am sensitive to knowing when to keep going on something and then also when to say, "OK, it's time to stop; that's enough." I might spend six months working on things to get it as perfect as I can and then other guys might accomplish this in a couple days because they've been doing it for 30 years.

The motorcycles I make are a collection of decisions. It's like this for anybody who makes things. I see certain things on my bikes that you wouldn't see. Why would you see them? You are not intimate with the process of making this thing. For example, on one of my bikes I recently finished the fork stops and they were not my favorite thing on there. I should have done something before I painted the bike. For me it represents a compromise. For you? You don't even notice what I am talking about.

Most people are not sensitive about making things. Most people just buy things. But for people who are sensitive to the process of making, they have paid attention to other makers. Or maybe they had a teacher. And this teacher has showed them how to do something properly. You don't just go out and throw something together. You have been taught a process and techniques. This way, when you do break the rules, at least you understand what you have done.

For me, it is important to learn about form— to understand about making good forms and then manipulating these forms. Like with a gas tank on a bike—there are definitely certain shapes I like but I want to appreciate these forms and to know about them and where they came from. For me, this kind of knowledge is an important part of the making process. I am not at a place where I want to make some crazy gas tank shape. At this point I don't need for my things to scream out CUSTOM. This kind of impulse is not important to me right now. I am more interested in things that are more mellow or nuanced. Not, "Wow, look at that crazy gas tank!" I don't want to make things that scream at you. I like the idea of making things that have a dialogue with people who might know about bikes. There are certain kinds of people who I want to appreciate what I make.

Fenton bike

Neil Fenton

Fenton workshop

Walt Siegl Ducati build at 2010 Brooklyn Invitational

Walt Siegl Ducati build at 2010 Brooklyn Invitational

Walt Siegl Ducati build at 2010 Brooklyn Invitational

Walt Siegl

The history of this whole thing means something to me. If you think that you came up with all of this stuff by yourself you are kidding yourself. It's been done and you just don't know about it. I don't like it when people do knock-offs, but there is nothing wrong with being inspired by different things. A complete knock-off just to make money is bullshit, but if there's something you like, chances are you won't make it the exact way anyways. I really like Hugh's [Mackie] race bikes. They are beautiful because they are functional. Walt Siegl is someone I look at. Everything he makes is done so well. Cole Foster is also somebody I pay attention to. These builders are important to me. I pay attention to the way they use form.

I always thought the paint jobs on old dragsters were very appealing. The letters were big and the car bodies were long. It was a lot more graphic and that has always interested me. As a kid I'd sit and watch drag racing on Wide World of Sports and that whole thing just impressed me. I lived in California and of course I saw Mexican Lowriders with crazy paint jobs. But I was into BMX bikes and they get thrown around a lot and all scratched up so that influenced me not to get too precious about things. Like when I finish painting a tank, I wouldn't be too happy if somebody scratched it, but then again, there is a sense of relief when something like that finally happens and the whole thing isn't precious any more.

With me, this whole issue of preciousness has something to do with me as a kid when I was surfing. You'd get a new surfboard and it's your most precious thing and you surf like a pussy and then as soon as you get one ding in it and you repair it, this changes things and then you are really ready to surf. You are way looser and you don't care anymore.

There is something going on now in New York with people building machines. People know about the guys in this garage. People know we are making bikes. We make bikes here and then they go off to different places. I'm finishing up a project and then it will go out to California. I will ride it around here a little but ultimately it isn't going to be seen here too much. There is definitely something going on here now in New York. The nature of the streets influences the way we all make things. It's nice to have something compact so you can get through traffic. It's nice to have brakes. There's a whole thing here about the cost of living. It's so expensive to live here. This changes the nature of New York machines. You see a lot of old Harleys. There are probably a lot more Triumphs because of Hugh [Mackie]. Everybody's bikes get beat up. Parking on the street brings in a whole new thing. But there are a lot of Ducatis and KTMs. They get parked in the street and they get beat up, too. That's just the way it is.

This area of Brooklyn is a mix of industry and artists. It is a good place to have a garage. These are the people I hang out with and I'm productive with. We trade off skills and share ideas. But for the same reason I got into skateboarding and surfing, I am not really a part of a group or anything like that. It's just a group of friends. I have never really had heroes or things I identify with. I have never been a member of a club or a team of any kind. But it means something to me to work in a space with these guys and we all do great stuff together.

I like old style stuff. In the old days, if you had a bike you learned how to work on it because it might be a hundred miles to the dealership. So, you learned how to do things. Sometimes I really start dwelling on things. I think about the shapes of these machines. There is a sensuality to them. It is overt and also subconscious. I mean, what's a motor? It's a lung. It breathes, and if you think about it, the whole thing is based on

Neil Fenton repairing upholstery sewing machine

an animal. You need fuel, you need energy; it needs to breathe and it transfers that energy. It propels itself. These things are beautiful. You can see everything on it. The old ones had all these shapes and curves to them. These shapes didn't necessarily need to be there but it looked nice.

During the past year my attitude about all this has changed a little. Before, I was learning how to make everything, and now that I can actually make a few things, I am concentrating on how they should really look—the flow and the form. I see myself progressing. I don't know, maybe I am just getting older.

Neil Fenton, summer 2010

John Copeland

I ADMIRE THE PROCESS OF HISTORY AND THE EFFECT OF TIME ON MACHINES

Brooklyn

John Copeland in his garage space

Of course there is some correlation with my painting and my motorcycles. I tend to build up the surfaces on my paintings. There is physicality to them. I have ideas of where I want the surface to go. It is process oriented for me. I am interested in and sensitive to the process of making things. In a way, for me, there are similarities between the processes of building a bike and making a painting. With a bike maybe there is an issue of function and form, but I think there is also an issue of content and thinking about the process. A lot of the making of things, whether it's a painting or a motorcycle involves making something and then stepping back and deciding what's going on.

I admire the process of history and the effect of time on machines. Motorcycle designs just didn't materialize out of thin air. They are the product of a historical process. I only really work on and build old stuff. I've never owned a bike that was newer than 1978. For me there is a lot to see in the development of these machines. It is important for me to be aware of what has been done before. There is definitely an evolution of what people have done. There is that process of how people respond to the forms and then push them in certain ways. For a while all these people were doing these really wide-tire bikes, then they moved on to something else. A lot of trends, people push them to the extreme and then go back to the middle. The fact that a bike needs to work puts a certain set of limitations on it.

Bikes certainly have traditions and a set of forms and a vocabulary just in terms of the parts they use. A lot of the things that I do are traditional in some way, and most of the bikes I like are from the late '50s to the early '70s. My Panhead is a '59 and my Shovel is a '67. The dual-carb Pan-Shovel is a mix of years. The generator bottom ends are probably my favorite. I'm not doing restorations, and basically, anything could provide a good basis to start a custom bike, but I have been stuck on the old Harley stuff for awhile. Maybe I'll end up doing newer stuff soon, I don't know. I'm not opposed to doing a newer motor, but I like this early time period. There are all sorts of things you can do with a motorcycle in terms of fabrication, and the motor, but you have to start somewhere. I am not going to build from absolute scratch, make my own cases. At least not yet. Most everyone starts from something.

These days I am pretty much working with Harley Davidsons but I have built a lot of Triumphs. When I was fifteen my uncle got me an old Jap bike—a Suzuki GS 750E that some guy had tried to outrun the cops on. It was impounded and he'd gotten it at a police auction. It didn't run, so I worked on that till I figured it out; taught myself to ride it. I just wanted to ride and wrenching on 'em was just as fun. I used to take my bicycles apart, too, same mentality. Repair, reconfigure, make it your own. That Suzuki was my first bike. I forged my parent's signature on my learner's permit. I wanted to get into a Harley or a British bike but there was always a money issue.

In high school I had taken all the art classes available and I also took all the auto shop classes they offered. The shop class was a work training type thing. Two hours every morning and then you had to set up an internship. So I got them to let me do the internship at a local independent Harley shop. Two mechanics and an owner; it was called Two Wheels. These guys ran on old bikes. I worked there for a while but I was just a kid. But being around it and listening to those guys, I learned what I could. Right before I left for college, Fred Wright, the older mechanic at the shop pulled me aside and said he wished I wasn't leaving. He wanted to really teach me everything I needed to know. I was honored he had asked me; as much as I wanted to stay, I had already made the decision to go to art school, and needed to get the fuck out of where I grew up. Both those guys had gone to Art Center in the '60s. I moved to Oakland that summer, I went to school in Oakland/San Francisco and after finishing my degree I moved out here to New York. I got rid of the Suzuki when I moved, bought a Triumph and redid that a few times. Then Neil [Fenton] and I got another Triumph to build up and sell. A long, 9-foot chopper, girder fork, big devil tail sissy bar; it was a funny bike.

We started buying cheap Triumph projects, building them out and selling them to pay for some of the bigger tools—a TIG welder and a milling machine. I started getting more and more into fabrication.

John Copeland's garage bay

John Copeland working

John Copeland's arms

John Copeland working on 2010 build

Neil Fenton

After I got my Panhead, I started working more and more with the H-Ds. I had always had my eyes on Harleys. My high school girlfriend's uncle had a '61 Panhead, rigid frame, super traditional '60s chopper. For me at the time, that was the coolest thing I had ever seen. And when I worked at that Harley shop both Fred and Mike were heavy into the older machines. Lots of Evos in the shop for repair, but their personal rides were mostly Pans and Knuckles. They rode them every day to work. I was obsessed with this yellow Knuckle Fred had. Mike used to talk about the shapes in the motor, polished aluminum over chrome. So that's probably where I started being fascinated with that era of machines. It was just a matter of eventually doing well enough so I could buy something to start with. Triumphs are incredible motorcycles and great for bombing around the city but not as optimal for long distance rides. Visually, the Harley is a more beautiful motor for me. It's bigger and there's a lot more you can do with it. They fit me a little better physically—the size of the motorcycle.

Part of what I enjoy about working on bikes is the literalness of it. It is creative but it is a different animal. I don't have to worry about what it's trying to say in any direct psychological way. It's just building a bike. I want it to look a certain way proportionally but there is also a function to it. It has to work. And I really enjoy the engineering of it. Either it works or it doesn't. There isn't as much of the banging one's head against the wall that can happen with art. There's plenty of things you can do for a look but they've also gotta function.

I like building motors. Figuring it out and designing parts. The problem solving aspect of it is totally different than working on something like a painting. If something isn't running right I have to figure out why. There is a tangible or literal reason for everything. It's not some abstract thing to work through. There are aesthetic questions about the look of a bike, but it's a lot simpler, do you like it, does it all work together, does it take away or add to the bike? Motor combinations, trying new things, I enjoy pushing those boundaries when I can. I like trying to do things that haven't been done, but you know it's all been done one way or another. But that's not an excuse to stop. You can always push something further.

Bikes can change a lot as you're doing 'em; sometimes what you thought would work is terrible once you've gotten into actually seeing it on the bike. In terms of ideas, I make a lot of things and some of them get changed and some of them go into the scrap pile. I try to challenge myself with certain things, just trying to keep learning. That's the nice thing about machining, fabrication, motors, there is always more to lean; you can always get better at something. The more you learn, the more you realize there is to it. It's a good challenge to keep moving with 'em, I can't keep doing the same thing over and over again. Both mechanically or aesthetically. That Triumph I had, I think I changed it at least six times. I changed my Panhead a lot of different ways, too. Everyone has their tastes though, and that evolves as well.

For me, this process of changing things can be very subjective. Something looks wrong—a sense of proportion. I guess that I have developed a style with the bikes that I build in one way or another. The Shovelhead I bought is pretty much a bone stock '67 Shovel. And I am slowly starting to redo things on that. I can't fucking leave that thing alone, but I guess it's that way with everything. If something looks too bulky or heavy or it doesn't perform right and makes it sluggish, or out of tune—it's got to go. That's the chopper sensibility.

This sense of the chopper has changed over the years. Particularly now that information travels so quickly. It has good and bad aspects. I've met a lot of good people. But I try not to pay too much attention to what else is out there, I do the same thing with my work. It can be trouble, being too conscious of what other people are doing. It can affect your decision making.

With a chopper there are a limited number of elements: frame, motor, gas tank, oil tank, brakes, handle bars. The way all those things balance. But there are myriad ways to do it. That's what I think I love about bikes. Seeing what people do with this basic form. There is just something that looks kind of right about a bike. A lot of people try to push things as far as they can for the sake of doing it, the biggest wheel, or the longest fork or whatever, it's all a kind of balancing act for it to work. There are a lot of people out there with fabricating talent, but they have no fucking taste. This is not to say I think I have great taste, of course that is a really subjective thing to say, but there is a lot of horrible shit in the motorcycle world. There is more horrible than great. I guess it's that way with most things.

There are particulars about American machines. Harleys and Indians and domestic bikes are a lot different than European bikes for a reason. The roads are different, there is a different terrain; things are more spread out here. I think this contributed to the development. A lot of guys will say, "Yeah, I want to get a bike and ride across the country." This sounds good, but to actually do it is a whole different thing; long distance takes a lot of endurance. I really like riding late at night. I get on my bike and ride around the island some nights, just to clear my head. That's part of what I love about motorcycles, when you are riding, you are totally in the moment. You have to fucking pay attention or you're gonna get killed. Best way I can describe it to people is like bombing hills on a skateboard. When I lived in SF we did a lot of that. You're going too fast to stop and you've gotta have a line picked out, expecting everyone who can to pull out in front of you. Riding a bike is kind of like that. You are in the moment. You are not thinking about your problems.

I don't really make bikes for other people. I have done it in the past, but that's not the reason I build motorcycles. I mostly just do it for myself. I have a tendency to be a perfectionist and it can get a little nuts. I take my time to do everything to my standard. I would find the process too consuming if I was building for other people. It would become endless, and there is something nice about not having to compromise, not having to build something to suit anyone else. I ride with a small group of guys. We share ideas and tech things between us. These are very important and creative relationships. I am very happy that this has evolved but that wasn't always the case. Neil [Fenton] was the only other guy I knew with a bike and we became friends. Slowly, over the years other friends have gotten bikes. Wes [Lang] got a bike a few years ago and Jeffro [Jeffrey Schad] had been doing his own thing and then he came into our shop. I only got to know Keino and Paul well over the last few years. In the past it was always more of a private thing—people doing it on their own in small garages and shops.

This is why the WKITHOK crew and the Brooklyn Invitational show we put together are so important to us. We are all into this in a personal way and felt like no one else was doing anything, so we might as well put together a proper bike show. This is not a club or an MC at all. We're just all good friends. We all have this one thing in common: riding and building these bikes. Hanging out.

This is how the Brooklyn Invitational Show came together. I was working at the shop while Jeffro was there working and we started talking about just doing our own show. At the time there wasn't any local

Meeting of the White Knights about 2010 Brooklyn Invitational event

bike event happening any longer. We saw it as a great way for people to showcase their projects and to showcase some of the talented people we had met. We also wanted to make a statement about New York and the East Coast, at least for the first show. Feature people who we respect. We kind of curated it the same way we would curate an art show. We wanted to maintain some control over what was going on. Who we think is doing good work. The motorcycle thing here was and is very small, at least it seems that way. It has really only become popular in the last few years. The TV shows and all that has increased the interest in motorcycles. But in New York there are really only a handful of custom shops. I like that its small and I like going on rides with friends. New York is hard; it's a fucking chore to keep everything going—pay rent. It's expensive. Our group of guys helps us to stay clear about things; good friends are really important. There's some healthy competition with bikes which

Copeland and Schad builds parked out front of garage

Jeffrey Schad and John Copeland in front of garage

John Copeland, 2009 Panhead build

John Copeland, 2010 Shovelhead build

keeps it fun. This is New York. People come here to do their thing, and there are a lot of talented people here. That's what I like about our garage. The people who work here are talented, motivated, and ambitious. We aren't sitting around watching TV. We are doing something.

I like that small scene here in New York. We have found a group of like-minded people. I don't think about it so much as being privatized but there's something about the process of learning about bikes and the way they work that you have to come to yourself. A sensibility. And I think that to do this correctly means it's going to take time. Today, everything is immediate. Life is based on immediacy. What's in, what's trendy. I'll get these fucking shoes and this fucking bike. But for these people there is no sense of spending time and figuring things out. For me it's all about the learning process of figuring things out. Like my paintings—they look the way they do because I have been making paintings for fifteen years. The way these paintings look is a part of something. They wouldn't look like this without the work that went before them. I have been making decisions over those years. It's the same with my bikes. I make them based on what I have been learning and making over the years. Trying things out and making things that did and didn't always work. There is something to be said about taking the time to learn this stuff. It's not about the impulse to show off. That's not what it is about for me. I share it with a couple like-minded guys and leave it at that.

I keep a bunch of old design templates around. I have a few of French curves that I look at from time to time. These are templates of very graceful curves that people have used for making engineering or architectural drawings. Years ago when you would be sitting down making a drawing of a motor or a casting, these templates were a set of matched proportions in terms of scale and measurement. I am definitely sensitive to the issue of form; particularly when it comes to working on old motors. Yes, we can change and modify things for our specific purposes, but we are stuck with these old transmissions and motors. And there is something really beautiful about the proportions of these old motors. I do feel that the subtleties of these shapes and proportions have become slightly lost over the years. Industrial design from the late twenties to the seventies has always been very interesting to me. You look at an old Harley motor and the way the case has been shaped is very old world. The tolerances, the way the casting has little lips and flourishes. The weight of the case metal. It's as thin as it can be.

Chopper Dave Super Freak Panbead, photo taken at 2010 Brooklyn Invitational event

Chris Lindig Shovelhead, photo taken at 2010 Brooklyn Invitational event

Jeffrey Schad's High Lil' Pony: Triumph 650cc, photo taken at 2010 Brooklyn Invitational event

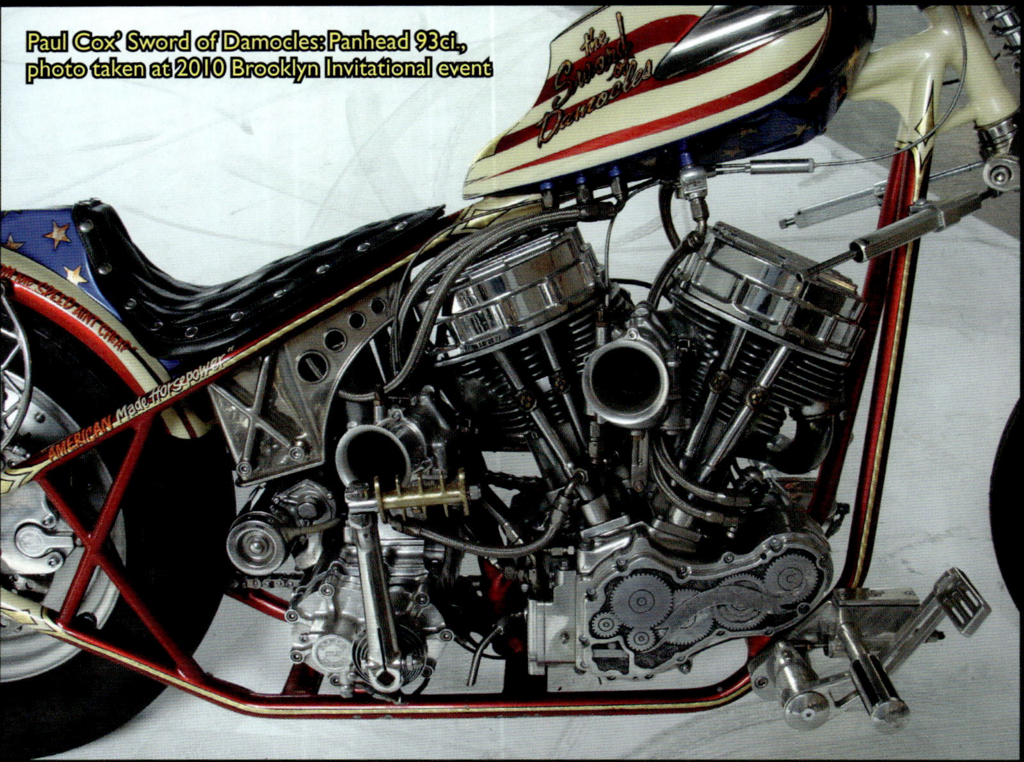

Paul Cox' Sword of Damocles: Panhead 93ci., photo taken at 2010 Brooklyn Invitational event

Max Schaaf Shovelhead, photo taken at 2010 Brooklyn Invitational event

Nowadays, with a new production motor, the shapes and designs look computer generated to me. These old engines have some soul to them. You can see the hand. You can see that hands have designed and made them. These motors have been around for a while in various forms. I like the fact that the motorcycles started with drawings. Somebody was working on a piece of paper and shaping actual materials. Even though it's machined, there are a lot of organic qualities to these motors. And this isn't quite the same with the newer motors. You can still build a beautiful bike around an Evo motor, but the old stuff is closer to my sensibility. The stuff I make feels right to me. Even as a kid I always gravitated to the older things. Growing up in California there isn't that much that is really old.

I love old buildings, old machinery, all this kind of stuff. My grandmother had an antique shop when I was a kid. I have always been curious about old things. I don't want to get romantic; it's just what I like. These kinds of things look like somebody cared about it and made it. It's not perfect. As much as we all strive to make these things perfect, they are never perfect. They are made by hand and there are things that are not exact.

I'm trying to attain a balance in the things that I make. The paintings and the motorcycles. My motorcycle projects are about forms and being able to experiment with things. Developing my eye is one of the most important things to me. There is structure going on in my work. I am sensitive to using form in a certain way. Little details. When I am making something, I know when it feels right. If something is a hair off, I'll work till its right. I don't know, you can drive yourself crazy, but that's part of the whole deal. The pipes on my bike look right to me. On a different bike they might look stupid. I like subtle details in things. There is a sense of general form and proportion that is really

Mike Davis Panhead, photo taken at 2010 Brooklyn Invitational event

Matt Davis Panhead, photo taken at 2010 Brooklyn Invitational event

Shinya Kimura Knucklehead, photo taken at 2010 Brooklyn Invitational event

John Copeland in his painting studio

important to me. If something is a little too big, a little off, people won't notice it but that shit drives me fucking insane. I guess this kind of thing is difficult to nail down and I don't know where it comes from, but it is important to me. I guess this kind of thing develops over time. Different people and influences. This kind of thing evolves with us as people.

New York City is a very important place, in terms of working on my bikes and art, for a lot of reasons. There is a group of people out there working on things and we don't necessarily know each other or each other's names, but it is important for me to know that they are out there. It is important for me to be around people who are motivated. All the guys in this garage feel the same way. We have a friendly and respectful camaraderie and sense of competition. It's healthy and fun because everyone respects each other. Being in New York, surrounded with old buildings and the streets and the history matters to me; even if not in any literal sense. If we were in some gray, generic, industrial building that was built three years ago I don't think it'd feel quite the same. The visual appeal of a place like New York is very important. There was a standard when New York was built; I don't know, but it seems like there was a greater general level of craft. There was a standard when old Harley motors were made. One helps me appreciate the other if that makes sense. This place spoils you in a lot of ways, I can't imagine working and living in any other place.

L Train Morgan Avenue stop

BROOKLYN INVITATIONAL

Lock Baker tank fabrication, '49 Knucklehead, 2009 Brooklyn Invitational

Lock Baker, '47 Knucklehead, 2009 Brooklyn Invitational

Andy Camay Shovelhead, bike in background is Kevin Orangers' Panhead, 2009 Brooklyn Invitational

Rich Phillips build, 2009 Brooklyn Invitational

Paul Cox's "The Butcher," 2009 Brooklyn Invitational

Keino Pan-Shovel build, 2009 Brooklyn Invitational

Bill Dodge build, 2009 Brooklyn Invitational

Jeff Wright's The Hammer of God:
100ci Shovelhead, 2010 Brooklyn Invitational

Matt Davis' Panhead, DICE, 2010 Brooklyn Invitational

Andrew Ross drag bike, 2010 Brooklyn Invitational

Max Schaaf Shovelhead, 2010 Brooklyn Invitational (he rode in from Oakland)

Mike Davis Panhead, 2010 Brooklyn Invitational

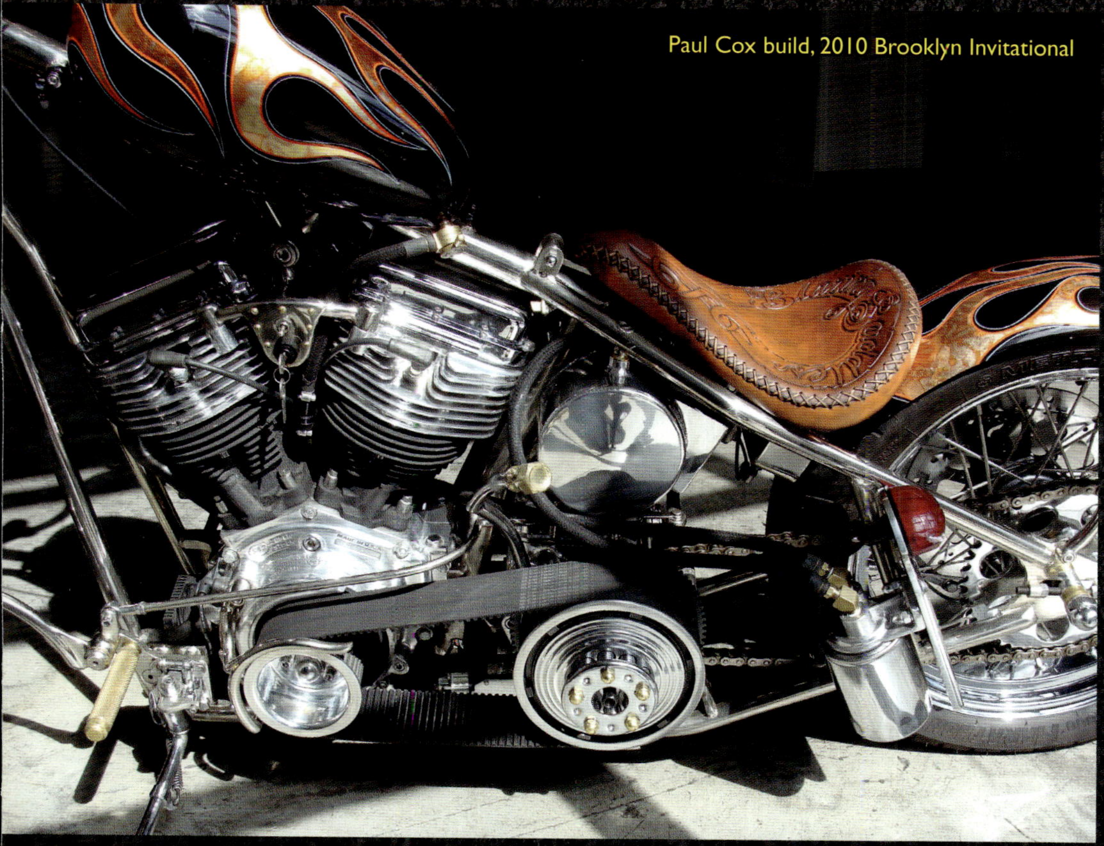

Paul Cox build, 2010 Brooklyn Invitational

Shinya Kimura, 2010 Brooklyn Invitational

CONCLUSION

Mel Bernstein, c.1967

The stylized motorcycles and cars included in this book represent an ongoing process of cultural awakening. Originally, in post WWII America, as the automobile and motorcycle became more accessible, mostly young men and some women turned to these mass-produced symbols of middle-American pride and accomplishment and reshaped them into more precise and highly unique statements about youth and power. The stylized machines became a vocabulary that was phrased within a grammar of profound countercultural change. Inside of a decade an influential mystique emerged that experimented with its own set of codes and strategies for making fast and noisy wheeled machines.

These machines and their innovators traveled around America and broadcast an outlaw message that encouraged high-speed behavior and a willingness to experiment with a risky expertise. This new set

Bonge with builds

Bonge with builds

of values took root and in turn reflected America's regional diversity. During the mid-1940s, New York City emerged from its eighteenth-century legacy and stubbornly fell into step with the automobile age. Young people there had a lot of unfavorable obstacles to contend with but they answered the call to make fast cars and bikes. Styles emerged in the five boroughs that reflected the racial and ethnic diversity of the people living there, and over time notable creative innovators established nuanced reputations. This process has a unique history in New York City and it continues today in personalized workshops throughout the five boroughs. Talented mechanics, artists and craftspeople from different generations continue to design and fabricate machines that take cues from the past at the same time that they pursue a vigorous innovative impulse into the future.

Michael McCabe
New York City, 2012

1927 Roadster pick-up build by Bonge

1959 Old's motor rebuild by Bonge

NY horse power